YANK
DOWN UNDER

A Drink and a Look Around Australia
(Through the Eyes of an American Local)

TIM SWEENEY

Copyright © 2023 Timothy Sweeney
www.TimSweeneyLive.com

First Edition

Cover design by Natalia Olbinski
Typesetting and internal layout by Antonina Konopelska
Photographs by Tim Sweeney and Andre Caron

Paperback: 979-8-9879547-0-6
Ebook: 979-8-9879547-1-3
Hardcover: 979-8-9879547-2-0
Audiobook: 979-8-9879547-3-7
Library of Congress Control Number: 2023911471

These are my memories, from my perspective, and I have tried to represent events as faithfully as possible. To maintain anonymity of people, some details and names have been changed.

The web addresses inside this book were live at the time of publishing. A selection of websites and publications used for research can be found in the bibliography section.

Thanks to Mom, Dad, and Chris
for all your support and all the witty banter at the dinner table.
And for the encouragement to move to Australia.
Dad, I'm sorry this took so long.

CONTENTS

Before I begin, I'd like to acknowledge the Traditional Owners of the land on which I traveled to write this book. And pay my respect to Elders past, present, and future.

I undertook these travels over the course of eight years. The traditional owners have taken care of that land for tens of thousands of years.

A NOTE FROM THE AUTHOR

The stories on the following pages stem from travels taken over the course of eight years. Many originated as short blog posts on my old website. At the time of publishing, I did my best to verify that any businesses, restaurants, vineyards, or local watering holes mentioned are still in business and go by the same name. I have noted where I learned otherwise. I would recommend using the internet to confirm the current price of things like tours and ferries where they are included in the story. The book was written to be read in order, but the sections are titled so that you can hop from section to section and use it as a guidebook if you'd like. Finally, I italicized the *Aussie slang*, but you'll figure that out.

Enjoy the stories and thanks for reading.

PART I:
G'DAY AUSTRALIA

The iconic Sydney Opera House from the Sydney Harbour Bridge

Chapter 1: Spectacular Sydney

"G'day, mate! You 'right there?"

That's what the rugged, relaxed Sydney police officer standing to my left said to me as I alternated my gaze from the broken luggage handle I was holding to the street signs above me.

I looked back at him blankly. My brain was moving slowly and he appeared decidedly un-busy, but delightfully cheery for 7 a.m., like he was approaching the end of an overnight shift. Or perhaps everyone seems more upbeat than you after you disembark from a fifteen-hour flight. It took a few seconds, but eventually it dawned on me that he was asking if I was all right.

"G'day," I mustered back in unconvincing Aussie speak. "Yeah, I'm good, thanks. Can you tell me the way to the Darling Harbour Hotel?"

The copper was happy to point me in the right direction and quick to inform me that the grip to my rolling suitcase had broken off as I dragged it off the curb while exiting the subway station.

"Yeah, mate, just walk this way two blocks," he said. "Then walk down the hill and make a right."

"Perfect. Thanks very much. Is it a long way with this thing?" I asked, nodding toward my fifty-pound bag, which now had the metal extension device permanently protruding awkwardly from one end.

"Nah, mate. You'll be 'right. You Canadian? Or American?"

The potential to offend a Canadian by assuming that he or she might be American has somehow trained Aussies to ask first if you are Canadian, despite the overwhelming odds—on population numbers alone—that you will be American. Everyone needs something to be offended by these days, even Canadians.

"American," I replied.

"Where ya from?" he asked.

"Near Boston originally," I said.

"Been to America. Loved it," he replied.

"Nice. I like it, too. Which parts?" I asked.

"New York, Las Vegas, and L.A."

"Good time?" I felt compelled to ask, though I knew what was coming.

"New York was amazing, mate. LA was hard to get around. Vegas is crazy."

"It is for sure," I said.

"Have a good one, mate," he said. "Enjoy 'Straya."

And so I was into it. *Straight away,* as the Aussies say. The lingo, the friendliness, the relaxed attitude, the good-natured ball-busting, and the same answer about going to America and seeing New York, Vegas, and LA that you get from half the Aussies you meet. I didn't know it, but it was the perfect introduction to the land down undah.

About eighteen months after this first visit to Australia, I would relocate to Melbourne and spend nearly three years working there. Given the opportunity to work and live abroad, I adopted a personal policy of saying yes to just about any opportunity that popped up (within reason) because…well, Australia. I went to as many pubs, concerts, Sunday markets, pubs, sporting events, beer gardens, parks, pubs, and cafés I could find the energy for. Did I mention the pubs?

On random Saturdays, I took "tourist walks" to places residents probably never visit. I drove an hour and a half and paid $25 to sit in bleachers and watch tiny penguins run ashore on a flood-lit beach. I stayed out late singing "Horses" by Daryl Braithwaite while drunk people ten years my junior bounced off of my shoulders and spilled Carlton drafts all over me. I sweated my ass off in the Northern Territory while looking at thousand-year-old drawings of kangaroos and scouring the water for crocodiles from a tin boat. I ate kangaroo, stepped over a poisonous snake on a golf course, nearly drove into oncoming traffic on three occasions, almost ran into a kangaroo on my mountain bike, and even went to a few museums…when it rained and I couldn't think of anything else to do. Not a big museum guy.

In short, I was a resident with a tourist mindset, which, it turns out, is a fun way to go through life.

Truth be told, I took a job in Australia because it was a paid opportunity to live abroad in a place that had always fascinated me. My job was to market Callaway golf clubs and golf balls to Aussie golfers, as I had been doing in Southern California for the six years prior. Occasionally, I even got paid to chase—or, more accurately, search for—said balls across revered pieces of Australian turf and into nearby forests. If you've ever found a shiny new Callaway marked with a "T" in the state of Victoria, you're welcome. If you ever found one in the front seat of your Holden Commodore or living room, it was Tom, Terry, or Trevor.

Over the journey, as they say Down Under, the lens through which I viewed the culture became more local—and so did my vernacular—but certainly not native. I started saying things like: "you'll be 'right," "good onya," "how ya going?," "how ya traveling?," "righto," "give me a spell," "she's tidy," "no drama," "pull your head in," "what a shocker," "full-on," "what a ripper," "having a perv," "time to pull the pin," and, my personal favorite, "onya bike, son!," which basically means "get the hell out of here!" (I cleaned up that last one.)

I didn't talk that way on purpose; it just sort of happened because this is how Aussies communicate. And no, I never asked for a Fosters or mentioned putting shrimp on the barbie. No one says those things in Australia. Really. No one. Somewhere along the way, I started jotting down notes about everything I experienced and the characters I came in contact with. Those notes evolved into what follows on these pages.

I first visited Australia in 2011 when my good mate and colleague Leighton Richards and his bride Laura invited me to their wedding. I'd become friends with Leighton because I was the one tasked with entertaining him during his lengthy business trips to California over the years, whether with a round of golf or a "quiet" evening out. I was the only US colleague who took him up on the wedding invitation. The rest were too busy, too lame, or too married to fly fifteen hours and dance to INXS at the reception. I was too single not to. A year or so later, Leighton and another character, Scott Jungwirth, offered me a job in Callaway's Melbourne office and I said, "Sure, I'll have a go." As I learned in an Aussie improv class, when you say, "Yes, and..." the possibilities are endless.

That very first journey from Los Angeles to Sydney had gone as smoothly as could be expected once we got off the ground. We boarded an hour late, sometime around 10 p.m. Pacific Coast time, then sat inside the plane without air conditioning on a hot early autumn evening waiting for the machine that starts the plane to be…what's the word…available.

If I had my druthers, sweating profusely prior to take-off would not be my preferred way to start a journey across the Pacific, but it was less ideal for the young Sydneysider in the middle seat to my left. He had chosen, for no reason I could fathom, to wear leather pants for this journey. I can't imagine dressing like Gene Simmons or another member of KISS for a fifteen-hour flight, but the travel tip here is to always bring backup *jocks* and change into something comfy right before you board a long-haul flight.

Once airborne, the flight itself was surprisingly easy to tolerate. It's so long that you resign yourself to the fact that you will be there for the better part of a day and you relax. I actually found it easier than many of the six-hour cross-country redeye flights I used to frequently take from San Diego to Boston. Plus, the screen in front of me had more entertainment than I had in my apartment. It wasn't Montreal for a bachelor party weekend, but you couldn't get bored if you tried and you were less likely to catch a sexually transmitted disease.

Three movies, half an Ambien, two glasses of red wine, five hours of sleep, and one entire season of *Entourage* later I arrived in Sydney at 7 a.m. local time. An entire day on the calendar had gone missing, giving my father the perfect excuse to drop this dad joke in response to the email I sent when I landed.

"Tim, the internet must be extra fast down under," he replied. "I received your email Monday at 7:52 p.m., but you sent it on Tuesday at 10:52 a.m. What a time warp! Please send me tomorrow's lottery numbers. Thanks. Have fun."

At least you'll understand where the bad jokes come from.

I didn't care about my day that had gone begging somewhere over the Pacific. I was in Sydney, Australia, and this all seemed a little bit surreal. Right down to the broken suitcase and the cop with the dream of a stand-up comedy career. I thanked the cop for directions, set off in the direction of the hotel, checked in, took one of the most refreshing showers of my life, and then attempted to saw off the metal bars sticking out of my suitcase. I failed.

Like it does for most Americans, Australia had always seemed so very far away, and not just physically. My parents were not international travelers until later in life. When I was a kid, we took the type of family trips that you take when you grow up in New England suburbia—summer weekends to visit my father's aunt and uncle on Cape Cod or a few ski weekends in New Hampshire. We went to Disney World in Orlando once and visited my aunt and uncle in the Tampa area. We even trekked randomly to The Catskills of upstate New York one time, though I can't recall why. All I remember from that trip was a brief, random encounter with Bill Murray when my father stopped at a local liquor store to grab a six-pack and Murray happened to be walking out. When my brother and I stuck our heads out the window to sneak a peek at a real-life celebrity, Murray walked by and rubbed our freshly buzzed heads, prompting my father to mention that we might be ready for a role in *Stripes*. (Look it up, kids.)

We had everything kids could ever need. The Sweeneys just weren't global. Mom and Dad worked, saved, and took us to an endless amount of our sports practices and games all over Massachusetts, and we traveled when time and money allowed. To be fair, fewer people were global in the '80s and '90s than they are now. Or I was just unaware of these people. My aunt and uncle took me on a trip to California when I was 16, and that felt like being in a movie. As my parents aged—as we've all aged—the world shrank, and it shrank for them, too. In retirement, they put aside money for cruises around Alaska and Hawaii. They toured around Italy with their retired friends. Dad even came to visit me during a semester in London, and we jumped to Ireland for a week together. Mom had to stay behind for fear that my brother might throw a party and burn the house down.

In my early thirties, when I lived in California, the four of us laughed and bickered like the Griswolds on a road trip from San Francisco to San Diego. A decade or so later, my parents and brother came to visit me in France and we road-tripped into Switzerland and Italy. It was fantastic to witness my parents seeing the things I got to experience, mostly because it was their efforts that led to my opportunities. Still, as a kid, seeing the world was not something I took as a "given" someday.

My first extended look at Sydney was watching the 2000 Summer Olympics on television. Athletically, the highlight of those Games was Australian Cathy Freeman's victory in the women's 400-meter race. Freeman, an Aboriginal woman, delivered a gold medal after being anointed a sort of unifying symbol for the entire host nation on the world's biggest athletic stage. There's nothing like the media perpetuating a storyline about how the racial unification of your homeland hinges on your ability to run one lap around a track faster than anyone else in front of 100,000 screaming compatriots and a global TV audience. It remains one of one of the most clutch performances in Olympic history.

Aside from Freeman's grace *under the pump*, what I remember most about watching from the US was how NBC Sports went in and out of each Olympic commercial break with scenic footage of the host nation as if the Aussie tourism board had made up the shot list for them. The closing ceremony was a giant party with an endless parade of Aussie celebrities that included Paul Hogan, Greg Norman, and Elle Macpherson, all singing along to "Land Down Under" by Men at Work. It looked like a blast, but it also looked just out of reach for a young man watching from the US. I remember wondering how I might somehow go there...someday.

Now, with the excitement of my new surroundings temporarily overcoming my sleep-depravation, I was going to make good use of my first morning Down Under by heading out for what some Aussies refer to as a *dingo's breakfast* — a drink, a piss, and a good look around. Mostly, the first and third of those three.

I had agreed to meet up late that morning with an Aussie who was a university classmate of one of my close friends. I hadn't seen Duncan in nearly a decade, but he was a local now, having returned to Sydney a few years earlier upon finishing his studies in the US. The last time I saw him was at a house party full of PhD candidates who were studying molecular biology at the University of Colorado in Boulder, including my close friend from my undergrad days, Jason Stumpff. They were doing things like trying to find cures for cancer by studying the protein in one fruit fly for the next five years (I'm paraphrasing here because I still don't understand what they were doing).

On the evening of this Boulder house party, Duncan spent most of his time standing behind a small bar in the basement consulting a Bartender's Bible to determine the name of the drink that fit the next customer. At one point, he latched onto something called the Dingo because it was the most Aussie thing he could find in the book. The dingo in real life is a wild dog that inhabits parts of Australia. The Dingo in a Bartender's Bible is a drink consisting of rum, whiskey, amaretto, orange juice, lemon juice syrup, and grenadine, but Duncan was using whichever of those he could find behind the bar and then ad-libbing the rest. The ad-libbing part does wondrous things for your hangover. So does drinking six of them.

For the next three hours he went around handing out Dingos to anyone who would take one while yelling, in the most exaggerated Aussie accent you can imagine, "The dingo will eat all your babies!" The line was in reference to a tragic Australian case in which a two-year-old girl was taken from a tent by a dingo in 1980 and never found again. Her death, and the subsequent trial of her parents, captivated Australia throughout much of that decade, though none of this seemed to be the point of his drink-slinging. The purpose, I think, was to destroy everyone's night and next day. And, from what I recall, it was a resounding success. If you're thinking "that's the perfect guy to give you a tour around an Australian city," that's what I was thinking, too.

We started with a quick lap around Darling Harbour. The most entertaining part of this tourist-targeted area was a sort of animal park mall called WILD LIFE Sydney Zoo, which felt more like a big pet shop where you can't buy the animals and wouldn't want to buy the reptiles. For $35 AUD (Australian dollars), we strolled through small indoor and outdoor areas filled with attractions like an outdoor kangaroo viewing area, a room where "the most venomous snake in the world" lay behind a small pane of glass, and an outdoor koala exhibit where you could learn fun facts about those cute and cuddly creatures in the trees. Fun fact #1: The very first solid meal a baby koala eats is its mother's stool. It's true. Momma bear produces a special paste called pap to pass important bacteria onto her young that will allow the little one to digest the leaves it eats. I suppose once you eat Mom's shit you've got the stomach for just about anything. As a kid, my mother actually washed my mouth out with soap when I had a bit too much to say. It was miserable, but I'm glad she didn't know about the koala thing.

Without a doubt the star attraction of the non-petting zoo was Rex, the fifteen-foot saltwater crocodile. The zookeepers mentioned that we were all fortunate to be there for Rex's feeding, which only happens three times per week. I'm not saying they are telling fibs or saving cash on chickens, but I wouldn't stand on the edge of Rex's tank on Tuesday morning either. My gut says Rex is not on a self-imposed diet and that he would eat whatever you dangled above his dome any day of the week. Watching him use his tail to launch most of his giant body up out of the water made it clear that Monday afternoons in Sydney were not the time and place to be a dead chicken dangling four feet above the tank of a zoo-kept crocodile. Sadly, Rex passed on to the great crocodile farm in the sky in 2016, but there's a new croc on the premises these days if you want to stand by the water holding a bag of KFC.

Like any crocodile feeding would, this one made us thirsty. So Duncan and I adjourned to a waterfront bar along Darling Harbour for a couple of pints. I had slept five hours in the last thirty-six and I felt like I had just done a forty-eight-hour shift on an Alaskan crab boat from *Deadliest Catch*.

A couple of *quiet ones* (beers) seemed to perk me up so we decided to continue the tour with a stroll across town toward Circular Quay at Sydney Harbour, the glorious waterfront area that is home to the Sydney Opera House and the Sydney Harbour Bridge. As we made our way through the financial district, it was clear that it was not entirely uncommon here for lunch hours to be extended into entire afternoons *on the piss* (drinking). Men in suits were knocking back cold ones at open-air pubs at 3 p.m. I surmised that they had either left work early or took lunch and never went back. "They seem to not take work too seriously" was my first thought, and "How do I get a job here?" was my second. Prophetic, I suppose.

I'm not sure if the alcohol had any effect on the way people were walking, or how I was walking, but as we moseyed down the street I was having more trouble than usual determining which side of the sidewalk I was supposed to be on. Everyone who came at me seemed equally conflicted. They drive on the left, UK-style, and on something like an escalator you always went to the left, which I nearly learned the hard way at the train station. Yet, the same rule didn't clearly apply to sidewalks. The first prisoner ships from England had arrived in nearby Botany Bay more than 200 years earlier, yet in the two centuries that followed no Aussie seemed to have made that simple declaration of where to walk when someone approaches you. The result for me was performing an awkward dance with every fifth or sixth oncoming stranger to avoid crashing into each other's face. My inner monologue was on overdrive as I attempted to sort this out. "You're going right? Okay, I'll go right. Oh shit, now he's going left."

I continued this afternoon tango with the unsuspecting residents of Sydney all the way across town as Duncan and I caught up on where life had taken us in the ten or so years since we had been in the same company around our mutual buddy, Jason. Most notably, he had survived a kidney transplant and competed as a swimmer in something called the World Transplant Games, which is the same thing as the Olympic Games except for the notable caveat that you need to have survived some sort of organ transplant in order to be a participant. While strolling through Sydney's business district, we covered the fact that he had beaten one Estonian in a four-man race to earn the bronze medal.

A few minutes later, we arrived at The Rocks, the cobblestoned laneway section of the city that rises from the shore of Sydney Harbour. The Rocks was once the slum of Sydney, home to prostitutes, gangs, and, later, an outbreak of the bubonic plague. In the early 1900s, the New South Wales government bought back many of the houses stretching from Sydney Harbour to Darling Harbour. To improve the area and rid it of the plague, many of the homes were demolished. Later, even more were demolished to make way for the Sydney Harbour Bridge, which opened in 1932. In the mid-1970s, after much protesting from locals who had generations of family history in the area, The Rocks was conserved and restored. Today, the area is a major tourist destination with shops, pubs, and restaurants filling old buildings made of hand-carved sandstone bricks.

Most of this information was shared to me by Duncan, who is one of those people who takes a certain pride in both his home city and his homeland, and in knowing much about each of them. I find this to be a good thing, as long as people aren't bashing mine. The United States could stand to have more people who know a bit more about the country they grew up in. There are residents in my native Massachusetts who probably think Lexington and Concord, where the first shots of the American Revolution were fired, are the pet dogs of Ben Affleck and Matt Damon and that Paul Revere was a New England Patriots quarterback.

Sydney Harbour Bridge and the Sydney Opera House

Australia didn't become the Commonwealth of Australia until 1901, so I suppose you could argue that there isn't a ton of history to memorize. Still, without me having to probe much at all, Duncan explained the current events of Aussie government, native plants we saw, native snakes at the non-pet shop/indoor zoo, and the overall demeanor of crocodiles, though everyone seems pretty well versed on that. One of the most fascinating topics was Australia's high-speed internet progress, which I happened to catch on a C-SPAN-type of network in my hotel room that morning.

Due to the vast open spaces of Australia, some of the country did not yet have access to high-speed Internet. This seemed incredible to me. It also provided a nice broad (if not hazy) base of truth from which I could continue to crack bad jokes to Leighton about how they still used rotary phones and that their lives would change considerably when this newish thing called the WORLD WIDE WEB landed on the fine shores of his homeland. His response, predictably, was always simple and direct: "Piss off, mate!"

At the top of The Rocks, high on the hill, Duncan led the way into a pub called The Glenmore, which also had a splendid rooftop bar with a view of Sydney Harbour. I enjoyed it so much that the Glenmore has since become a regular stop for me on subsequent visits to Sydney. The sun poked through after a partly cloudy day, lighting up the seascape below. Across the water, about a mile away, was the Sydney Opera House. A cruise ship was docked on the near shore, and ferry boats to Manly Beach checked in and out of the Circular Quay terminal. It is, without debate, one of the most spectacular cityscapes in the world—so modern, so open, so shiny, and so sunny. It felt like we were standing over the place where the beach meets business.

In Sydney, the harbor doesn't feel like the place where the city ends; it feels like part of it. Even if Sydney's cost of living lies somewhere between absurd and ridiculous, it's easy to feel a little envious of someone who takes a ferry from the beach into the city for work each day. I have friends who've had similar commutes in places like Boston and New York, but it's not the same experience when the windchill factor is "negative a hundred."

We strolled down the hill and, at Duncan's suggestion, made a quick stop at Sydney's longest continuously licensed pub, The Fortune of War, which has been serving drinks in The Rocks since 1828.

A *schooner* (half pint) later, I got my fourth wind and, with two of Duncan's female friends joining us, we carried on for a touristy cocktail on the patio of the Opera Bar, which sits in the shadow of the Opera House, the most iconic landmark of the city and perhaps the country. With the sun going down, the Sydney Harbour Bridge was aglow across the water and the day that would never end was finally nearing the finish line. Exhausted and starving, we all hopped a taxi back toward my hotel and grabbed dinner at a Malaysian restaurant I couldn't find again even if you threatened me with time in a Malaysian prison. My first full day in Australia was in the books. I didn't know it at the time, but it would be the first of many.

Coastal Walk from Bondi to Coogee

Chapter 2: Sydney Beach Life

A solid night of being absolutely comatose set me straight for my second day in Australia. After a quick workout at the hotel fitness center to ward off the jet lag, I set off in the direction of The Rocks and strolled across the Sydney Harbour Bridge, which afforded a memorable view of the harbor. Above me, thrill-seeking tourists made their way to the upper reaches of the bridge as part of Bridge Climb Sydney. Dressed in their blue jumpsuits, guests latched into safety lines and followed a guide along catwalks to the top of the bridge for a 360-degree view of the city that tops out 440 feet above the water. At the time, the experience to climb the more than 1,300 steps to the top would set you back about $200, plus whatever you'd normally pay for a new pair of underwear. Walking across the lowest part of the bridge next to the passing traffic (161 feet above the water) was free and good enough for me.

Because I had seen what was behind me, I continued across the bridge and landed in the harborside town of Milsons Point, with exquisitely landscaped houses on small pieces of property that cost an absurd amount of money. Much of the neighborhood looked back across the harbor at the city, and the streets of Milsons Point all smelled like fresh flowers. It was overwhelmingly pleasant, so I kept walking like a weirdo wandering through a neighborhood until I found the Milsons Point train station. After one train change back in the city, I was en route to Bondi Junction. From there, it was about a mile-and-a-half walk down a long, busy street to the famed Bondi Beach.

As I walked, several groups of twenty-something women in various forms of beach attire—mostly bikini tops and small cutoff jeans that looked altogether uncomfortable to walk in—would periodically pass in the opposite direction speaking a variety of languages. I was *doing it tough*, as the Aussies would say. That's sarcasm for: life is good. Much of the daytime population in the area appeared to consist of young backpackers living in paradise for the summer. I wanted to be them.

The ocean came into view on the last steep downhill into town, and Bondi Beach itself was all you might expect. It stretched across a wide inlet and there looked to be 200-plus feet of sand from the back sea wall out to where small waves rolled ashore. To the right was the famous Icebergs Club, with its saltwater swimming pool abutting the ocean. Waves crashed over a seawall into the pool while locals swam laps back and forth. I have no idea how they got the ocean to stop coming ashore for a few days while they built the pool wall, but it must be some sort of engineering marvel. At the near end of the beach, above the sand, skateboarders dropped into two empty pools and stylishly launched themselves into the air. It was a lively, youthful scene that made growing up in my perfectly quaint hometown seem completely unfair.

The streets were lined with bars, restaurants, coffee shops, and touristy places to purchase mementos of your visit. I ordered a beer at an open-air restaurant/watering hole as an excuse to pay the bartender for the local knowledge I was about to solicit from him and because I was about to piss myself. After a quick sandwich, I plopped down in the sand of Bondi, took a swim, then read my guidebook in the sun and rested my feet. An hour of relaxing can often feel like a waste of time to me when I'm exploring a new place—yes, I have to work on this—so I packed up after thirty minutes and began tackling the coastal walk to Coogee Beach.

The bartender at my lunch spot, who it's safe to suppose had never served a Dingo to anyone, gave me the travel tip of the week when he recommended the 6.5-kilometer coastal walk from Bondi to Coogee. He assured me it would take "about an hour," but it ended up occupying the rest of my afternoon because I couldn't stop taking photos.

From Icebergs, the coastal walk travels past a monument to something called Black Sunday, commemorating the tragic events of February 6, 1938, when a set of freak waves swept ashore. About 250 people had to be rescued, including many who were swept right off the beach, which was populated by some 35,000 people that day. Thirty-five thousand people…at the beach! The number of people involved is staggering: 150 people had to be rescued, five drowned, sixty others nearly drowned, and thirty-five were brought to shore unconscious. Black Sunday would have been considerably blacker if more than seventy surf lifesavers (lifeguards) weren't on the beach readying for a race. They used their rescue devices to save hundreds of lives, including dozens of people who had to be resuscitated on the beach.

You can imagine the emphasis placed on life around the sea in a country where it is said that 85 percent of the total population

Bondi Beach

live within thirty miles of the coastline. Nowhere is this swimming, surfing, life-guarding culture more evident than in the communities along the coastal walk from Bondi to Coogee. It's not uncommon to see surf rescue teams doing their best Mitch Buchanan imitation, conducting training sessions on various beach craft in their way-too-small red swim trunks (aka *budgie smugglers*). Junior lifeguard training, rowing, sea kayaking, scuba diving, and surfing; it's all happening everywhere here.

On this particular day, permanent structures like the Black Sunday Memorial were joined by a collection of temporary artwork as part of something called Sculptures by the Sea, which turned the first mile and a half into an outdoor art exhibit. Sculptures by the Sea has been going on since 1997 and it was, for me, a case of being in the right place at the right time. The things artists had done to integrate their work into the surroundings were captivating.

My favorite was a sculpture of a table and four chairs, with all of the flat surfaces made of bright green sod. It was sitting in just the

31

right spot overlooking the sea: the perfect place for your morning coffee, except you'd have to mow your table and chair every few days. If you were my father—or, more accurately, his sons—you'd have to mow it methodically so that all the mowing stripes went in the same direction. You'd also need to have the mower set to the optimum height so as not to burn the grass, but not leave it too long either. Do I sound bitter? I'm not bitter.

The general vibe of those first two kilometers was fantastic. Locals milled about on a beautiful spring afternoon to see what had been created on their regular walking/running route, and tourists snapped photos of the artwork against the backdrop of what is a marvelous, rugged coastline. Even without the sculpture show, the entire coastal walk is a little slice of heaven. As you walk, you get the feeling that people who live here might not have the same everyday problems and stresses you do. That's ridiculous, of course, because they do, but it feels that way. Fit people with Aussie, American, German, and Scandinavian accents ran by smiling and chatting. The concrete walkway, a little wider than your average sidewalk, guides you along over rocky scenic overlooks and down to quaint beaches, each with their own distinct character, and it continues like this for four miles.

Between Bondi and the next beach, Tamarama, the path wound along a high overlook area called Mackenzie's Point. Tamarama Beach, like all the beaches in this area, is dwarfed by Bondi, but it makes up for its lack of size with stunning beauty. Not far from the beach, the ocean is choked on both sides by the rocky coastline. Farther out, surfers dodged rocks to paddle into waves. Along the shore, scuba divers bobbed around in the chilly spring water.

A few more minutes of walking brought me to Bronte Beach, a smallish area that backs up to a green park. At the south end of the beach is a spectacular lap pool that blends into the surrounding rocks. Across the road were a handful of cafés. Sluethy internet research by yours truly revealed that there is a dangerous rip current here called the Bronte Express, which sounds more like something that would give you diarrhea than sweep you out to sea. A sort of rock pool toward the south end of the beach let young swimmers frolic around in more protected waters. I bought an ice cream from a vendor near the park, sat down on a bench on the edge of the sand, and let the cooling onshore breeze wash over me. *If I lived here,*

I would sit here every night with an ice cream cone, I thought, before correcting myself with the knowledge that life would crop up most days and I probably wouldn't.

A little farther on, I came upon Waverly Cemetery, which extends a few hundred yards up the hill and offers a spectacular view of the Tasman Sea to its inhabitants. It has to be the greatest piece of real estate occupied by dead people this side of the United States Capitol building. Inching closer to Coogee, I found another secluded piece of beach heaven called Gordon's Bay, which can only be accessed via the coastal walk. Here, the sea stretched inward to form a turquoise cove, and a handful of small, weathered boats were rested on wooden racks just above the sand. The differing character of each beach along the walk was striking. Though they are just a couple of miles apart, Gordon's Bay would not look out of place on Cape Cod, while Bondi looks more like Southern California.

Bondi to Coogee Coastal Walk

Walking past a memorial to the 202 people (eighty-eight Aussies) who died in the 2002 Bali, Indonesia nightclub bombings forced me to bury any self-pity that I had for my sore feet as I neared the end of my two-hour stroll. I reached Coogee Beach around 6 p.m., much later than planned, and immediately found a comfortable bar stool at some kind of establishment that allowed for onsite sports betting. I ordered myself a well-deserved pint and caught up on American football highlights that were playing on the bar's TV.

Despite the magic of the last few hours, I was frustrated that the long walk had thrown my plans for the day out of whack. I had seen less than I had intended, and for a few minutes that annoyed me. When I pulled out my phone and flipped through my photos, reality set in. Why was I worrying about some imaginary schedule? I can't remember where I was hoping to go after the coastal walk, but the day was so delightful that the hours slipped away, and that was a good thing. What you learn over time is that the best days while traveling are often the ones that go off-schedule or are hardly planned in the first place, and Australia would teach me this lesson over and over.

Because I was super eager to ascertain just how sore my feet could get, I decided to hoof it some more the next morning just in case I never made it back. It was sunny and already uncomfortably warm as I climbed a hilly street away from Darling Harbour toward Hyde Park, a green space in the middle of the city with huge, canopied trees offering cooling shade. From the park I set off in the direction of a place called Harry's, which I was told served the best Aussie meat pies in town. That took me through another park area called The Domain, which was filled with people jogging, playing soccer, and, of course, kickboxing in the sun…because that's what normal people do in the sun on a Wednesday afternoon; they kickbox. It was about noon now and there was some sort of corporate challenge running race going on all around me as I headed down a long flight of stairs to sea level in the direction of Harry's.

Harry's Café de Wheels is essentially a food stand set inside a trailer and it is a Sydney staple. At last check, there were ten locations, including one in China, but the one I was heading to was the original spot in the chic harborside section of town called Woolloomooloo, a former naval yard. Harry's has been around since the late 1930s when, according to their website, a "ripping bloke" named Harry Edwards opened a food caravan near the entrance to the naval dockyard.

He enjoyed much success serving sailors, soldiers, *coppers* (cops), and other late-night carousers until he closed the business in 1938 to join the Australian Army during World War II. When Harry returned to Sydney in 1945 he looked around and saw that there still wasn't a place to get a late-night *feed*, so he reopened the caravan. This time he added Café de Wheels to the name because the city council insisted that food caravans move at least twelve inches per day. No matter where they are, city councils are forever passing ultra-important laws such as these.

Harry sold his business in 1975 after operating it for thirty years, but the history of the little caravan that could is littered with interesting tales. In the 1970s, Elton John held a press conference from inside Harry's. Evidently, the Rocket Man wasn't going to let the sun go down on his Aussie visit without a meat pie from Harry's. Colonel Sanders from Kentucky Fried Chicken even stopped by for a few pies sometime in the '70s. Harry's website claims to have served pies to an impressive list of important people that includes Frank Sinatra, Sir Richard Branson, Russell Crowe, Kevin Costner, Brooke Shields, Olivia Newton-John, Jerry Lewis, Billy Crystal, Pamela Anderson, and Anthony Bourdain. Given this level of popularity across such a diverse range of clientele, it seemed only natural to add Tim Sweeney to that esteemed list. I had to try one of Harry's meat pies. Okay, two. I had to try two. And I may have tried three.

As meat pies go, Harry's are as good as they get, and my visit to the small trailer on the edge of Woolloomooloo would begin a long love affair between me and the Australian meat pie, which might be the equivalent of the American hot dog, only much better. If you went to an Australian Rules Football match or a rugby match or choose to attend all five days of a cricket test—and why you would torture yourself like that, I don't know—you would eat meat pies as if you would eat hot dogs at an American sporting event. At a stadium, pies are normally single-serving size, about the circumference of a couple of cupcakes, and your choices are usually a beef pie (my preference) or a minced meat type of situation.

Pie specialty shops like Harry's are scattered around Australia and New Zealand, and normally offer a much larger variety. At Harry's, you can choose beef, chicken and mushroom, seafood, or even veggie. Named after the founder, the signature Harry's Tiger pie is beef-topped with layers of mashed potato and mashed peas, plus gravy. I ordered one of those, along with a second beef and mashed potato pie, took a seat on a stone wall nearby, and proceeded to have my mind blown and my belt stretched.

Harry's Café de Wheels

When I could stand up, I decided to take a stroll around Woolloomooloo, which is evidently home to some famous Australians. Minutes later, I somehow found myself strolling through a dilapidated housing project where everyone seemed to be home at one o'clock in the afternoon on a Thursday. It wasn't far from the shiny condominiums of Woolloomooloo, but it was a world away. With a camera in one hand and wearing a backpack and ball cap, I couldn't have announced my presence better if I screamed, "Tourist approaching!" No one gave me any trouble, but the curious glances seemed to say, "No one walks through here who doesn't have to, so why would you?"

Eventually, I found my way back past Harry's and grabbed a third meat pie for the road, which was not the best idea I've ever had, especially considering I soon had to climb back up the hundred or so stairs I had descended earlier. If you made note of "relish the unplanned days" as a travel tip following my afternoon on the coastal walk, be sure to jot down "refrain from eating meat pies while climbing stairs" right underneath it.

Gravy oozed out of the crust with every bite as corporate challenge runners struggled past, eying my meat pie as if it was Gatorade. By the time I arrived to the shade and chirping birds of Sydney's Royal Botanical Gardens, my meat pie had been replaced with indigestion. I felt like I do after Thanksgiving dinner...digestively destroyed, but grateful. I staggered through the gardens, then continued slowly through the park and along the harbor, where scores of joggers were out enjoying the sunshine and making me feel guilty. Again, I'd like to point out that it was a weekday and no one seemed in a real hurry to get back to the office. *Good on them*, I say.

The jogging path/sidewalk led directly to the steps of the Sydney Opera House, which is the result of a global design competition launched in 1956 to construct a national opera house that would sit on Sydney's Bennelong Point. The winning designer, a Dane named Jørn Utzon, was somewhat unknown at the time of his winning submission—as if you know him now—although he had studied in the United States and Mexico for a short while, coming in contact with Frank Lloyd Wright and other notable architects and designers of the day. His design for the opera house was unlike anything of the era and remains highly revered in architecture circles today. It was eventually completed on October 20, 1973, but not without a bevy of challenges, complications, and damaged relationships. Utzon, in fact, never saw his design completed. After a falling out with the New South Wales government in 1966, he flew out of Australia and never returned. Probably because it would've taken him twenty-four hours to get back. Today the Opera House attracts 8.5 million visitors every year, making it the most visited attraction in the country. That might be because Rex the crocodile died. More than 1.5 million people take in more than 2,000 shows each year at the Opera House. The entertainment has ranged from opera (imagine that) to Jimmy Buffett.

A few minutes later, when my feet felt like they might again be capable of supporting my body weight, I ambled 400 or so meters over toward the ferry terminal to figure out how to get to Manly Beach. There are at least two ferries—the regular ferry and the fast ferry—that will take you to Manly from Circular Quay, the main departure point in Sydney Harbour.

"If you want to ride the fast ferry, you can't buy that ticket here," said the clerk on the other side of the ticket window, without me asking a single word about the fast ferry. "We don't operate that ferry. It's run by another operator."

37

This didn't seem to be the best way to sell me anything, but I admired his candor, so I engaged him further. One of the enjoyable things about traveling in Australia is that if you deliver wit, you are likely to be given it back. This is amplified if you do so with a grin that gives away the fact that you are intending to be a smartass. Aussies call this "taking the piss." For example, if you ask, as I did, "So how fast is the fast ferry?" you will get a retort you deserve, just like I did. "It's fairly fast, mate," the clerk replied.

And we both shared a chuckle through the glass. By the time Captain Up-Sell told me that I would knock a whopping eight minutes off the thirty-minute journey by purchasing the more expensive "super-fast" ferry ticket from another vendor, he had earned my trust. I purchased my $13 ferry ticket aboard the slower ferry from him and hopped on. Banter counts for something in my book. At least eight minutes.

Ferry approaching Circular Quay, Sydney

The ferry cruised out of Sydney Harbour under partly cloudy skies, especially in comparison to the previous days, but I didn't care. Even a slow ferry ride to the northern beaches is worth your time and money if just to see the harbor from, well, the harbor. The ferry cruised out past the Opera House, the busy harbor bridge towering above.

Thirty minutes later we landed at the Manly ferry terminal, and I commenced the five-minute walk to the beach. Manly Beach itself was a narrow slither of sand that backed up to a sea wall, but it seemed to stretch on forever. The road along the beachfront was filled with surf shops, burger joints, restaurants, and bars that weren't yet crowded this early in the season. I walked from shop to shop and along the beach while an approaching storm cloud kept the crowds away. A few minutes later it began pissing down with rain, so I did what you do when you are without an umbrella or rain jacket: found a place to drink beer and eat a lamb burger. My late lunch finished, I stepped out into what had eased to a light rain and made my way back toward the ferry station. It wasn't the best day for Manly.

On the ferry ride back, the rain returned and sailboats tossed and turned on a choppy sea until, suddenly, the sun appeared. Back on land, I made my way from Circular Quay up through The Rocks, weaving in and out of the small laneways until I popped out next to something called the Australian Hotel. Based on the signage and throwback façade—or maybe it was just old—I thought it might be a pleasant place to take part in an honest-to-goodness Aussie happy hour. I was right.

The Australian Hotel looked like the type of place where soldiers would hang out on leave in the 1940s. It was established in 1914, so maybe they did. I grabbed a barstool a few steps from where the afternoon sun splashed through the open doorway and chose one of the fifty or so beers on tap. As if they knew I was coming, the Australian Hotel also had a happy hour deal on chicken wings for the bargain basement price of $3.50. I couldn't think of a better way to end the day until "Land Down Under" by Men at Work came on the bar's stereo. My life was turning into a movie. Outside, people sat at tables and enjoyed their cold beers in the sun. I sipped on my pint and overheard conversations in four or five different accents as the work crowd began to roll in during the four o'clock hour. My chicken wings arrived, the beer was cold, and a classic '80s tune about a guy eating a Vegemite sandwich was blaring on the stereo. Sydney was all that I had hoped it might be. It was only day three, but Australia was growing on me.

UNSOLICITED ADVICE: SYDNEY

MUST DO:

So much to say here: **The Rocks**, **Circular Quay**, the **Opera House**—all the obvious stuff. The **coastal walk** from Coogee to Bondi or vice versa. If you don't have time to walk it, go for a run there. It's a place you will always remember... After the meat pie from **Harry's** you'll need the run, but skip the stairs... **The Glenmore** might be just a pub, but I tend to go there for at least a drink when I'm in Sydney. Sipping a beverage at sunset from the rooftop while looking down on the harbor is a pinch-yourself moment for an out-of-towner. The nighttime view and ambiance is festive, too... On a subsequent visit to Sydney, I took a ferry from Double Bay to the Beach Club Hotel in **Watsons Bay** for dinner on the patio, which was one of those things that seem normal in Sydney, but nowhere else. You can get there by ferry from the major ferry landings in town... A **ferry ride** somewhere is mandatory in Sydney.

UP TO YOU:

Walking around **Darling Harbour** was just okay. You can see it quickly, but it doesn't deserve a ton of time due to its touristy feel... Other areas like **Double Bay** are great for brunch or nightlife and pretty people... If you play **golf**, there are a number of spectacular courses not far from the airport. Bonnie Doon, The Lakes, Royal Sydney, The Australian Golf Club, and New South Wales (where I once watched whales breach while standing on a tee box) are all spectacular, but will cost you a small fortune to walk on... On a subsequent trip to Sydney, I splurged with my hotel points and got a **room with a view** (if I craned my neck ever so slightly) of Sydney Harbour. If you can do it, do it.

NEXT TIME:

I never made it to the **Blue Mountains**, which are just a couple of hours away by train. Having spent a lot of time in big mountains around the world on my skis and on foot, it was never at the top of my list during a visit to Sydney, but people say it's a memorable trip, even for a day... I've also never tasted wine in the **Hunter Valley**, though my Sydney friends tell me it's a great day out, or more... I had bad luck with weather on the day I took the ferry to **Manly Beach**, but some of my Aussie mates say it's a "better beach" than the southern beaches toward Bondi. That's hard to believe, but I'd like to go back on a nice summer day to see what all the fuss is about.

PART II:
TROPICAL NORTH QUEENSLAND

Floating above the Great Barrier Reef

Chapter 3: The Great Barrier Reef...and more

I heard somewhere that the Great Barrier Reef is the largest structure on earth made from living organisms. It's the size of California, has around 1,500 species of fish, depending on whom you ask, and is visible from space. California is too, so I suppose that makes sense. The easiest way to visit the Reef is to get yourself to Cairns in Far North Queensland and hop aboard one of the various tour boats that will haul you out to the reef for a fun-filled day (or more) of snorkeling, diving, and frolicking about like a piece of chum.

So with great expectations, and more than a little trepidation due to enchanting programming like Discovery Channel's "Shark Week," I headed off to Cairns. Home to roughly 150,000 people, Cairns is popular with young backpackers and built on tourism thanks to that reef just off the coast. A charming waterfront is the hub of the town, and several large hotels overlook the marina. The Daintree Rainforest sits in the mountains above town, and the summer climate could be safely classified as humid as all hell. The folks strolling the streets looked to be in equal numbers tourism employees, Indigenous Australians, pasty white tourists from abroad wearing Panama Jack hats with socks and sandals, and twenty-something backpackers having the time of their lives. As they do all along the Eastern seaboard of Australia, *heaps* of young people from around the world arrive in Cairns on bus tours of all kinds. They see the reef, spend a few nights at a hostel drinking and attempting to fornicate, then continue on their merry way to the next stop, where they will do the same things, sometimes even with the same people.

By most standards, Queensland, especially Far North Queensland, is a place of extremes. It boasts spectacular coastal areas and a reputation for citizens who are just a little bit different from their more "refined" southern neighbors in New South Wales. Right or wrong, venturing beyond Sydney or Melbourne often made me feel as though I was getting to know Australia on a deeper level, and—though it's touristy and hardly "the outback"—Cairns was that first time for me. All my research told me that Queensland offered the climate, wildlife (of both the land and sea variety), and retirees of Florida with the natural disasters of California on steroids, though that is not how they summarize it on VisitQueensland.com or the vibe they are going for on the @queensland Instagram page, funnily enough.

It has all the same types of natural disasters and storms you get in most tropical climates—humidity, huge rainfall, wild floods, wind—except here those things tend to happen on the most ridiculous scale you can fathom.

In a twenty-day stretch in January 2011, for example, Queensland was hit with biblical floods that wiped entire towns off the map, killed dozens of people, and resulted in three-quarters of Queensland being declared a disaster zone. Queensland is two and a half times the size of Texas, so that's a fair bit of disaster. I remember watching a television show that described in great detail how that January 11 rainstorm swept in off the East Coast and dropped four inches of rain in an hour on Toowoomba, a hilltop city in southeastern Queensland. When the water rose through town and toward residents in the Lockyer Valley below, one water gauge measured a ridiculous eight-meter rise (twenty-six feet!) in twenty minutes. Johnny Cash wrote an entire song about water that was only "Three Feet High and Rising." No one would have believed a song called "Twenty-Six-Feet High and Rising."

The flood turned into an inland tsunami, which sounds horrific, that washed away entire towns. It was tragic. On the coast, where the water was headed, a large portion of Brisbane, Australia's third largest city, was left underwater. A resilient bunch, 50,000 "Brissy" locals showed up the next day, many with shovel in hand, to get the city back on its feet. With southern Queensland in recovery mode a thousand miles away, the far north part of the state, including Cairns, was bracing for tropical storm Yasi, which made landfall in February as a cyclone, which is the name for a hurricane in the South Pacific and Indian Ocean. (In the northern hemisphere, hurricanes rotate counterclockwise; cyclones move clockwise in the southern hemisphere. That meteorology lesson should come in handy if your home is ever rotating off its foundation.)

Yasi was not just your ordinary hurricane, but rather a "mega-cyclone"—a category five storm with winds reaching up to 175 mph, stronger than those of Hurricane Katrina in New Orleans. It covered an area so large that it would have enveloped most of the United States. A hurricane ABOUT THE SIZE OF THE US is what the narrator on this TV show said. Once you've boarded up the windows, where exactly do you drive to in order to avoid that—South Africa? When all was said and done, the eye of the storm passed just south of Cairns, with the towns farther south along the coast taking the brunt of the damage. Somehow, compared to four inches of rain, the inland tsunami, and the floods a few weeks earlier, the category five hurricane the size of America was evidently the tamer part of that summer.

Thankfully, the weather pattern during my trip to Cairns was far less eventful. On my first morning, I awoke early to a clear day, quickly threw on my board shorts and—pay attention, this is important—APPLIED MY FIRST LAYER OF SUNSCREEN. From my hotel, I strolled a mile or so along the waterfront, stopping briefly for a tasty plate of scrambled eggs and toast from a takeout window, then continued to the marina to find the *Ocean Freedom*, the boat I'd be spending the day on. As one of the first onboard, I had time to meet the crew, who introduced themselves one by one. It was immediately apparent that they enjoyed what they did, probably because it didn't involve sitting at a desk all day thinking about how they'd love to someday go to a place like the Great Barrier Reef.

The first paying customer I met was a twenty-three-year-old Irish plumber from Galway named James. A brawny rugby player with a receding hairline, he had just landed in Australia earlier in the week with his friend Erin, a chatty and friendly young woman who rolled her eyes and chuckled at James' harmless antics. Because the Aussie government has made it easy to obtain short-term working visas, James and Erin were planning to work and travel around Australia for the next year. That's how appealing it is to escape the constant rain of Ireland. The palest people on the planet were packing up and moving halfway around the world to do things like pick onions under the blazing Australian sun. Like many of the boat passengers, James and Erin were staying at a youth hostel in Cairns.

"We are living with this weirdo who sleeps on plastic bags and goes around picking things up with a napkin," James said to me roughly three minutes after I met him. "This is a man who should not be living near other humans! I woke up this morning, looked him straight in the face, and said, 'How ya?' and he said nothing. Well, feck you, you ignorant prick. Someone says hello to you, you acknowledge them."

James was fired up. I jokingly suggested that the plastic bag would at least make it easy to dispose of his body during the night should he start snoring, an idea James seemed to ponder a bit too seriously.

Erin and James fit the profile of most of the people onboard the *Ocean Freedom*. It was predominantly twenty-somethings from the Netherlands, Norway, Sweden, Germany, France, the UK, and Ireland. There was hardly an Aussie among them. In fact, although the Great Barrier Reef sees nearly two million visitor days per year, a surprising number of Australians I met in my time Down Under have never been there. It's a three- or four-hour flight to Cairns from where much of the population resides in the southern half of the country, but Aussies are a well-traveled bunch, and being a well-traveled Aussie means a three-hour flight is nothing. Most people just seemed more inclined to take their holidays overseas for weeks at a time than in their own enormous backyard, often because it's less expensive to travel abroad than domestically.

For an outsider like me, one of the great benefits of wandering around Australia was that it afforded me the chance to experience a number of "firsts." My first Aussie meat pie, my first time seeing a chicken fed to a crocodile, or even how a kangaroo reacts when struck in the face by a golf ball at close range—accidentally and off of someone else's club, I should add. (They shrug it off and hop away, if you're wondering. They're all muscle.) Today, I would experience my very first scuba dive and, as locations go, taking your first scuba dive on the Great Barrier Reef might be the equivalent of losing your virginity to an adult film star. Although, my first dive did last twenty minutes, so that comparison might be a tad ambitious. I mean, for some people.

After a forty-five-minute ride across calm waters, we arrived at the first of two snorkel/dive spots, and the pristine beauty of the reef came into full view. The water was a spectacular turquoise color that I'd never seen. Beneath us, the reef seemed to stretch into the distance forever. As one of ten or so customers who had paid an extra $150 to go scuba diving, I was herded to the front of the boat for a fifteen-minute group tutorial on how to not die while doing this activity. Convinced—but not really—that I would be safe, I joined the rest of the group for a thirty-minute snorkeling session until it was my turn to dive. After PUTTING ON MORE SUNSCREEN, popping on my mask, and scouring the boat for size 13 flippers, I jumped into the warm but refreshing Coral Sea.

This seems like a good time to point out that I was well aware that I would be spending much of the day facedown in the ocean in a part of the world where the sun is particularly potent. It's not as if I wasn't warned. Random strangers in Australia will go out of their way to tell you how powerful their sun is if you happen to mention that you might be out in it for an extended period of time. It's as if they think no one else has a sun...the same sun, in fact. "Mate, make sure you put sunscreen on," they'll say in an almost prideful manner. "We have a hole in our ozone layer. No, seriously, a HOLE in our OZONE." My primary goal for the day was to not end up looking like a tomato...sorry, "tomahatoh."

If you haven't taken part in many underwater ocean activities—and outside of falling off my surfboard, I hadn't—the first few minutes of snorkeling on the Great Barrier Reef is somewhat surreal. Despite being miles from land, the water is shallow enough to stand in during low tide and so unbelievably clear that you can see the bottom when it's fifteen meters deep. On one hand, it feels odd to hop in the ocean so far from any land and swim around without knowing what's down there. On the other, it's comforting to know that there are sixty other tourists in the water and odds are good that someone looks tastier than you.

Underwater at the Great Barrier Reef

The reef itself is an astounding pallet of colors that only nature could create. Multicolored fish appeared from all directions, barely bothered by the fact that humans were swimming among them. They were the type of tropical fish you normally only see in a fish tank at an expensive restaurant, with zebra-like patterns, bright yellows, and fluorescent blues. Sea turtles floated by as if they were putting on a show for another batch of visitors. It was mesmerizing.

I'd swim thirty meters thinking I'd seen all there was to see, then swim a little farther and see something totally new. It's one of those experiences that cause you to somehow heighten your senses in an attempt to process everything you're taking in. I caught myself thinking: *This is it! I'm on the Great Barrier Reef. How did this happen?* You can't help but smile. It was nearly impossible to think of anything else going on in my life. No emails, no inkling to look at a cell phone, not even a thought of where I might be in a few hours' time. You just soak it all in, engrossed in your surroundings. Fully present.

It was from this blissful state that I was abruptly jolted by the sound of a boat buzzing by me at what I deemed to be a high rate of speed considering the tourist population bobbing in the water. I looked up to see the captain of the *Ocean Freedom* at the helm of a small watercraft. A tall, bronzed figure with cool sunglasses, he was yelling something I couldn't quite decipher until he slowed the motor.

"Tim! Tiiiiim! Where's Tim?"

Is he yelling for me? What have I done now? I pulled the snorkel from my mouth and yelled back.

"Yeah, I'm Tim."

"It's your turn to dive, mate. Didn't you hear us yelling for you?" he said in a somewhat chastising tone.

"Umm, no…because I'm SNOR-KO-LING. You know, with my head in the water? You told me to come back in thirty minutes."

"It's been thirty minutes, mate."

I was so "present" I'd lost track of time.

"Really?" I said. "Sorry about that."

"No worries," he said. "We've been yelling for you for a while now. You couldn't hear us?"

"No. Sorry. I had my head in the water. Where it's hard to hear anything above the water when you're, you know, a human."

"Yeah, we were yelling pretty loudly."

"Right. Yeah, I had my head under the water," I repeated, not quite following why this was so hard for a scuba boat captain to comprehend.

"Right. No worries, mate. Hop in."

And so, with fifty-nine people peering up from the water, we commenced the short and slightly embarrassing one-minute ride back to the *Ocean Freedom* in what they had earlier termed the "rescue boat." Back aboard the Freedom, I suited up for my first scuba dive, which would be a guided, twenty-minute trip during which an experienced diver would be close by—holding onto the back of my vest, in fact—at all times. I strapped on the tank trying to remember the details from the fifteen-minute safety chat we'd been given earlier.

"If you get in trouble, do this," they said. I'd already forgotten what THIS was, but I was sure I'd have no trouble signaling trouble.

Hold your nose and pop your ears on the way down.

This means OK.

This means UP.

This means DOWN.

Go like this to remove water from your goggles.
And this means SHARK. (The guy used his hand to make a fin on top of his head. I remember this part distinctly.)

Right, and in the event the shark signal is invoked, the panic on my face will be my signal for: "I got the shark signal loud and clear."

There were several other important tips to digest, all of which would ensure that my lungs would not explode upon resurfacing, resulting in a lonely, painful death in front of fifty-nine strangers, a small crew, and one boat captain who didn't understand that humans can't hear from underwater. Pleasant thoughts. The most important tip was a simple one: remember to breathe normally through the mask. Evidently, lots of first-time divers have a bad habit of holding their breath because that's what your brain tells you to do underwater. From what I understand, your lungs then fill with air when they shouldn't and bad things ensue. Noted.

To my surprise, any nervousness I had prior to the dive dissipated immediately when I jumped off the back of the boat. The first dive was over a large, vibrant coral area. Small schools of fish swam around us as if we were part of the landscape. My guide was a confidence-inspiring Kiwi bloke named Alastair in his late twenties. If there is a central casting for dive masters, he was cut from it—tanned, long hair, and rather chill. Once settled, he showed me bits of coral, picked up things along the ocean floor, and handed them off to touch and feel. At one point he handed me a sea cucumber. So, yes, it would be accurate to say I did a tandem dive connected to a dude holding onto my vest while we passed the cucumber back and forth. We only went down about twenty feet on the first dive, but it offered a completely different perspective than snorkeling. I came back to the surface both wanting to do it again, and with my lungs intact, which was a bonus.

Between dives, over lunch, I applied MORE SUNSCREEN. The opportunity to meet people from around the globe is one of the added perks you don't consider when planning an adventure to a place like this. The conversations were interesting and multi-lingual. It was like being on a company outing with the United Nations. After lunch, a pretty French girl I had been chatting with in a group offered to apply more sunscreen to an area of my back she saw me struggling to reach. I accepted her offer. I'm smart like that. She was traveling on her own through Australia, eventually making her way down the East Coast to Sydney. I could not reach parts of my back. It was destiny.

When we got to the next dive spot, which was a deeper area, Alastair told me we'd be looking for some reef sharks that hide out in one area of the reef below. Twenty minutes of diving under my belt and now we're *seeking out* sharks? This activity has a steep learning curve.

"I suppose if the sharks get angry or hungry, I only have to get out of there before you, right?" I joked. Alastair showed me the large knife that was strapped to his leg.

"Yeah, mate," he replied straight-faced, "but I could just pull this out and cut you. They like that sort of thing."

We both laughed. Me nervously.

In retrospect, it was amazing how my own mental approach changed after one dive. Only two hours earlier, I was slightly apprehensive and wanted no part of anything with a dorsal fin. Now, I found myself hoping we'd see a shark—preferably a small, friendly, toothless one by itself that had just eaten, but still a shark would be cool.

Because I could see everything around me, I felt safer diving than I did on the surface. For example, I've never been bobbing on my surfboard and said, "Gee, it would be nice to see a shark out here today because I may never see one again."

We never saw any sharks, and I'm not going to pretend we did to make it more interesting, but Alastair gave me a little more leeway on the second dive. I was allowed to swim around on my own as long as I stayed close, which added another element of freedom to the whole experience. We went down about thirty feet, swam into a couple of small caves, and observed some sea rays. Alastair was great at his job, which, in addition to keeping me alive, was to act as an underwater tour guide via signals. It was easy to see how people get hooked on scuba diving.

On the way back to Cairns, I chatted more to the cute French girl. She spoke perfect English, which went well with her perfect abs. I also made sure to apply MORE SUNSCREEN (or maybe she did). At some point, I walked to the railing for a better view and chatted with the woman who was second in command on board. She told me that they'd seen plenty of hammerheads, tiger sharks, and even saltwater crocodiles in the area where we were diving and snorkeling. On the list of things you do not want to encounter on a snorkeling trip, a saltwater crocodile is ahead of the shark from Jaws. Because the water is so clear, tour boats can rely on helicopter tour operators above to let them know if a large shark or croc is swimming in the area. When they do, they cancel that dive spot and move along to another location, which seems good for business. Tourists don't search Google for "reef cruises who have only lost a few people."

By the time the boat was back in the marina, everyone onboard looked like they had just stormed the beaches of Normandy. The sea and the sun have a way of exhausting people, and the fact that the final two hours of the trip were spent imbibing Coronas at a healthy clip under that hole in the ozone layer wasn't helping. Still, the plan was to rally for a night on the town with my new friends, so I went back to my hotel to nurse my brutally sunburned back. The French girl was nice, but she was shit at applying sunscreen.

When I awoke after a thirty-minute *kip*, I noticed through a wandering, half-open eye that it was now 7 p.m. Twelve hours from now, I was scheduled to be picked up from my hotel for a one-day tour of the nearby Daintree Rainforest.

The smart thing to do was find some food and retire for the night... but what fun would that be? (That's a statement; not a question.)

The inspiration to pry my body from what was a blissfully relaxing and pain-free position came from an unlikely source, my brother Chris. Three years my junior, he has a unique ability to motivate others when he senses that a good night might be coming to an end earlier than HE expected. My fondest (and most blurry) memory of this was in Las Vegas some years earlier when, at around 3 a.m., Chris managed to convince me that it was ludicrous to consider turning in for the night rather than visiting one last bar a mile off the Strip that a bartender told him "gets really good around this time." He also has a way of personalizing the plea, as if going home to sleep would mean missing a golden opportunity to fortify the family legacy together.

"We don't even live in the same city," he'll say. "We don't get to hang out that often. If you want to go to sleep, that's cool, but how many times are we gonna be in Veehhgasss together?"

"All right, get a cab!" is what you end up saying back to him.

Now, with my back and shoulder looking exactly like the tomato I feared they would twelve hours earlier, I asked myself, "How many nights will you ever spend in Cairns, Tim?"

One painful shower and aloe bath later, out I went into the humidity in the direction of any place that could provide sustenance. If I was going to meet up with a throng of alcohol-fueled twenty-five-year-olds with less experienced livers than myself, I would do so on a full stomach. In the middle of town, I found a corner shop that served palatable pizza by the slice, as well as tall beers and small beers. I ordered three slices of pizza and a beer in the size you're supposed to when confronted with such decisions. The young woman behind the counter pointed me in the direction of P.J. O'Brien's, the Irish bar where the boat crowd was heading. On first glance, it was just another Irish bar, the kind you find in every town on earth, with outdoor seating, dark-stained woodwork, endless beers to choose from, and big, uncomfortable wooden booths that encourage unrealistic posture. At 9 p.m. it was rather lame and empty. I was pondering going back to my room, taking another bath in aloe, and going to bed for my 7 a.m. pickup.

I'm not exactly sure when I recommitted myself to the night, but it might have been when the twenty-five-person toga party arrived at P.J. O'Brien's and the subsequent pole dancing contest commenced on the bar's backstage. Actually, yeah, that was definitely the moment. I'm certain of it now. It's coming back to me.

We were just a few quiet pints into the evening when the toga party arrived. Among the two dozen twenty- and thirty-somethings from Adelaide wrapped in bed sheets were several scandalous-looking young ladies who seemed eager for attention. Before long, two female dancers who worked for the bar climbed atop a platform that was rolled out for just such an occasion. They were dressed—if you can say they were dressed—in cowboy hats, cowboy boots, and jean shorts with inseam lengths that erred on the side of brevity.

When the music started they took to the poles like firefighters responding to a three-alarm blaze...but seductively. It was something to behold. In fact, I'm not even sure how I just remembered the cowboy hats. Spurred on by the two hired dancers, female patrons were now volunteering to take part in a dance-off on a small stage at the back of the room. The grand prize was something on the order of a $100 bar tab for you and your friends. I can't recall what the price of a drink was at P.J. O'Brien's, but based on what I saw next, $100 AUD must go a long way in Adelaide.

Three girls from the toga party took their shot at glory onstage, each finishing with fewer bed sheets on than the previous until the final contestant decided it was too warm to bother with any linens at all. She ended her performance with a pair of skillful scissor kicks that revealed her disdain for underwear. And then, I assume, she drank for free for the rest of the night. Your $100 winner, ladies and gentlemen. In a landslide.

Not surprisingly, this riled up the crowd, who now turned their attention back to the bar where Hired Female Dancer #1 and Hired Female Dancer #2 were beginning another round of routines. When they concluded, it was time for more patrons to take to the bar top. This time, the contest included guys who thought they could dance, and others who knew they couldn't but didn't care. Among this second tier was James, the Irish plumber, who decided to reveal his follicly endowed but badly sunburned chest and back while twirling his shirt above his head and gyrating his hips.

When things slowed a bit—and by that I mean when women stopped revealing their breasts and vaginas onstage—the boat crew decided to move on to Gilligan's, a noted lodging and entertainment complex up the road. With a large bar, pool tables, and a packed dance floor, Gilligan's is renowned as a backpacker hot spot in Cairns. Based on the fact that there were 200-plus people in there on a Tuesday night, the hostel/entertainment complex idea seems like a brilliant business model and is therefore used a fair bit in Australia.

Around 1 a.m., as I waited for the bartender to hand me another Bundaberg Rum and Coke, my voice of reason intervened for just a moment. I set my cell phone and watch alarms for 6:45 a.m. in order to be "ready" for my Daintree Rainforest tour the next morning, for which I had already plunked down something in the neighborhood of $140. About thirty minutes later, while waiting for another Bundy and Coke and attempting to read the blurry numbers on my phone, the French woman who had shown such genuine concern for my skin's well-being earlier that afternoon appeared next to me at the bar with a welcoming smile and a flirtatious touch. It was loud and difficult to communicate. Either she told me she was enjoying her time in Cairns, or she invited me to visit her family beach house in Cannes. The one in France.

At some point, she asked why I had not approached her at the Irish bar hours earlier. She must have been the one person who missed the exotic toga/cowgirl/stripper/chubby Irish guy dance-off that was occupying everyone's attention. I glanced at my watch one last time to see just how long I had before the tour shuttle would be arriving at my hotel. Plenty was the answer. Plenty.

Kuranda Scenic Railway

Chapter 4: Daintree Forest

My watch and phone alarms went off at 6:45 a.m. just as I'd set them to do in my moment of lucidity earlier that morning at the bar. I wanted to be dead. I don't mean that to be dramatic; most of us have had hangovers. But if you gave me a choice between doing something productive—like, say, dressing myself—and never coming back to life again, I would have at least considered option B following that alarm. Since advising anyone to stay away from French women seems mildly hypocritical, the Aussie travel lesson here is to simply stay away from Bundaberg Rum. And if you must have it, stay away from it in drink quantities above, say, eight, nine, or twelve. Come to think of it, that's fair advice for most anything. An even dozen is generally enough of most things in life.

When I arrived downstairs the bus driver was in the lobby asking for a guy named Tim. That's twice in two days, if you're scoring at home. In a daze, I walked to the bus, put my hand on the right front door handle, and saw the driver smiling back at me.

"Did you want to drive, mate?" he asked, as I tried to open his door on the wrong side of the bus.

"No," I said, dropping my head despondently. "That would not be good for anyone."

I went to the wrong side of vehicles a lot in Australia. Even after a couple years of living and driving there, I would occasionally walk to my own passenger side door expecting to drive. Even if no one was with me, I'd normally attempt to play it cool by looking inside for a few seconds as if I was searching for something, then close the door and walk around to the driver's side and go on my way. It was as if I was trying to convince myself I hadn't forgotten that the steering wheel was on the right.

There was no playing it cool now. I walked around the front of the bus, climbed in, and plopped myself in the third row against the window. It was a small bus with ten or so people on board, all of whom, it can be safely assumed, had done far less damage to themselves in the previous eight hours of their lives. In hindsight, and without the hangover, it can also be safely assumed that they had far less fun. At the moment, this was hardly comforting.

59

We headed off in a northerly, slightly inland direction toward the Daintree Rainforest, which was about twenty minutes away. To my delight, the day was overcast with a light mist dampening the air. It was soothing weather for the type of hangover that makes you want to give up drinking for the rest of your life. The Aussies would say I was feeling "a bit dusty," but that would not be doing it justice. "Still slightly inebriated" would be more accurate.

Before too long we pulled into the parking lot, departed the bus, and made our way through the gift shop, where I successfully avoided buying any toy crocodiles or children's coloring books featuring a multitude of reptiles that can kill you. I found the largest bottle of water they sold, paid them approximately $678 for it, and quickly made my way to the loading station of the Skyway Rainforest Cableway, which would take me into the World Heritage Listed Daintree Rainforest. The Daintree covers about 450 square miles, 75 percent of which is tropical rainforest. That's an area about the size of Sydney, but with one opera house fewer and no Harry's meat pies, sadly. At an estimated 180 million years old, the Daintree Rainforest is generally regarded as the oldest continuously living rainforest on earth by people who regard things like that.

Ferrying passengers 7.5 kilometers above the dense green canopy, the Skyrail gondola is a wonderful way to see the rainforest. A one-way ride to the Kuranda Terminal, the third stop on the hop-on, hop-off journey, takes about ninety minutes. It was just what I needed at the time—tranquil, stress-free, and, most importantly, quiet. It was like being on a ski resort gondola, except ice pellets weren't waiting to smash me in the face when the doors opened at the top. Instead, the balmy overcast day created a mystical scene. A light fog drifted on the gentle breeze as we skimmed just a few feet above the treetops of the dense green vegetation below. I expected Sigourney Weaver to appear through the trees below with her mountain gorillas, Digit and Bert. (That's a *Gorillas in the Mist* joke, if you don't watch movies from 1988.) Looking back in the distance, the flat coastal land we'd left behind at the loading station stretched to the edge of the sea. Out there somewhere was the Great Barrier Reef. Despite my mental haze, the enormity of the place caused me to straighten up and take it all in. It looked rather spectacular; the opposite of me.

The second stop on the Skyrail was called Barron Falls Station, which afforded a view across at, you guessed it, Barron Falls. With a small herd of retirees and families, I ambled slowly toward the observation deck, where the earth dropped off sharply beneath our feet. In the distance, water cascaded over the large, rocky face of a somewhat tranquil Barron Falls down to Barren Gorge 900 feet below. The green tropical backdrop provided the perfect contrast to the white water falling over the rocks. A quick YouTube search will show you that in the dry season (April–November) the falls can slow to a near trickle. After substantial rainfall during the wet season (December–March), however, the falls look like something out of one of those insane flood videos that you see on the nightly news from faraway places like, well, Queensland. Today, in early November, the water rate was somewhere in the middle, the overnight rainfall providing a temporary glimpse of what the coming months might look like. It was an impressive sight, and the sound of rushing water was almost soothing for a guy moving from a drunken headache to plain, old exhaustion.

From Barron Falls, the skyrail carries passengers a few more minutes to Kuranda, the end of the line and home to what is billed as "The Village in the Rainforest." It's also home to the Kuranda Railway Station, from which my train back to Cairns would depart later that afternoon. Kuranda has a number of tourist-related activities like bird, butterfly, and koala exhibits and the "world famous" Kuranda markets, which are so famous that I had never heard of them until now and it's likely that you haven't either. Most of the activities are probably best left for families. They will cost you some coin and, to be honest, having my picture taken with a koala in captivity, getting in touch with butterflies, or hand-feeding a kangaroo weren't on the to-do list today. I could barely feed myself.

I took a leisurely stroll—yes, there's a theme here—around Kuranda, checking out the markets and taking stock of the boomerangs, bracelets, and various trinkets. There wasn't much worth carrying around with me, which is how I generally gauge the importance of a purchase while traveling. On one street, an Aboriginal man played the traditional didgeridoo—a long, wooden wind instrument that was born in this part of the world some 1,500 years ago and sounds a bit like a trumpet, though that is a horrendous description of the sound. He had mates, too, and they performed a traditional dance in front of him in the street. A small crowd stood and watched for a few minutes, then moved on or made a small donation.

The Aboriginal culture has deep roots in this area. The Djabugay people have lived in the area for more than 10,000 years and always

considered it ideal for fishing and hunting. The area that Kuranda now occupies was called Ngunbay, which means "place of the platypus." I guess they went with Kuranda because Place of the Platypus was hard to fit on coffee mugs in the gift shop. Personally, I think they misplayed that one; I'd have bought a coffee mug from Place of the Platypus.

In the late 1800s—which must seem like yesterday from an Aboriginal standpoint—white men began to access the area for gold and tin mining, using the walking tracks of the native rainforest people. In 1886, the new residents began constructing a railway line from Cairns to Heberton, sixty miles away. Conveniently enough (for them), they did so along one such walking track. As you might imagine, this did not sit well with Djabugay people. Their land was now being over-hunted by the men who were busy building the railway line, leaving the locals without much food for themselves. The Indigenous people exhibited their displeasure by spearing some of the intruders, killing their bullocks (oxen, not testicles for you Brits) on a number of occasions, and taking their food. In the mid-1880s, at a place called Speewah in Far North Queensland, a settler named John Atherton sent troops to exact revenge for the death of a bullock, which seems somewhat irrational. The Speewah Massacre of the local Aboriginal people, as it became known, was not an isolated incident in what is hardly the proudest period in Australian history and certainly not the most talked about.

Prior to white men arriving on their doorsteps, the population of the Indigenous rainforest people in the Cairns area was estimated at between 4,000 and 5,000. By 1900, the number of white men was far greater than the locals, whose population had rapidly declined. Soon after coffee became the area's first cash crop, in the late 1890s, the Indigenous people began working on plantations in the Kuranda area. By the early 1900s, many of the local rainforest people found themselves living on the outskirts of the white settlements, unable to live the mobile lifestyle of hunting and fishing that they had become accustomed to for centuries.

To give you an idea of the plight of the locals in this region, consider that the Kuranda.org website explains much of what I just relayed above, then closes with this sentence: "The land around Kuranda has been home to the Djabugay Aboriginal people for more than 10,000 years and this vibrant Indigenous culture continues to thrive today."

Barron Falls, Kuranda

As I watched them perform dances in the streets of Kuranda for ten tourists at a time, I wondered if the Djabugay people might have a slightly different definition of what it means to thrive.

After grabbing a sandwich at an open-air café, I spent another hour meandering around town while simultaneously re-hydrating myself with expensive bottles of water. In the early afternoon I made my way to the Kuranda Railway station to catch my train back to Cairns. The station itself looked like something out of an old World War II movie and seemed out of place in the rainforest. A fair amount of stairs led down to a singular platform that was surrounded by lush green vegetation. It felt as though I had stepped back in time by about 75 years. Train conductors walked back and forth along the platform and tourists milled about, some eating ice cream that looked like it had revived them after a day of too much time spent on their feet. I wondered if Indiana Jones might suddenly come running along the platform, trailed by three angry Nazis in military garb. The place piqued my interest straight away and, for the first time all day, I had a mild spring in my step that lasted a solid three minutes or so. I plunked myself down on a surprisingly comfortable bench and waited for the "All Aboard" call.

When the train rolled out of Kuranda, my expectations of the ride back to Cairns were somewhat limited. The vegetation around us seemed too dense for the Kuranda Scenic Railway to be all that scenic, and I'd already had the bird's-eye view of the rainforest from the skyrail. But the train ride that followed was perhaps the most surprising part of my trip to Cairns and the Reef, aside from the Frenchie. I should preface my effusive praise with this bit of information: much of my excitement related to the interior comfort of the train cars. Each one was equipped with big red couch-size seats, beautiful wooden walls, and tinted windows that slid up to allow the outside air to flow in and made for easy photo taking. It was an ideal place to lie down and let the last of my hangover fade away.

Shortly after departing Kuranda, we made a sweeping left-hand turn that provided a perfect view of Barron Falls from the other side of the gorge. The train stopped for five minutes so passengers could hop out and take photos from an observation point, then continued on for ninety minutes through the rainforest. We crossed through open green fields and across bridges that must have been hell to construct in this harsh environment, then dove into pitch-black tunnels and emerged into the brightness of the day on the other side. It was delightful. When we finally rolled into the station in Cairns in late afternoon, I had a hankering for my pillow.

After waking from a short slumber and applying yet more aloe to my lumbar region, I rallied myself once more to meet my new friends from the previous day's reef adventure. They were eager more fun because they were twenty-three years old and had slept until noon, then lounged by a pool for five hours. Tonight's meeting place was a second-story watering hole called The Woolshed, not far from last night's Irish bar-turned exotic dance club.

For a quarter-century, The Woolshed has prided itself on a guaranteed party seven nights a week. When we *rocked up* around 10 p.m., most of the bar's patrons were dancing on top of large wooden picnic tables. If my experience is any indication, table dancing is as popular as snorkeling in Cairns. A throng of patrons was stacked two-deep at a large bar along one side. At the back was a small secondary bar where a spectacularly gorgeous blond woman of about thirty was slinging drinks. Her outfit used a limited amount of material and did an effective job displaying what I believe—but cannot say from personal experience—were two after-market breasts and an impressive abdominal section that had seen the inside of a gym once or twice. By ordering a beer from her, I ascertained that she was American. By spending a couple of minutes speaking to her about the accent we had in common, I ascertained that she was married to the guy standing at the end of the bar, who quickly came over to introduce himself as the manager of The Woolshed.

They were both very friendly and in town on some kind of working holiday. Their plan was to spend six months in Cairns before moving on to their next stop. Together they'd see Australia, presumably making enough cash along the way to break even. Seemed like a pretty cool thing to do as a young, married couple, presuming you are able to remain a married couple for the duration of such a trip.

I was running out of steam by 11 p.m., but hung around The Woolshed long enough to realize that the scene was as out of hand as it was the night before—minus the dance-off, the nakedness, and the poles. The Most Australian Guy of the Evening Award went to the bloke who courted the *lovelies* by walking up and down the picnic tables on his hands, while his feet walked along the ceiling. Yep, you read that correctly. He was doing a handstand with his feet pressed against the ceiling...and walking. If I wasn't so busy being confused, I'd have been impressed.

As the bar crowd emptied into the pedestrian mall outside about an hour later, I saw the barroom gymnast using his skills to impress more ladies on the sidewalk. This time, he was doing a handstand with a slice of pizza in his mouth. To increase the degree of difficulty and his score with the Russian judge, he began to eat the pizza *upwards* while doing a handstand. "Well, there's a first," I said to anyone who would listen. His display of arm and shoulder strength was surpassed only by his esophageal aptitude. Talk about a guy who had it all.

When he ceased being inverted I seized the opportunity to engage him in conversation. He asked where I was from, what I was doing in Cairns, and what I thought of his inverted pizza digestion skills.

"Very impressive," I said. "You are an innovator."

"Righto, mate," he said, not paying attention at all.

"So where are you from?" I asked.

"Townsville, mate," he replied, with what seemed like a heavy dose of pride. "It's about a four-hour drive south of here. Ever been, mate?"

"No. Can't say that I have," I said, anxious to hear more.

"Don't go," he said. "It's a shithole."

And then he took the last bite of his pizza and walked away. On his feet this time.

UNSOLICITED ADVICE: THE REEF

MUST DO:

Get to the **Great Barrier Reef**, obviously. I mean that's why you came here, right? If you don't consider yourself adventurous enough to **snorkel or scuba dive**, spend a few bucks and take a boat ride anyway. You might change your mind on the snorkeling part when you get there. I've never seen water and marine life like it. If boats aren't your thing, take a helicopter or plane ride over the reef... If boats, planes, and helicopters aren't your thing, how the hell are you ever going to get to Australia?... The **gondola ride above the Daintree Rainforest** was a very original experience... If you stay in Cairns, and you are (or look) young enough to blend in, do yourself a favor and experience the **backpacker nightlife**... Whatever you do, wear sunscreen and bring aloe.

UP TO YOU:

The **gondola ride** and the **Kuranda** railway ride back to town were good, but I didn't see the need to spend much time in Kuranda itself. Locals will tell you it's a tourist trap and you'll find yourself killing more time than you need... If you do the **Skyway to railway option**, see if you can arrange for less time between the end of the gondola ride and your departing train back to Cairns. You really don't need more than a couple of hours in Kuranda unless you love pouring over touristy items like necklaces and boomerangs.

NEXT TIME:

I'd do a day on the reef to start, then a day on the railway to let my sunburn calm down, then go back out on **the reef for a second day**, covered in SPF 4,000,000... Plenty of Aussies skip Cairns altogether and head to **Port Douglas**, about an hour up the road, where there are fewer backpackers and more upscale resorts and beaches. If drinking until the wee hours with backpackers is not your thing, Port Douglas offers a slower, less frat-party feel, so I'm told. I'd go there next time, since I'm more mature now. I think... I would also consume less Bundy rum and Cokes, maybe.

PART III:
BYRON BAY VIA THE GOLD COAST

Point Danger Lookout

Chapter 5: The Goldie and Beyond

The great thing about renting a car in Australia, I learned, is that you can drive it like you own it. Because for the rate they charge, you should. When I finally finished getting screwed over with add-on fees at the car rental desk of the Brisbane Airport, it was time to head south toward the Gold Coast and, eventually, to the beach hamlet of Byron Bay that evening. I'd flown in from Melbourne for a Christmas holiday that felt decidedly un-Christmasy to a guy who grew up in New England.

Brisbane, about a nine-hour drive north of Sydney, is Australia's third largest city and, like most Aussie metropolises, has a rapidly growing immigrant population. Something like 26 percent of the residents of Brisbane were born overseas and, as of 2016, 16 percent spoke a language other than English in their home. With more than 2.4 million inhabitants, there is a legitimate economy and all that fancy big-city stuff in Brissy, and it's known for its warm, sunny climate, except when it's stormy as hell.

The tourist mecca just south of Brisbane is called the Gold Coast, known in these parts as The Goldie. Orlando, Florida is the closest American comparison to this part of Southern Queensland, and not just because they call it "The theme park capital of Australia." Sea World, Movie World, Wet'n'Wild—there are endless things for tourists to spend their money on besides just their rental car. Since I had the entire afternoon to get to Byron Bay, about two hours south, I decided to hop off the highway and drive what should have been a helicopter but looked and felt an awful lot like a Nissan Sentra through the coastal enclaves of The Goldie.

After about forty-five minutes, I exited the highway at Brisbane Boulevard and headed east toward the coast. The road ended in a bustling town called Southport, which is home to Sea World, a giant mall, a number of marinas, and a rather scenic intracoastal waterway. Expensive boats passed back and forth carrying excessively tanned occupants while families who can't afford boats gathered in an area called the Broadwater Parklands and looked at the people passing by in the boats. It was about eighty degrees on December 21st and I couldn't spot a cloud.

In the water were huge inflatable slides and platforms that

looked like something out of a bad Japanese game show where people get hurt running on inflatable things covered in oil or Jell-O. Ropes stretched across the waterway cordoning off the Aquasplash Water Fun Park from the non-paying folk. Hundreds of kids who will grow up unaware of how strange it is to have their Christmas break in the middle of summer were flinging themselves on, over, and off of the man-made features. Basically, it looked like a blast and I wanted to be twelve years old again.

I'm nowhere near twelve years old so, instead of pulling off the shirt, jumping in with the kids, and then being put on some sort of neighborhood predator watch list, I drove up the road and found an uncrowded parking lot, which seemed like a good place to stop and sink my feet in the sand along the banks of the waterway. I spent a few minutes watching a handful of yachts pass by, then hopped back in the car and headed a few miles down the road into Surfer's Paradise, the heart of the Gold Coast.

The Goldie is a stretch of overbuilt coastline that consists mainly of high-rise hotels with balconies overlooking the ocean. Surfer's Paradise is the center of all that. Today, the roads were packed, as I assumed they would be in the days leading up to Chrissy, as Aussies call it because they abbreviate everything. For me, Surfer's Paradise, or Surfer's (see...abbreviated), is one of those places that looks and sounds a lot cooler on TV or in magazines than it actually is in person. It's not its fault, really. Certain places get built up by years of banter, travel brochures, or airline magazines. The name Surfer's Paradise also sets the bar quite high. I mean, a paradise for surfers? How bad could it be?

To be clear, I'm not saying it's "bad." It just wasn't my speed. For many who travel through Australia in their twenties, Surfer's is a highlight, and I can see why. For me, seeing Surfer's for the first time reminded me of my first trip to Venice Beach near Los Angeles. As a native East Coaster, I expected it to look just as it had in the movies and in that flashy intro to the *Tonight Show with Jay Leno*. Years later, I felt an immense letdown on my first stroll around Venice Beach. The most memorable part of the day was when a six-foot-eight African-American man with an enormous Afro roller-skated past me wearing MC Hammer pants with a five-foot-long boa constrictor draped over his shoulders.

Surfer's Paradise wasn't as startling as Venice Beach in real life, but it did afford the rare opportunity to see more tank tops and tattoos than you do in an NBA game. Still, if you come for the fun and the sun, there are plenty of both. This is why Aussie *schoolies* (high school-aged kids) jet away here on their spring break graduation trips to let their hair down after twelve incredibly arduous years of, you know, school. Not medical school or even university-level schooling, mind you, just high school. Think: Daytona Beach, but lower the drinking age by three years. Depending on your personality, that notion will either scare you or make you wish you went to high school in Australia.

How wild does spring break get on the Gold Cost? Based on news reports I watched, many spring breakers had taken up a curious sport called "balcony hopping," which is just what it sounds like: a very bad idea. It consists of drunken teenagers climbing over the balcony railings of their high-rise hotel room and then hopping across and over a railing onto the next balcony, which would be a bad sport to find out you are not very good at the first time you played. If your room and the connecting hallways is, say, on fire and a guy carrying a hose and wearing tall boots and a funny helmet has instructed you to jump to the next balcony so that he and his mate in the big red truck with the ladder down below can save you, by all means, jump! Doing it after ten Carlton drafts and seven Jägermeister shots ups the degree of difficulty a tad. According to reports I watched and read, this practice has been something of an epidemic at certain periods of time, resulting in a number of teenagers plummeting to their deaths.

I settled for a less risky afternoon agenda and, after a lengthy effort to secure a *car park,* went in search of a late lunch in Surfer's. Eventually, I bellied up to the bar at an Irish pub called Kitty O'Shea's on the main pedestrian mall, just across from the beach. A Northern Irish lass named Leann was kind enough to brew me a batch of iced tea while I eagerly awaited the arrival of the first honest-to-God steak and cheese sandwich I'd seen in months.

Thirty minutes later, as I finished my meal, two tall, attractive blond women in their early twenties walked behind the bar, broke out four or five bottles of Southern Comfort, and set up shop within arm's reach of me, not that I was calculating my reach. They were "promo girls" dressed in skin-tight red dresses with Southern Comfort logos on them. As luck would have it, they were in need of a taste-tester to determine whether they were mixing the correct amount of Coke with the Southern Comfort. If you've ever wondered when the phrase "90 percent of life is just showing up" applies, this would be just such a time.

Gold Coast

In order to assist, I agreed to stay a few extra minutes and lend my experienced pallet to the task at hand. They started by pouring me a Dixie cup-sized drink of mostly Coke, which I kindly advised them needed more Southern Comfort. Then they poured me another small drink...and then another...before we arrived collectively at the most accurate SoCo to Coke ratio for the rest of the bar patrons to safely imbibe for the remainder of the afternoon. Comforted by the knowledge that I had done my job, a broad grin washed across my face. As omens go, the trip seemed to be off to a promising start. After completing the SoCo Taste Test, it was time to hit the road while I was still within the legal limit. I'm referring to my alcohol intake, not their ages, but I feel obliged to share with you that no laws were broken in either case.

Heading south, the road took me through small but bustling Gold Coast beach suburbs like Burleigh Heads, known to surfers the world over. From there, the coastal towns became less commercial, almost quaint. Coolangatta, at the southern point of the Gold Coast and the last town in Queensland, is as gorgeous a spot as you'll ever see named after a shipwrecked schooner from 1846. Across the state line into New South Wales is Tweed Heads, which shares its economy with Coolangatta, according to the worldwide interweb research I just did.

Burleigh Heads

78

After driving around in Coolangatta, I pointed my vehicle straight up a steep hill toward the beach and was glad I did. At the top was the Point Danger Lighthouse, which I assumed meant I was at Point Danger. *Be careful*, I thought. The dots were all connecting now with the danger and the shipwreck and stuff. The view looking down from the lighthouse toward Flagstaff Beach to the south is likely on postcards in the local gift shops. Just beautiful. The beaches around this area are home to some of the greatest surf breaks in Australia, leading me to believe that this may be the actual paradise for surfers, not Surfer's Paradise up the road. The water was predictably dotted with surfers as the last few hours of sunlight crept over from the inland mountain ranges to the west. In the distance, beyond a rock jetty, the Tweed River emptied into the Coral Sea and a weathered fishing boat chugged its way out to the open ocean. I sat down on one of the surfboard-shaped park benches, breathed in the ocean air, and took it all in.

Then a dive-bombing seagull nearly shit on my head. It was time to finish the drive to Byron Bay.

Byron Bay sunset

Chapter 6: Byron Bay and the Art of Chillaxing

At the bottom of the stairs that take you into Byron Bay's famed Beach Hotel bar was a Taekwondo-fighting, hot dog street vendor. I know he was a Taekwondo fighter because he told me. I know he was a hot dog vendor because he was cooking and selling hot dogs.

"Hi. How are you?" I said to the wiener man in a friendly tone on my way out of the bar at 11 p.m.

"Hey!" he replied, somewhat angrily.

"Those smell good," I said, and ordered one. "So how long have you been doing this? I bet you have some stories hanging outside this place."

"Seven years. Why?" he snapped back.

"Well, I've never been here before," I replied. "Just curious if you might be able to tell me how the place has changed over the years."

I had guessed—erroneously, it seemed—that a street vendor in Byron Bay might be the friendly salesman type you see hawking sausages outside ballparks in many American cities. I had surmised incorrectly.

"This is my friend's business," he said. "I just operate it for him. I have three jobs and I sleep three hours a night."

"Three hours? That must be exhausting," I said, trying to stroke his ego.

"You don't need more than three hours a night, mate," he told me. "The dumbest thing man has ever done is put a fucking watch on his arm."

"No, actually, the dumbest thing a man has ever done is engage in conversation with a hot dog vendor in Byron Bay," is what I wanted to say, but thought better of. Before I could ask more about his philosophy on time, he continued.

"I started taking Taekwondo to protect myself," he told me for no reason that I could decipher.

"Ahh, how's that going for you?" I asked. "The Taekwondo?"

"People fight like the place they are from," he said, shifting the conversation again. "Middle Europeans don't really want to fight."

Uh-huh.

"Russians want to cut your head off," he added.

Okay then.

"And North Koreans want to kill you!"

"Is that right?" I asked, hoping he would continue. He wouldn't, and ended the conversation by handing me my hot dog and making it clear I could now leave.

With that, I adjourned toward another live music venue, munching on my very average hot dog while keeping an eye out for angry North Koreans.

My conversation with the Oscar Meyer man was hardly indicative of the personal encounters I had in Byron Bay over the course of four summer nights at Christmas. But, in addition to being a small piece of paradise, Byron Bay is home to an eclectic mix of people. Many of them are temporary visitors: backpackers heading up or down the coast, surfers paddling into some of the best breaks in Australia, or families and couples from Sydney, Melbourne, and Brisbane looking to slow their lives down for a few days. Some are Taekwondo-fighting hot dog vendors who don't believe in wearing a timepiece.

This will sound ridiculous, but visiting Byron Bay for a few days over Christmas with no real plan except to relax and enjoy the perfect weather was a somewhat scary notion. I have found it difficult to sit still since I could walk (I never crawled, my mother says). Beach vacations have always seemed like a bit of a waste of time. I could be, you know, off doing something. Still, I had heard good things from everyone I'd asked, so I took the advice of the roadside sign that welcomes visitors to Byron Bay: "Cheer Up. Slow Down. Chill Out."

Cape Byron, which juts into the ocean next to Byron Bay, is the easternmost point of Australia. A picturesque lighthouse tops the point, and scenic walking trails crisscross beneath it, but no one really talks much about that. I think that's because there are really three things Aussies tell you about when you mention that you're heading to Byron: the laid-back lifestyle, the unbelievably diverse mix of people, and the spectacular beach.

Although checking into a hotel in Byron Bay is basically like taking over Jimmy Buffett's life for a few days, don't get the impression that a trip there has to be all about sitting on your ass in the sand. There are waves to surf, shipwrecks to dive, trails to hike, kayaks to rent and paddle, and restaurants to eat at and bars to drink at. Byron Bay's closest major city is Brisbane, which is two hours up the road if you don't stop and taste test Southern Comfort on the way, but it's also about nine hours by car from Sydney to the south. Europeans first came to Byron in 1770, but Aboriginal people have been coming here for thousands of years. (Sounds familiar, huh?) Throughout much of its history Byron was a poor working town, first revolving around a timber industry and later dairy, specifically butter. And who doesn't like butter?

Following the closing of the factories in the 1950s and '60s—maybe not everyone likes butter—long-boarders (that's surfers on longboards) flocked to Byron Bay, which gave the area its start as a tourist destination. When Nimbin, a hippie settlement about ninety minutes west into the mountains, hosted the Woodstock-style Aquarius Festival in 1973, an alternative crowd began flocking to the area as well. Today, Byron hosts several festivals each year, the biggest of those being the Byron Bay Blues Fest, which attracts major global artists and throngs of music fans over five days each April.

The hippie and surf cultures may have survived through the years, but it's evident that the money came, too. On the outskirts of town, expensive-looking homes overlook the ocean and, though there are a number of dive bars in town with talented live music acts, there are also enough high-end dining alternatives to please the most discriminating pallet. You expect to find cultures and classes meshing in large cities, but I haven't seen many small towns where people from such different backgrounds and economic classes mix so obviously on a day-to-day basis like they do in Byron Bay. Turns out, hippies like the beach and former hippies turned wealthy ex-beach bums still love to surf.

After a relatively low-key Saturday night, I awoke Sunday morning to a perfect ocean breeze gusting through the screens of the balcony door and windows of my hotel room. The sun was shining and the day was on its way to a summery, but not sweltering 85 degrees F. I grabbed a newspaper and made for a local café called The Rocks at Aquarius, which was attached to a backpacker hostel. Nothing feels quite like vacation to me than eating an omelet while reading the news-

Byron Beach

paper under a sun-drenched umbrella. It really is the little things.

Feeling nourished, I hit the town to observe what weekend life was like. My first impression was that Byron Bay is what you picture Australia to be if you've never set foot on the island. Shirtless skateboarders cruise the streets. Young, tanned international students stroll to and from the beach in bikini tops and jean shorts (women) or tank tops and board shorts (men). Surfers sit in coffee shops or open-air bars and chat about where they paddled out earlier that morning. It was obvious straight away that Byron Bay is a place that makes going back to your real life very difficult.

Around noon I headed down to the main beach that abuts the town. The water was refreshing but not cold, and moderate shore-breaking waves that were perfect for bodysurfing kept visitors happy. The beach itself was perfect. It was about fifty yards deep from the water's edge and it had sand, water, and sun. All the things you need from a beach. To the east (I think) on my right was the lighthouse. From there, the bay curled in and stretched for what seemed like miles to the west and north.

There were plenty of transient twenty-somethings, but also some slightly more mysterious older folks. Not far from my beach towel, a tall thirty-something man in tiny Speedos meditated and then began to contort himself in and out of yoga poses. In Byron you are not considered "weird" for doing things like this. Or you are, but no one cares. Behind me, a fifty-something gentleman with a metal detector, headphones, white socks, sandals, and most assuredly no sex life walked within a couple feet of where I was lying with his metal detector. It was as if he thought I was an unburied treasure lying in the sand waiting to be discovered.

"Yes, sir, your metal detector is going off because you put it over my cell phone, which is inside that bright orange backpack."

I thought I was on candid camera and was becoming annoyed before I considered that perhaps he was just trying to find the keys to his mother's basement, where he must live. The loitering bloke from *Revenge of the Nerds* was my cue to leave. Slightly sunburned and fully parched at 3 p.m., I headed for the nearby Beach Hotel, which has a huge outdoor patio that looked across the street to the main beach, as well as another covered open-air space with a stage. I used the beachside entrance to avoid being on the receiving end of a Taekwondo-style ass-kicking and landed some prime real estate (and a barstool) at the bar, along with a cold, refreshing beer. Because I was planning to spend the afternoon sitting on the beach, I'd left my wallet in my room and brought just $50 cash. When a fantastic band called Sticky Fingers, with a dynamic lead singer named Lisa Hunt, took the stage and blew the room away, I suddenly had a problem: How could I make my $50 last the afternoon? The answer, which I came up with all by myself, was easy: Don't eat.

As Ms. Hunt channeled her inner Aretha Franklin, I proceeded to mount a strategic, but most enjoyable $50 assault on the bar. By 6 p.m., the place was packed, the crowd was going crazy, the band was on fire, and I was relaxed, let's say. What could be better than a good daytime party...by the beach...in Australia...with live music...and a whopping $50 burning a hole in your pocket? Well, $60, of course. Or even $70. Seventy dollars would have been perfect, actually.

I woke up the next morning glad that I had only brought $50 to the beach and, after only one day in the sand, was already feeling slightly antsy. So, after another stellar breakfast under an umbrella, I decided I ought to get a little value from the Nissan. Like a lunatic, I drove away from the coastline up into the mountains above Byron to the west.

My destination was a place called Minyon Falls in Nightcap National Park, which seems like the perfect name for a national park in Australia. The drive was as adventurous as I hoped, and then some. A short detour a few miles out of Byron put me temporarily well off track, though it was hard to get frustrated amidst the scenery of the rolling green hills. After a few minutes I was back on my way, winding up roads that passed through farmland, dense forest, and, eventually, across dried-out creekbeds. The roadside water depth sign at the creekbed crossing reached to roughly double the height of my car. I was glad it was the dry season.

At some point, the road turned from pavement to a rougher mixture of concrete remnants and dirt that must have been cobbled together two decades earlier and given little attention ever again. There was enough room for one and a half cars, but not two. I bounced along slowly, certain that the extortionate rental agreement would in no way cover any real harm to the Nissan.

It was around this time that a large tie-dye colored bus careened around the corner at approximately 50 mph. The driver showed no signs of slowing down. With my choices limited, or at least obvious, I veered to the left edge of the road as far as I could without my wheels rolling off the shoulder and into the woods. As he sailed by, I caught a glimpse of the driver's face, which displayed neither remorse nor fear. Instead, he was grinning from ear to ear. The bus itself was a sight to behold. It looked like a hippie commune on wheels, straight out of Woodstock and the summer of '69. Above the windshield, the word "Nimbin" was permanently painted in letters that could not be amended for travel to other destinations. This bus went to one place and one place only. It was adorned with peace signs and flowers of every color. I think it said "Be Happy" across the back or side, but I can't be sure on account of the fact that a trail of dust and the scenes of my life passing by obscured much of my view.

Nimbin, where the bus was coming from, is a small village about forty miles west of Byron that is known for its willingness to allow/encourage the open use of recreational drugs. It gets its name from the indigenous Widgibal people whose Dreamtime (the term for Aboriginal spiritual beliefs and existence) refers to the Nimbinjee spirit people protecting the surrounding area. Many call Nimbin the drug capital of Australia and, if everything I've heard is true, second place is a long way off.

This all started in 1973 when a group of hippies, university students, and proponents of what politicians might call an "alternative lifestyle" gathered in Nimbin for the Aquarius Festival. When the festival ended, many attendees stuck around and formed communes. Over the years, Nimbin has attracted artists, writers, poets, students, and various other people who love to smoke weed. Today, while growing, selling, or possessing marijuana is illegal in New South Wales, it is openly sold and used in Nimbin. If you are wondering how a place like this exists, we're on the same page.

The best Nimbin story I have ever heard was from a former American co-worker and friend of mine named Scott Goryl, who spent a semester studying in Sydney in the early 2000s. On one of the weekend getaways Scott and his classmates often took to Byron Bay, they got wind of something called The Hemp Olympix taking place in Nimbin and decided it was not to be missed. They hopped aboard something called Jim's Alternative Tour from Byron to get there. The Hemp Olympix is exactly what it sounds like if it sounds like a bunch of stoners pretending to be Olympians taking part in drug-themed "sporting" events while high.

One of the best things you can do with regard to researching Nimbin is take a gander at this tribute to sport on YouTube. The Hemp Olympix, with an X, take place during the Nimbin Mardi Gras, which has its own website, by the way. The Olympiad boasts events like Joint Rolling, the Bong Throw and Yell, the Growers' Ironperson competition, and the Tug O' Drug Peace, a tug-o-war that used to pit stoners against the local police force. Though, according to the Nimbin Mardi Gras website, the police became too embarrassed losing to "the stoners" each year and did not participate in recent years. The Growers Ironperson event is a triathlon of sorts. It involves competitors carrying a forty-five-pound bag of fertilizer, then a bucket of water and then a crop of cannabis, obviously in a nod to the local marijuana growers of the region.

As one might expect of such a prestigious sporting competition, there are categories to consider and heats to get through in order to progress to the finals. The joint rolling competitions, for example, feature several sub-categories; it would be an injustice not to share them with you here. All of these descriptions are taken from nimbinmardigras.com. I couldn't make them up. The Speed Roll—which sounds like an event made for the Jamaican 4x100 relay team—requires competitors to roll a standard three-paper joint as fast as they can. "Joints must include a cardboard filter or will be judged incomplete," the website says. In the Artistic Roll competition, participants must "roll the most beautiful joint within 10 minutes with as many papers as you like." For the Roll in the Dark event, "athletes are blindfolded." And, yes, they refer to them as athletes. Finally, the Adverse Conditions Roll is "dependent on weather conditions on the day and the judges' creativity."

When I asked Scott for some insight into his day at the Hemp Olympix, he went searching for his Aussie travel journal in the garage, but found the excerpt from this day to be "woefully lacking details or any useful insights," which was not surprising. He didn't mention if it was also Dorito stained and stored away with his bronze medal in Speed Rolling.

"From what I recall, there were stunningly impressive achievements on display, but an event on that scale organized by people with very short-term memory lends itself to a fair bit of disorganization, as you might imagine," Scott told me. "And a lot of snack breaks! The Bong Throw and the Ironman event seemed exceedingly dangerous to participants and bystanders alike. My most vivid memory was sitting on a grassy hill overlooking a joint-rolling contest based on artistic and creative merit. The winner, if you can believe it, rolled a rocket launch pad the size of a shoebox. I'm not sure exactly what one is supposed to do with a structure like that, but along with the rest of the stunned crowd I applauded the effort nonetheless."

Modern-day Nimbin has a reputation for more hardcore drugs than was the case years earlier. I was told that a stroll down the main street in Nimbin today would reveal drugged-out heroin addicts with needles in their arms. Investigative-minded though I may be, that wasn't how I wanted to spend a day of my time in and around Byron Bay. I've seen *Trainspotting*. Instead, the plan was to hike around a majestic waterfall, but as the great American philosopher Mike Tyson once said, "Everyone has a plan until they get punched in the face."

When the Nimbin bus was well out of sight and I had gathered my two left tires from the shoulder of the road, I started up the hill again with renewed resolve. A few kilometers up the road, I entered Nightcap National Park and the road became more of a dirt/rock path for cars. I bounced on through the thickly wooded landscape past the first small parking area to a turnout near the top of the falls.

When I strolled over to the lookout for my first glimpse, nothing was falling. The normally 600-foot Minyon Falls was more like the Minyon Trickle. It looked like someone had forgotten to completely turn off the kitchen faucet. I lost a game of chicken to a stoner bus driver for this? I focused on the fact that the view was still impressive. Fanning out to my right was a sheer cliff—or *escarpment,* in Aussie, if you want to make it sound more dangerous—where water would normally cascade onto the rocks below. At least the cloudless day meant I could see almost all the way to Byron to the east. After spotting a few people lounging in a pool at the base of the cliff, I decided this was where I needed to be.

I snapped a few photos, jumped back into the car, drove to the lower car park, and began the two-kilometer hike on the Minyon Grass trail to the base of the falls. As with any bush walk in Australia, there is a healthy level of trepidation involved because you never know what you might see/die from. I wasn't sure how many poisonous spiders or snakes inhabited the area so I followed within earshot of a young couple doing the walk in sandals, bathing suits, and towels. This couple and the people I had seen from above seemed to be the only other humans inside the park. Presumably, everyone else was enjoying the live band at the Beach Hotel Bar in Byron at the moment, which is where I should have been.

The walk descended gradually into the forest for the first 500 meters and then leveled out until I had to scramble over some rocks to a small pool at the base of the "falls." It was refreshing after the humid walk. The dark gray wall of the cliff stretched impressively upward to the observation point above. I hung around for a few minutes to cool off, but without the falls it was less of an experience than I had envisioned. Recognizing that I was playing third wheel to the happy couple, I made myself scarce and headed back toward the car, closely eyeing the leaves for any sign of movement that I was certain not to see anyway. The noise of a rare-sounding bird spooked me a couple of times, but otherwise the walk was without incident, and the drive back was pleasurable thanks to a late afternoon glow that highlighted every bit of color from the surrounding hills.

I made it to Byron Bay in time to catch the last thirty minutes of daylight on the beach and a memorable sunset. At the east end of the beach, the lighthouse was flashing as its light revolved. To the west, the last few rays of sunlight crept over the inland mountains, silhouetting them perfectly against a light blue sky. There was no place else to be.

That evening I treated myself to a steak on a second-floor balcony restaurant overlooking the main street, then chased live music around town. First stop was the Northern Hotel, which also had a second-story balcony straight out of an old western film. Next was the Railway Friendly Bar, known simply as The Rails. Both places had solid live music by local and traveling artists. The Rails is an open-air establishment housed in an old railway station that claims to have had live music seven nights a week for thirty years. It's a unique place in that it's part hippie hangout and part biker bar. Being that it's in Byron, the bikers all seemed pretty chill. I didn't see any Hells Angels.

I retired to my hotel room and had one last cold beer on the balcony. A perfect ocean breeze cooled the night air as I thumbed through a Byron Bay Visitor's Guide pamphlet and pondered what I would do tomorrow. When I looked up, a spider big enough to carry a jockey inched up the wall across from me. I figured this meant I was four or five feet from being *brown bread* (dead), so I stood up, stepped in from the balcony, closed the sliding glass door behind me, and went to bed.

Cape Byron Lighthouse

Chapter 7: Byron. Why Leave?

When I strolled up to the entrance of the famed Byron Bay Hot Bread Kitchen the next morning, there was a twenty-five-year-old bicycle parked outside with a sack of fresh oranges in its rear basket and a small dog in a second basket on the handlebars. It was sunny and 75 degrees on Christmas Eve morning and the terrier seemed as relaxed as any human in town.

Located close to the Great Northern Hotel, where I'd listened to tunes the night before, the Byron Bay Bread Company claims to "only sell what we'd eat ourselves." A family owned and operated business that has been serving its goods here since 1982, the Bread Company "employs a team of 36 local people." The food was outstanding and probably why they could afford to stay open twenty-three hours per day. Also—and I'm hypothesizing here—being open twenty-three hours a day in Byron means you can cater to young backpackers who congregate here in the wee hours when the munchies set in.

After a relaxing hour on my hotel balcony reading the local newspaper with my tasty cakes and a morning tea, I mustered the energy to head out for a coastal walk toward the picturesque lighthouse I'd been eying for a couple of days at the eastern tip of Byron. I started along the beach with the idea of linking up with the Cape Byron Walking Track. Within a few minutes, I was sweating like a whore in church and my sunscreen was running down my face, but it was a spectacular summer day.

Along the beach, families took cover from the sun under overhanging trees a few feet from the sea. As I neared the end of the beach, the tide was rising and a small, knee-deep channel began to form between the sand and some stairs that ascended to something called the Fisherman's Lookout. I waited for a lull, darted across a few semi-submerged rocks to keep my *runners* dry, then climbed the steps to the point. Fisherman's Lookout offered a bird's-eye view of a full lineup of surfers as they bobbed in the sunlight waiting for waves. They were forced to take turns with dolphins who would appear out of nowhere to ride a wave toward shore for a hundred meters and then quickly head back out to sea before rejoining the lineup and grabbing another wave.

I lingered at Fisherman's Lookout long enough to slow the perspiration on my brow, then retreated across the water and joined the paved walking track that was more stairs than path. I followed the stairs uphill longer than I would have liked and then around to the easternmost point of Australia. The Cape Byron Lighthouse lorded over, and the trail had various lookout spots along the way to pause and gaze at the sea. From September to November, you might even see whales off the coast as they return south for the warmer months.

Between the lighthouse and me were a few hundred more steep steps, which were starting to become annoying. At long last, I reached the beacon of the night, which was decked in a fresh coat of bright white paint and sharp blue trim around its base. It didn't seem as tall (only seventy-four feet) as it looked from far away. Built in 1900 and 1901, the lighthouse was operated by a lighthouse keeper until 1989, though (we can safely assume) not by the same guy the entire time. Today it's automated by a team of IT guys working out of a call center in India. Not really, but it is automated. At night, the famous revolving light shines brightly over Byron and draws roughly a half-million visitors to the lighthouse each year. The original light, interestingly enough, was a kerosene burner.

You can visit the Maritime Museum in the former Lighthouse Keeper's office from 10 a.m. to 4 p.m., or you can go looking for a drink of water like I did. Once hydrated, I strolled through the parking lot—yep, it seems I could have driven up there, but what fun would that have been when you love stairs?—and debated my next move.

The coastline far below stretched around the point and then continued south in the form of a lengthy-looking beach that was pretty well deserted. The quick route back was down the driveway toward a cold refreshment and some lunch in town. That seemed too easy, so I veered off the road and down into the trees along a dusty trail that I figured would eventually take me to the beach. After five minutes of ambling along through the trees congratulating myself for pushing on in the direction of additional adventure, a sudden movement to my right halted me in my tracks and scared the shit out of me. "What the hell is that?" I asked out loud to no one else. A five-foot-long lizard of some kind was staring me down from six feet away under the trees. Its tongue slithered in and out of its mouth as we locked eyes. Is it going to attack? Is it afraid of me?

Should I run for my life? The reptile seemed harmless enough, but this is Australia, where they probably have killer butterflies.

The creature, I later learned, was a goanna, a species of monitor lizard that is protected in Australia. They can grow up to eight feet in length with long tails, sharp teeth, and claws, all of which I am glad I was unaware of at the time. They are weary of humans and generally scamper away. Those last two facts would have been great to know before we locked eyes.

I shuffled away somewhat carefully and quickly before my mind started racing. If there was a lizard, surely there could be other reptiles here. Like a big, super-poisonous King Brown snake that might bite me and kill me just a few hundred meters from the help of a tourist-infested parking lot above.

The surf lineup in Byron includes surfers and dolphins

95

I slowed down, told myself to relax, and even enjoyed a few more encounters with the seemingly unimpressed goanna population of Byron Bay, as well as a strange abundance of Brush Turkeys in the area. The beach ahead of me is called Tallows Beach, and it was as deserted as it seemed from above, possibly because everything I read about it said it was not patrolled. Either that or the goannas had scared the tourists back in the direction of their cars. The beach stretches roughly six kilometers to the south and is known for great bird watching. I'd seen enough wildlife so, after a few minutes, I high-tailed it back along the road in time for a late lunch and to prep for Santa's arrival that night.

Christmas Eve in Byron Bay, which happened to be my last night there, was spent bouncing from what had now become a few of my "old haunts"—The Rails, the Beach Hotel, and even a newer, trendier spot whose name I didn't catch because it was the last place I went to. It was packed with a mix of visitors on their Christmas holiday and young people who had grown up in Byron Bay and were returning for family time. While waiting for a drink at the crowded bar, a twenty-something next to me struck up a conversation. He had grown up in Byron Bay and was now living in the south of France working on super yachts in some sort of electrician/boat mechanic expert capacity. Whatever he did, it seemed as though he had life pretty well *sorted* at the moment. He advised me to take a drive through some of the neighborhoods just outside of town on my way back north to Brisbane in the morning.

On Christmas morning I hit the Bread Company to give myself one last tasty cake, hopped in the car, and then did as the young world-beater instructed, meandering through the residential streets of Byron Bay for fifteen to twenty minutes as crumbs fell into my lap. The leafy boulevards were lined with large, modern houses that sat on generous pieces of property. For whatever reason, I didn't expect to see such newness. It was clear—in my mind anyway—that the Byron Bay surf bums of the '70s had grown up, landed big jobs in Sydney, and then bought swanky second homes in Byron, completing the final stage of the "Australian Dream" or something like that. Or maybe the longtime locals had just been nudged out of town by later-arriving out-of-towners.

I was giving serious thought to how all of this often plays out; how places like Byron or nearly every ski town I've ever been to slowly morph into shiny places that the people who started coming to them in the first place don't really want to be in anymore. Just as I was getting philosophical, I spotted a gathering of people about 300 meters up the road. Creeping closer, I saw about a dozen pale asses jogging down the road. They were wearing red Santa stocking caps and other red and green holiday garb in the form of socks, caps, and shirts. Everything except shorts or pants. More mostly naked individuals were standing in front of a backpacker hostel cheering and waving at the only car in the neighborhood, me.

As I rolled by, they serenaded me with "Happy Christmas" shouts. I waved back and then spent the next few minutes laughing to myself as I jumped back on the highway toward real life. Spending the Christmas holiday on a solo mission to Byron hadn't been as gratifying as opening Christmas gifts as a kid with Mom, Dad, and my brother, but when I called them a few miles up the road to wish them a Merry Christmas Eve back in snowy Boston, I had my own (Charles) Dickens tale to share, if you will pardon the pun. My father laughed heartily and my mother giggled her giggle. They were, of course, a little disappointed their eldest son wasn't there to share a few stories and devour Mom's fantastic Christmas Eve chicken wings. I told them what I had experienced, the general feel of the place, and how it seemed like perhaps I was visiting it as it was changing personalities.

"If a bunch of twenty-somethings think it's an acceptable place to go streaking down the street on Christmas morning, it sounds like maybe it hasn't changed that much," my father pointed out. And he was right, as usual.

UNSOLICITED ADVICE: BYRON BAY

MUST DO:

Now that I'm back, I find my mind wandering back to the late afternoon moments I experienced in **Coolangatta** and **Burleigh Heads**, south of Surfer's Paradise. If I had it to do over, I'd spend a day there, or more... Once in Byron, walk at least out to the point at the eastern end of the beach. If you adore stairs, or at least can tolerate them, walk up to **the lighthouse** and check it off the list. Or just drive to it... **The Beach Hotel in Byron** on a Saturday afternoon, with live music blowing the roof off the joint and a summer breeze blowing through, was a quintessential Aussie experience. Don't miss it. And bring more than $50.

UP TO YOU:

Surfer's Paradise and the **Gold Coast** was not my favorite part of the trip, as you might have gleaned, but if youthful beachside partying is your thing, the Goldie is your spot. Some people love it and I'd imagine it's much more fun when you're in a group of at least two... There's a reason I gave you my friend's account of **Nimbin**. The near-death experience with the hippie-loaded bus was as close as I got, and that was close enough... The hike to the **Minyon Falls**/Trickles was unspectacular at this time of year; I should have gone **surfing**.

NEXT TIME:

I wish I had planned a day in **Brisbane**. I've heard good things about Bris-vegas, as some people like to call it, and one less day in Byron would not have been a dealbreaker... Someday, I will go to Brisbane and experience the **State of Origin** rugby series between New South Wales and Queensland. Each year they face off in the three-game series and the atmosphere for the matches in Brisbane is the stuff of legend.

PART IV:
THE TOP END

Darwin waterfront

Chapter 8: Darwin

I should have known that Darwin would be a little different when, on the twenty-minute taxi ride from the airport to my hotel, I spotted a quaint Aboriginal Art Store in a small strip mall. *Isn't that cool?* I thought, like a tourist would. *This is legit Australia.* And then my eyes panned to the storefront next to it: "SEXYLAND. Australia's largest range of FUN products for adults!"

I didn't know it at the time, but in a way this side-by-side existence of the Aboriginal art store and Sexyland was the perfect microcosm for what they call the Top End: 50,000 years of civilization existing side-by-side with the finest representation of modern society.

The Northern Territory (NT) of Australia, of which Darwin is the capital, is exactly that—a territory. The locals just call it The Tear-a-tree. This makes sense because the only other Tear-a-tree is the Australian Capital Tear-a-tree (ACT), where the federal government "operates" from in Canberra. The rest of Australia is made up of six other chunks of land worthy of being called "states." Lucky them.

At more than 500,000 square miles, the NT is bigger than South Africa and six times larger than the United Kingdom. Behind Western Australia and Queensland, that still only makes it the country's third largest state/territory. Much of that land is uninhabited desert in the southern part of the Territory, where temperatures can climb over 110 degrees F during the summer months and droughts can last years. That might explain why, despite accounting for 17.5 percent of Australia's land area, the NT had a population of only about 250,000 people in 2019, roughly 1 percent of Australia's total population. With 30 percent of the people who live in the Northern Territory being of Aboriginal descent, The Tear-a-tree has the largest Indigenous population of any state in Australia. To put it bluntly, the landscape is not the only thing that changes when you go from a place like Melbourne or Sydney to Darwin; the facial complexions do as well.

The Indigenous population of the NT includes people of Aboriginal descent and Torres Strait Islanders from the group of small islands between Australia and New Guinea. Beyond that, Darwin itself has more than sixty different ethnic cultures represented among its population, including a large percentage of Greek, Mandarin,

Filipino, and Thai. As of 2016, 30 percent of the city's residents spoke a language other than English at home. And some of the white folks who speak English up here might actually be even harder to understand.

The flight to Darwin from Melbourne takes four and a half hours. It's worth making the journey during the day if only to get a bird's-eye view of the Aussie interior, which could be mistaken for Mars, though I have never flown over the latter. Red clay stretches as far as the eye can see before jagged, toasty-looking rocks jut up sharply from the earth. Much of it looks very much like human feet have not seen it for decades, though feet have, in fact, walked upon it for thousands of years. As you approach Darwin, the red clay-colored earth gives way to thick green wetlands, almost like the mangroves you might see dotting the waterways of Florida.

Darwin, which sits on the Timor Sea in the tropics, is actually closer to Asia than it is to any other Australian capital city. To drive to it from any place you might have actually heard of takes more than a day, and it's a good bet you won't see much on the way. Alice Springs, a central desert town to the south that people in Darwin seem to speak of as some sort of neighbor down the street, is fifteen short hours by car. That's not a neighbor you can call for a cup of flour or a spare egg when you're making a birthday cake for little Jonno. Still, if you ask someone in Darwin where they grew up, they might say something like, "Yeah, just down the road in Darwin, mate," while pointing over their shoulder with their thumb. It would be like someone in New York saying they grew up in South Carolina but acting like it was New Jersey.

The Top End, as the larger land area that encompasses Darwin is known, can feature downright abusive weather. The summer wet season delivers monsoon-type rains and cyclones that would merit the whole scary-graphic-with-a-dramatic-name thing on CNN. Like "Firestorm 2018" or "Arctic Blast 2017." According to a quick web search, Darwin's wet season rainfall totals look like this: December, ten inches; January, fifteen inches; February, twelve inches. Three feet of rain in three months! Basically, Darwin makes Seattle seem like the Sahara.

During the wet season, humidity is in the 70 percent range. If you're not a meteorologist, the average summer afternoon humidity in Florida is 63. During my visit in autumn, temps were in the 90-degree Fahrenheit range and Darwin's harbor beaches were empty.

I mean not a single soul was on them. Why is that, you might be asking? Well, because crocodiles and box jellyfish visit those waters, and both of them can kill you. Hold on, I'll go get the real estate listings for you.

Before you put down what you're reading, turn to your spouse, and say, "Honey, maybe we'll skip the Top End on the Griswold family vacation to the land down under," there is a bright side. For one, the winter dry season is warm and sunny. There. That sounds better, right? Secondly, the Top End is home to some of the richest natural beauty in Australia. Kakadu National Park, Litchfield National Park, and Katherine Gorge draw tourists from around the globe despite the considerable effort it takes to get to them. Even better, many of the scenes from the Australian Outback in the *Crocodile Dundee* flicks were filmed right here in the Top End. (If you're Australian, I fully understand that you just cringed at my use of that movie as proof of this area being worthy of a visit. I apologize.) If you're getting the impression that the Northern Territory is Australia's last frontier, that's a fair impression. And the residents appear to revel in that notion quite convincingly. Make no mistake: there is a slightly different vibe to Darwin and the Tear-a-tree.

Certainly, some of that is due to its unique, and formidable, history. There is evidence of settlements in the Northern Territory that date back 50,000 years, making it home to the oldest living culture in the world. A number of Indigenous cultures still exist and live off the land in a traditional manner. Half of the territory is considered Aboriginal land and there are still eighty Aboriginal languages being spoken. The prominent groups are the Yolngu—which originated in Arnhem Land, a 100,000-square-kilometer wilderness area in the far northeast corner of the NT—as well as the Arrernte, Warlpiri, and Pitjantjatjara in what is called the Red Center of the country. The Indigenous groups here were artists and hunters, establishing trade routes with the people of Indonesia, which surprised me to learn, though I'm not sure why. In 1788, when the first British settlers landed on the shores of Australia, there were roughly 300,000 natives speaking almost 250 languages. And I thought Switzerland was linguistically diverse. Google Translate must have been a Godsend in those days.

Darwin was the first and only successful attempt by the British to establish a settlement in the NT. The other three ended in starvation, which is a sure way to not be classified as "successful." Miserable conditions and a lack of proximity to other people—both viable excuses—were the main culprits. The city was established by an English chap named Captain John Lort Stokes in 1869. He named the harbor and the town after his former shipmate, a guy named Charles Darwin, whom you may have heard of. I think we can all thank him for not naming it after himself because flying into Lort Stokes would have sounded odd. Two years later, Alice Springs was founded...probably because it took them that long to get there from Darwin. By 1872 the Brits had set up cable lines, and by 1889 they added rail service. Two decades later they were mining, and a half-million cattle were being raised in the area.

On the afternoon I arrived, I took a leisurely stroll along Darwin's small, leafy Bicentennial Park, which sits atop a bluff overlooking the harbor. The only people around were two police officers chatting with three Aboriginal men who were trying to sleep in the park. A minute later, at a small information wall that detailed the history of Darwin Harbor, I came upon a group of fifteen or so American marines on their off day. They looked to be about nineteen years old and they were on their first deployment, stationed on a military base twenty minutes outside of Darwin. This is where they'd be for the foreseeable future, and they seemed as surprised by this as I was to see them.

They'd recently completed their training at Camp Pendleton in Oceanside, California, north of San Diego and not far from where I'd lived for seven years, so we chatted about life by the beach in Southern California. They asked me what it was like to live in Australia, what cities to visit, and if I knew much about Darwin. I did my best to pass along information that might be pertinent to a group of nineteen-year-old guys with minimal leave time, omitting museums and craft markets and focusing on Tuesday nights at P.J. O'Brien's in Cairns.

The young men I bumped into on the esplanade are hardly the first American servicemen to spend time in Darwin. For some, it was their final resting place. It's not well publicized outside of Australia, but Darwin has a rich military history. On February 19, 1942, the very same Japanese forces that bombed Pearl Harbor ten weeks prior executed a surprise air raid on Darwin that left 292 people dead.

The air raids that day marked the first time mainland Australia had ever been attacked by a military force. When they came, the Japanese meant business, striking with 188 planes that launched from four aircraft carriers floating between Darwin and Timor. The first wave lasted twenty minutes, but wrecked most of the town, disabled twenty-one ships, and blew apart much of the waterfront area at the

Stokes Hill Wharf in Port Darwin about a mile from where I chatted with the young marines. Two hours later, fifty-four planes returned. This time they targeted the Royal Australian Air Force (RAAF) base, which still exists in the same location just outside of town. In total, Japanese planes would drop twice as many bombs on Darwin as they did on Pearl Harbor. Just beneath the bluff where I met the young marines, the Japanese sunk the USS *Peary*, killing ninety-one American sailors.

The Japanese conducted sixty-two raids on Darwin over the next nine months until November 12, 1943. American Kittyhawk fighters defended the region, slowly but surely reducing the attacks. It was from the Top End of Australia that the Allies would then take the fight to the Japanese on the islands to the north. I learned all of this at a memorial on the waterfront and at the Defense of Darwin Military Museum, which is a great excuse to walk around in some air-conditioned buildings for a couple of hours when your sweaty underwear starts to stick to your crotch.

Darwin has had its fair share of trials and tribulations. The Japanese air raids were the worst days in the city's history, but a natural disaster three decades years later is a close second. On Christmas Eve 1974, category 4 cyclone Tracy blew ashore with winds reaching up to 135 mph. I don't care how many reindeer you have at your disposal, you're not stopping your sleigh on a rooftop in a 135 mph onshore breeze. As you might imagine, by sunrise Christmas morning there weren't many rooftops left for Santa and his team to land on. Eighty percent of the homes in Darwin were demolished and sixty-five people perished. In the days following the storm, 26,000 people were airlifted from Darwin and resettled elsewhere in Australia. Some never came back. It was like Hurricane Katrina in New Orleans, but it happened about a thousand miles away from anyone who could help. I was told by several people that the hurricane's destruction of Darwin, and subsequent rebuild, is a large reason why the city has a modern, thriving feel to it today, particularly along its waterfront.

After thanking the young marines for their service, I wished them well and continued on my sweaty way down the esplanade. From there, I took a brief stroll up and down the city grid, which doesn't take long, then headed toward Mitchell Street, one block away from my hotel. I'd read numerous accounts about Mitchell being the lifeblood of Darwin's social scene, but on this afternoon it was sleepy.

It seemed as though every third door on Mitchell Street was a hostel, a takeout food joint, or a restaurant. Every second door was a bar. I played the odds and popped into one of the latter, ordered a beer, and watched a bit of the Aussie rules football game that was playing on the idiot box. As a cold beer after a 5 a.m. wakeup and a stroll in the hot sun will do to a guy, this one made me sleepy, so I returned to my hotel, took one of the more refreshing showers of my life, and lay down for a short power nap in my air-conditioned room.

I woke up just after 7 p.m. and looked out the window to see the sun beginning to set spectacularly over the ocean, which I couldn't understand because I thought the sea was to the north. At any rate, I threw on a pair of flip-flops and stepped out in the direction of Mitchell Street, which was easy to find by walking toward the noise. The serene, nearly deserted scene of the midafternoon had been replaced by loud music pouring from clubs and drunken twenty-year-olds at outdoor bars talking at unnecessarily loud volumes to people twelve inches from their face. A handful of Aboriginal people, mostly men, stood in pairs on the streets and observed the chaos. Pedicabs, the most dangerous thing to happen in the vehicle industry since Roman chariot races, carted people who wanted to die up and down the street.

I took a lap of Mitchell Street to survey the scene, then found a place to grab a quick slice of pizza for dinner. At one end of Mitchell's main drag was an Irish pub—there is always an Irish pub—named Shananagins. It had an outdoor patio and a live band. It also had a clientele of people who looked more than twenty-one years old, so I went in.

Inside, large, burly men who looked like they'd been playing with heavy machinery all day drank copious amounts of alcohol. They danced—together, on a number of occasions—high-fived each other excessively, compared neck tattoos, and hugged one another as if they were shipping off to war the following morning. This constant drunken hugging and high-fiving is something that men of this generation seem to do a large amount of while intoxicated. I don't get it.

I would never cast a stone in the direction of those who are fond of a pint or two, but the people in the pubs of Darwin made me feel like a Mormon. Everyone was smashed. I couldn't begin to hazard a guess at the average blood alcohol content on Mitchell Street on a Saturday night but no one is going thirsty there, this I can assure you. At Shenanigans, I heard regular pearls of wisdom like: "Eating is for pussies, mate. We're going to the next bar."

On the dance floor, one big, burly bloke with an enormous red beard and straw hat bounced off his friends as he swayed to the music. Closer to me, a rather dapperly attired forty-something man repeatedly stumbled into anyone around him as he attempted to find his groove, or maybe it was just his balance he was after. Eventually the bouncer, an older gentleman in his fifties, grabbed the Weeble and escorted him out the door. Twenty minutes later, the same guy was back inside twerking, or whatever you call it. Still, the band was great, the people were nice, the drinks were cold, and the atmosphere was lively and fun, so I embedded with the locals for a couple of *quiet ones.*

Somehow, I struck up a conversation with two Dutch guys standing to my right. I think it was because we were all laughing at the guy being repeatedly thrown out of the place, then let back in. The two Dutch fellas had come to Darwin to work on something they referred to as the INPEX project. What they were doing was helping to build a gas processing plant that was on the receiving end of a nearly 900-kilometer pipeline, delivering the goods from a recently discovered field of hydrocarbon liquids off the coast of Western Australia. Officially termed the Ichthys LNG Project, it involved some of the largest offshore facilities in the industry. The pipeline was expected to connect the drilling fields to the facility in Darwin for forty years. In addition to having an exceptional number of consonants in its spelling, Ichthys represented the largest discovery of hydrocarbon liquids in Australia in four decades. Today, the project is up and running, with large vessels chugging out of Darwin carrying liquid gas to overseas markets like China.

According to the Dutchmen, they were two of the roughly 5,000 people who had found work on the project. At its peak, it employed 10,000 people. These guys were being paid $50 per hour and their schedule went like this: work for twenty minutes, rest for fifteen minutes, then repeat. So, technically, they were getting paid $50 an hour for forty-five minutes of work. They assured me that there were safety reasons for this. I don't know how difficult the work was, but it was clearly challenging enough that everyone felt the need to drink the day away that evening, which would make fifteen-minute power naps handy every hour at work.

By the time the house band in the bar launched into the Aussie rock ballad "Khe Sanh" by Cold Chisel, Shananagins was officially out of control. A short while later, I *put the cue in the rack* and called it a night.

The next morning I awoke with no clue how I was going to spend my day in Darwin. At first glance, the walkable portion of the city seemed to be awfully sleepy during the day and there just didn't seem to be much more to see. I had ventured to Darwin because it is a gateway to the Outback, and that part of my trip would take place over the following three days on visits to Litchfield and Kakadu National parks. With the day to burn, I did the most touristy thing I could have: I walked to the Darwin information center and leafed through several pamphlets to see if drinking alcohol in enormous volumes was listed as an official tourist activity in these parts. My suspicion was confirmed when I arrived at the tourist office to find the three old ladies behind the counter drunk as skunks at noon. Not really, but I did get a good travel tip. A sober sixty-something woman who worked there recommended I walk down to the waterfront for an afternoon swim and advised me to finish off my day with a trip to a place called Cullen Bay Marina to watch the sunset.

I fetched my swimming apparel and a beach towel from my room and headed in the direction of the waterfront. The walk took me through a quiet neighborhood and eventually over a pedestrian bridge that

Croc-free swimming at the Darwin waterfront

110

overlooked an ultra-modern waterfront, complete with a glass elevator that took me down to sea level. To the right was a string of bars and Asian and seafood restaurants that were humming with lunch time patrons. To the left was a wave pool where most of the children of Darwin were keeping cool. In front of me was a small saltwater "safe" swimming area that is patrolled by lifeguards and protected from the ocean (and crocodiles) by a sea wall. Water is pumped in from the sea and the quality is maintained by mechanical flushing and mixing, according to the waterfront website. There are even mesh screens to keep stingers from entering the lagoon and the water is dragged regularly, though the website also makes no promises you won't be hurt by something exotic.

One huge area was roped off for people swimming laps around four buoys. The rest of the lagoon was for recreational swimming. Next to it was a large lawn where people lounged in the sun. The whole area was unbelievably contemporary compared to the other buildings I had seen in town. High-rises were being built around the waterfront and would soon join several upscale condominium-type buildings that already overlooked the harbor, evidence of the census data that says Darwin is the fastest growing city in Australia. I came upon an Irish pub and settled in for lunch under a large awning. It was as pleasant an outdoor meal as you can have when it's 472 degrees Celsius / 882 degrees Fahrenheit.

After sweating through a burger, I strolled out to the wharf area, where I grabbed an ice cream and finished it in nine seconds as it melted down my hands, arms, and elbows. There was a tribute to the victims of the World War II bombing campaign on the site where much of it took place and a small gathering of people ambling around. After a few minutes of unsuccessfully scouring the ocean for crocs, I strolled back to the lagoon, took a quick swim, and sprawled out on the lawn for an hour.

The walk back to the hotel took me through a large pedestrian mall lined with shops and I was privileged enough to witness one of the most casual, brazen acts of theft I've ever seen. Like Michael Jordan gliding in effortlessly for an uncontested dunk, an Aboriginal man walked up to a clothing rack positioned just outside a shop's front door and, without breaking stride, snatched a pair of shorts from the rack and continued on. He looked right at me as he strolled away with the shorts stuffed under his shirt. Before I could process it all, he was gone. I looked around to see if others had seen what I thought

I saw, but no one was around. I hate thievery and found myself simultaneously taken aback and somehow impressed by the casual nature with which he pulled this off.

Though this was, of course, just a singular act, it fit with the stereotypical narrative I'd heard prior to going to the Northern Territory, which goes like this: "Aboriginals drink too much, don't work enough, and steal all the time. They even sniff gasoline to get high." The Aboriginal people's struggles are too complex to tackle in this space and have been chronicled by people far more qualified on the topic than me, but visiting Darwin was the first time I had any contact with Aboriginal people in Australia, and it was a bit of an eye-opener.

The issues of Aboriginal homelessness and substance abuse in Darwin were far more obvious than anything I saw in Melbourne or Sydney. Here, Indigenous men and women wandered the streets, hung out on street corners, slept in the waterfront park, and sold goods at the local market. None seemed to cause much trouble from what I could see, unless you were the guy whose shorts disappeared off the rack, but there seemed to be a large number of Indigenous folks without much purpose. When you venture into the national parks, where many Indigenous people live as their ancestors did for thousands of years before them, you get a glimpse of their fascinating culture up close. As the Australia.gov website points out, "The indigenous cultures of Australia are the oldest living cultural history in the world—they go back at least 50,000 years and some argue 65,000 years." In the coming days, I'd get a brief peek into that world, which is why I had come to this corner of the country.

That evening, I took a $10 taxi ride to the Cullen Bay Marina as instructed by the old bird at the tourist office. A modern village on a small intercostal waterway with gorgeous new homes and condominiums with big driveways, it is about as far from the life of an average Aboriginal as you can get. A hundred meters from the ocean (for safety's sake), hundreds of people relaxed under palm trees on a well-manicured grassy area and watched one of the greatest sunsets I've ever seen. It lasted an hour, but felt like three. A tall sailboat cut through the horizon a mile or so offshore and kids ran back and forth on the sand. Magnificently, the sky turned from orange to red to steely blue in less than an hour. I sat as still as I could and took it all in.

Florence Falls, Litchfield National Park

Chapter 9: Litchfield National Park

The drive to Litchfield National Park from Darwin is a relatively short two-hour jaunt by bus. Just follow the famed Stuart Highway out of town before turning off onto a country road that winds its way to the park entrance. If you're feeling adventurous, you can skip the turnoff, drive another 3,000 kilometers through a scorching desert, and end up in Adelaide on the south coast of Australia. I had pondered this sort of adventure via the Ghan—the train that runs between the two cities—as a means of returning to the southern part of the country, but time constraints didn't allow. Still, the research was entertaining.

Leafing through the web, I came across great pearls of advice for those looking to drive the length of the Stuart Highway. They mentioned that driving at night was perilous because you and your rental car could potentially become intimately acquainted with kangaroos, cows, camels, and horses along the road. Other dangers included road trains—big rigs towing three or four trailers—and running out of water during the summer months. Not your car running out of water, mind you, but you yourself not having enough to drink. Whenever hydrating while driving is a necessity for survival, you are either a professional race car driver or should think about splurging on a plane ticket. My favorite bit of advice was from the person who said to look out for enormous eagles that are busy eating roadkill and have a habit of flying toward you as they take off and could go straight through your windshield. And if all of those weren't enough to dissuade you, there was the obvious fact that you could simply die of boredom because it was going to look a lot like a desert for four days.

So, rather than deal with killer eagles and an exciting, yet unattractive camel vs. car scenario, I found myself bouncing along in an AAT Kings tour bus out of Darwin with forty retirees at 7 a.m. The one-day tour would hit all the key spots in Litchfield and return us after dark to the city that never sleeps…except during the day. It took me all of ten minutes to realize that the day would be a success because we had Warren at the helm. Warren, our silver-haired bus driver/tour guide extraordinaire in his fifties, would proceed to fill us with tidbits and anecdotes that could have well been false for all I know, but who cares; he was entertaining. A few minutes into the ride, we arrived at the first intersection.

"A right turn here would take us to Perth," Warren said, making it sound like just down the road. "In four days."

And the retirees oohed and awed. Very effective pregnant pause, Warren. *Well bowled*, mate.

The stories and interesting factoids kept coming. Darwin, Warren told us, had more than 100,000 residents at the time (an estimated 150,000 as of 2021). It was a transient population with backpackers who arrived daily and stayed for a couple of days or a couple of years. The new construction workers only added to the just-passing-through nature of the place.

We passed the RAAF military base as we headed out of town, the same one that the young Americans I met two days earlier had flown into. Warren told us a quick story of Wilbert "Darcy" Hudson, the Naked Gunner and first recipient of the Military Medal for bravery against the enemy on Australian soil. When the Japanese bombing of Darwin commenced on February 19, 1942, Darcy was in the shower. Upon realizing what was happening, the twenty-year-old gunner ran to the gun site dressed only in his towel, helmet, and boots. As you might expect, he lost the towel along the way. Unable to get a clear shot at the bombers from one position, he risked a serious sunburn and a whole lot more by running into an open field, from which he brought down the first Japanese plane. He passed away in 2002, never wanting much fuss made of his naked wartime heroics.

On we drove, passing the Darwin Correction Centre thirty kilometers out of town, and Warren's stories moved into the horror genre. He told us about an inmate named Bradley John Murdoch, who was sentenced to life in prison for the murder of English backpacker Peter Falconio. In July 2001, Murdoch followed Falconio and his girlfriend Joanne Lees, also a Brit, as the pair drove along a remote stretch of the Stuart Highway in the early evening. After signaling to them to pull over, he coaxed Falconio from the vehicle by telling them he saw sparks coming from their car. He shot Falconio and bound Lees' hands behind her back, but she escaped when he went to dispose of Falconio's body. Lees hid in the bushes for five hours, then made her way back to the road and signaled a passing trucker, who took her to safety. Her testimony and DNA evidence convicted Murdoch. Warren told us that he is constantly transferred back and forth between this prison and one in Alice Springs in order to keep him guessing because he was always planning an escape.

Farther on, Warren mentioned that 300 crocodiles per year need to be relocated away from populated areas in the Top End. They are brought to a crocodile farm where they are bred for leather, and one farm is home to more than 60,000 crocodiles, which seems downright terrifying. He said something about 85 square centimeters of leather coming from one crocodile skin and that a handbag made from croc leather would cost in the neighborhood of $20,000. We continued toward Litchfield with Warren explaining that cattle stations the size of Belgium in interior Australia send live cattle to the Top End, where they are placed (still alive) on ships and exported to ports across Asia. If I'm making this guy sounds like a fountain of information, it's because he was.

Just a few minutes before the entrance to Litchfield Park, we stopped for a morning coffee and a snack at the café of the Banyan Tree Caravan Park. It was a fairly rudimentary place where visitors could stay in cabins, chalets, and "budget" rooms, which seemed heavy on the budget side. As I sipped my morning tea with the senior citizens in front of the café, a man, his wife, and their two small children were fiddling around with their bicycles and small bike trailer that held the little *tacker*.

"Where you headed?" one of my bus mates asked.

"Exmouth," he replied, in a German accent.

"Where from?" the old-timer asked.

"Darwin," he said.

"On a bike?" the tourist asked.

The German nodded convincingly, as if he'd been on the receiving end of similar surprise before.

Exmouth is a coastal town in Western Australia, about 3,000 kilometers from where we were standing in 100-degree heat. Some perspective: The Tour de France is normally in the neighborhood of 3,500 kilometers over twenty-one stages, and the riders do it with support vehicles and a peloton of other skinny guys in Lycra. The German, who was a surgeon by trade, was doing this with a three-year-old, an eleven-month-old, and a wife who was either as crazy as her husband, madly in love, or being held against her will. They had already ridden from Sydney to Darwin, a cool 4,000 kilometers. Their strategy was to ride during the day and then find a place to

117

camp on the roadside or at places like the Banyan Tree Café. The eleven-month-old had been born during their travels, and the three-year-old had a small BMX bike because he was "now old enough to ride for some stretches of the journey." (The quotes are there so you understand that those are his words, not mine. Don't call the Child Services department on me.) In the event that the three-year-old got tired, which three-year-olds tend to do, they would put him and his bike in the carrier and forged on.

"If he does okay with the hills, we are going to do New Zealand next," the dad said.

Of course you are. Why wouldn't you?

The crazy German volunteered that he had also ridden across "Madagascar and Africa," but not with his children. "That would be too dangerous," he said without a hint of irony. "It's beautiful," he added, before finishing up his preparations and heading off on the next leg of the journey. And that was when I realized the craziest thing about his adventure was not that he was turning his kids into professional cyclists at the age of three, but that he was not wearing padded cycling shorts. He could have said he was riding a unicycle blindfolded across the Outback, but without padded shorts? Madness! Maybe he just doesn't want any more kids to tote around.

When the old folks finished up their 9 a.m. lunch break, we all boarded the bus and headed off on an educational and scenic jaunt through Litchfield National Park, which was established only recently, in 1986. The Wangait people are the Aboriginal owners of the land, which covers 1,500 square kilometers. The park attracts more than a quarter-million visitors each year, which is impressive because the location of the place doesn't exactly make it easy to get to.

Termite mound, Litchfield National Park

Then again, if the octogenarians I was traveling with can make it here, anyone can. After driving past the German family peloton, we made our first stop to see some twenty-foot-tall termite mounds where Warren offered a thorough seminar on the social behavior patterns, cultural values, and considerable engineering talents of the native termite population, all of which I forgot within three minutes.

From there, we drove to a place called Florence Falls and began a five-minute walk down a steep trail to the bottom of the double waterfall on the edge of a plunge pool. We had forty-five minutes to swim in an area that we were assured had no crocodiles lurking below. The fact that it was packed with kids and fellow tourists was a second assurance that no one was being devoured. It was a spectacular place, the type of thing you see in travel pamphlets or on Instagram and think: I'd like to go there someday and swim under that waterfall.

I jumped in and swam out fifty meters or so to the deepest part of the plunge pool where the water was cascading down from the rocks above. Despite the fact that other swimmers were not screaming or disappearing, it was difficult not to wonder if the park rangers might have missed one croc. I've always wanted to swim in a place like this, so I pushed that thought aside until Warren called us from the water like a parent to his children at dinnertime, except in this case most all of the "children" were grandparents.

Due to the heat, it took all of 4.7 seconds to dry off, until we worked up a nice, uncomfortable sweat on the short walk up the hill before returning to the frigid air conditioning of the bus. *These people are going to catch pneumonia*, I thought. From Florence Falls we drove on to Tollmer Falls, a double waterfall that plunges more than 100 feet off a cliff into a large pool below. By the way, as best as I can tell, Aussies call a cliff an "escarpment," which is another way of making an already dangerous-sounding word seem even more perilous and complicated. It also has Rs that don't get pronounced in Aussie-speak. Escaahpment. Sort of like a Boston accent, but far less impressive to the ladies, I've found. Warren said something about the area being home to rare ghost and orange horseshoe bats, but I couldn't see any. They are called ghost bats, so I suppose that's the idea. We stopped for lunch at a place called the Litchfield Café at the Litchfield Tourist Park, where there is evidently a shortage of people tasked with coming up with creative names for places. Before leaving the bus, Warren offered one of the more creative lunch invitations I've heard.

Florence Falls

"Please stay at least fifteen meters from the stream," he said. "Crocodiles can move about seven meters per second when they want. We are no longer at the top of the food chain out here."

"So how do you know if there are crocodiles in the water?" one retiree asked.

"It's a good sign if there are lots of people swimming," he deadpanned. "If lots of people are screaming and disappearing, there's a crocodile around."

This guy could be a cop in Sydney.

Firmly convinced that we were having lunch in Steve Irwin's backyard, we disembarked and enjoyed sandwiches in the shade with one eye on the river. I sat with a few of the oldies and chatted about where they were from, how far they'd come to get there, and what it was like to see the light bulb invented. One of the younger folks, a fifty-ish woman who had been traveling across Australia and New Zealand for four months, had taken a leave from her job in the US. Most were retired, nearly retired, or nearly dead and they had come mostly from the UK and the US. All seemed a tad warm and fatigued at the moment.

After lunch, we made our last stop at Wangi Falls, where we couldn't swim because the plunge pool just behind the iron fence had not yet been swept for crocodiles after the wet season. The heat of the day was exhausting for me, and it may have nearly killed some of the kind souls on our nursing home retreat. When we disembarked at Wangi Falls, my new travel buddies were all sitting on park benches fanning themselves with brochures, eager to get back on. If allowed, I'm convinced some of them would have taken their chances with a refreshing dip in the pool just to bring their heart rates down.

It was explained to us that most crocodiles move downstream in the dry season (May to October) as the water retreats, away from high ground areas such as Wangi Falls. The manner in which park rangers deem a body of water "safe"-ish for swimming seems straightforward enough. They shine lights on the pools at night and look for crocodile eyes and throw dead chickens in the water. If the chicken doesn't "get to the other side," don't go in. If the chicken stays uneaten, you will, too. In all likelihood. I'm not sure what happens if there is a crocodile that doesn't like chicken, but I'm *tipping* that means the first person in is lunch. There is actually a website, becrocwise.net.gov.au, that outlines when and where it's safe to swim in the Northern Territory. The first lines on the page offer what seem to be the key points:

It should be assumed that any water body in the saltwater crocodile's natural range in the NT is unsafe to swim, unless signposted otherwise.

Most fatal crocodile attacks in the NT in the past twenty years have occurred when people have entered the water outside of designated swimming areas.

If you read newspaper articles from 2017, crocs seemed to be as prevalent as dogs. That's because 2017 was the Top End's third wettest wet season on record. All that rain connected river systems that allowed crocs to move around to more places. In the first six months of the year, the Northern Territory Parks and Wildlife Commission captured 181 crocodiles, seventy-four more than they did in the first six months of the 2016. There were stories of people seeing crocodiles in bushes not far from their homes, which certainly would make mowing the lawn a more exciting chore. I'm not telling you these stories to make it sound like Australia is the scariest place on earth, though sometimes it feels that way. It's just what you hear a lot about when you are traveling in the parks of the Northern Territory. And we haven't even discussed the snakes yet.

Since we couldn't swim, those of us under the age of ninety-seven took a thirty-minute hike to the top of the falls for a nice view of, well, the falls. The short hike was a perfect way to finish off most of us before the sleepy bus ride back to the training ground for Alcoholics Anonymous that is downtown Darwin.

I woke up as the bus cruised into the outskirts of town, cleaned up at the hotel, and headed out for a rather tasty Italian meal at a small restaurant on Mitchell Street. A plate of lasagna hit the spot and I left a little room for a post-dinner beer at an open-air bar across the street. I grabbed a table and began watching whatever form of football was playing on the TV.

A few minutes later, a middle-aged Aboriginal woman sat down with me and struck up a conversation when her friends headed outside for a smoke. She asked my name and then, unprovoked, began to tell me her story. She was a divorced mother of an adult-aged son and she worked in the local supermarket in Darwin. As a child, she had been orphaned by her father and subsequently raised by a white, seemingly wealthy Englishman in Alice Springs. She later moved to Batchelor, a 500-person town 100 kilometers south of Darwin that we'd driven through on the bus as we entered Litchfield. Her son, she said, played professional Australian rules football in Adelaide. Realizing I was traveling solo, she even invited me to have a beer with her co-workers while they waited for the band to come on, which I did.

When that conversation fizzled I began chatting with a group of US Army reservists from Buffalo who were enjoying a twelve-hour layover in Darwin on their way to Exmouth, the same place the crazy German was going without padded bike shorts. They told me they were headed to Australia's west coast to build a communications tower, the purpose of which they had not been told by the US military. Among them were a high school English teacher and a fireman. Exmouth is home to a US Naval Communications Station, which I've since learned provides radio transmission to the US Navy and the Royal Australian Navy in the western part of the Pacific Ocean and eastern part of the Indian Ocean.

The town of Exmouth was built in the late 1960s to provide housing to the military members and their families who worked there.

122

I chatted for a while with the reservists about American sports and they expressed their extreme pleasure at being sent to do their work in Australia, which sounded better than other alternatives like, say, Syria at the moment.

Any more banter was put on the back burner when people in the room began screaming at the top of their lungs because some guy told everyone he had crabs. In a bowl. Yes, he had crabs from the ocean in a bowl and he was about to start the nightly crab races. On a large table in the center of a big room normally reserved for dancing, the crab league commissioner lined up six small crabs with numbers on their backs. The starting gun, or something like it, went off and away they went…in all directions…because they're crabs and they don't know they're racing. None of this mattered to the crowd, of course. It's human instinct to pick a favorite and then cheer for him or her. Even if it's a crab. Because it's Australia, money inevitably exchanged hands as the winner (eventually) crossed the finish line at the opposite end of the table. When the race was over, the commish quickly rounded up the crabs into a large silver bowl and whisked them away, back to the locker room, I presume.

They don't have any top-flight professional sports teams in Darwin, but after watching the fervor that enveloped the bar for ten minutes during crab races, I *reckon* they could use one.

Yellow Water Billabong, Kakadu National Park

Chapter 10: The Outback

At 6:30 a.m., the morning after a few quiet Carlton lagers, the last thing you want is a chatty tour guide. Yet here I was, having not learned my lesson, sitting directly underneath the audio speaker in a tricked-out 4x4 tour bus built to transport a dozen or so people. It was still dark and we were on our way to Kakadu National Park for a two-day Outback experience. The opportunity to see the Aboriginal Lands of Kakadu was the main reason I came to the Top End. At first glance, it looks like a brutally difficult place to inhabit, something like a mixture between the swamplands of Florida and the hot plains of Texas, but with far fewer golf courses.

Aboriginal people have occupied the land in Kakadu for 60,000 years, and between 300 and 500 still live within the park today, depending on who you ask. Like much of the Top End, it's a harsh, hot, beautiful environment with an intense summer wet season. The Aboriginal people lease the land to the government, which operates Kakadu and doles out seven-day park passes to visitors from around the globe. The cost is $25 for an adult during the tropical season (November 1 – May 14) and $40 during the dry season. Family passes are also an option.

As we coasted out of Darwin in the morning darkness, this romantic notion of what I was about to experience was almost enough to appease the headache that the most talkative tour guide in the history of time was delivering to the orb atop my neck. But not quite. It wasn't that Jack, our driver/guide, didn't say things I was interested in hearing; it was that he said them four times and never came up for air.

As we approached our first stop of the day for a bathroom break and a refreshment, he explained the reasoning behind his wish that we not bring dairy products of any kind back onto the bus, a simple enough request that could have gone something like, "Folks, my only request is that you please do not bring any products with dairy in them back on the bus."

And our response likely would have been, "Sure, Jack. No worries, mate."

Instead, he explained every possible scenario associated with the perilous act of smuggling dairy onto the bus.

"The place we will be stopping at has plenty of food and drink items," is how he began what would unknowingly become the modern-day Gettysburg Address. "I only ask that you do not bring on any dairy-based items."

That's where he could have stopped. Instead, he continued.

"Spilt dairy and a hot bus creates an aroma none of us want to be amidst for the next two days, folks. Let me assure you. Now, folks, let's say you decide that you'd like a coffee or a flavored milk or maybe a tea. Let's say you spill that coffee, flavored milk, or tea. We all spill things. It happens. Let's say we hit a bump. Now, folks, I do my best not to hit bumps, but sometimes they are unavoidable. If I hit that bump, you might spill even a little bit of your coffee, flavored milk, or tea. This bus will get to 50 degrees Celsius when it's parked in the sun, and this little bit of dairy would create a smell we just don't want to experience. So, folks…"

And on and on he went for another minute to basically tell us one thing: No dairy on the bus. I wanted to come back to the bus and say, "Is this yogurt and Frappucino okay, Jack?"

As good as Jack was as a tour guide, and he was outstanding, I am convinced he missed his calling as a solo radio host. He spoke for nearly three and a half hours without stopping. It was a truly impressive feat. He should have been sponsored by a throat lozenge brand. At one point he mentioned giving our ears a rest, which must have been an obvious reaction when he saw the blood pouring from them. Then, he abruptly changed his mind after a fifteen-second break and began talking again without pause for five more minutes.

He had a habit of saying things like, "When the rain ceases and stops…," which I know should not have irritated me, but somehow did.

"If it ceases, it will have stopped!" I wanted to yell.

Eventually, I changed seats to avoid the speaker above my head and Jack ran out of gas for five minutes here or there.

At any rate, he turned out to be an all-star tour guide with an adventurous attitude that vastly improved the trip. It was obvious he truly loved his job, and he was good at it. In his red tour guide shirt with his safari hat and calf-high hiking boots, Jack looked the part and had the local knowledge to back it up. I genuinely liked him by the end.

As a tour guide, you must achieve some sort of requisite level of Aboriginal knowledge in order to bring groups onto the Aboriginal land, and Chatty Jack had achieved this status in spades. We were a manageable group of six that included two young couples from Sydney and a late forty-ish woman. All of us moved at or near the same pace, which was crucial to what would be an activity-oriented experience.

Like Jack's vocal stamina, Kakadu National Park is impressive. It stretches roughly 120 miles north to south and more than sixty miles from east to west, covering nearly 8,000 square miles. About half the park is Aboriginal land and the traditional owners manage the park in partnership with Parks Australia. According to the Parks Australia website, Kakadu gets about 1.5 meters of rain during the three months of the summer wet season, enough to blanket one-third of the park in flood waters. The site goes on to point out that the park is half the size of Switzerland. It's not much smaller than my home state of Massachusetts, though the weather, the accents, and the inhabitants are all slightly different.

The Kakadu Park Visitor Guide I was reading on the bus said that the park is home to 68 mammals, more than 120 reptiles, 26 frogs, more than 300 tidal and freshwater fish species, 2,000 plants, and 10,000 species of insects. All of these things also make it different than Massachusetts. More than one-third of Australia's bird species make their home in Kakadu. The Aboriginal people have lived there for more than 65,000 years, making them the oldest living culture on earth. There are paintings here that are more than 20,000 years old. At about 2,000 years old, the Roman Coliseum is but a child by comparison.

We started our Kakadu experience at the northeast corner of the park, about as far as you can go in Kakadu before entering the massive wilderness area known as Arnhem Land, which covers 37,000 square miles of largely remote and unspoiled rainforest, woodlands, and coastline in the northeast corner of the Northern Territory. The traditional owners of Arnhem Land are the Indigenous Yolngu people, who have been there for more than 60,000 years. Depending on which part of Arnhem Land you're looking to visit, you need permits from the Northern Land Council and/or something called the Dhimmurru Aboriginal Corporation, which we did not have. Plus, there's plenty to do in Kakadu.

After making our way across Kakadu and crossing a few washed-out roads in our elevated 4x4, we arrived at Ubirr, about 150 miles east

Nadab floodplain, Kakadu National Park

of Darwin. Jack offered a word of caution to keep an eye out for snakes, a warning that seemed far too brief, in all honesty. I pulled on the most sun-shielding piece of headwear I own, lathered on some sunscreen, and discreetly poured all my smuggled dairy onto the bus floor where someone else had been sitting.

Moments later, we commenced a one-mile stroll along a well-manicured path. Jack possessed a ridiculous amount of knowledge on the rock art that makes Ubirr famous. It was like being led around an outdoor art museum in the heat by a docent in calf-high hiking boots and a safari hat. Some of the art was 1,500 years old. Much of it is what is called X-ray art depicting things like fish, wallabies, and lizards. Basically, stuff you draw when you're hungry.

The highlight was the farthermost point of the hike, where we made a short climb to a plateau called Nadab Lookout. As the Aussies like to say, "It was *just magic.*" Panning out beneath us was the enormous Nadab floodplain. It appeared somewhat dry-ish on the surface, but was bursting with color on account of the tall, green grass. The remnants of a waterway were easing back after the wet season, and low, threatening clouds were shielding us from the sun. According to The Talker, the location was used to shoot a scene in *Crocodile Dundee.* After a lunch break in the town of Jabiru, we made our way to stop No. 2, which required a change of vehicles and a new tour guide for the next few hours. Jack, I assume, went off to soothe his throat with raw honey and lemon tea.

The sky was turning ominous as the large, rickety van that would take us to the docks of the famous Yellow Water Cruise splashed through the flooded parking lot at the end of a bumpy road and came to a stop. Before jumping out, our driver, who would also be our boat captain, delivered stern instructions to remain in the van until he opened the sliding door, then told us to proceed straight to the "cage of death" without stopping in the parking lot.

"After last night's rain a fifteen-foot crocodile was sitting right up there in a puddle in the parking lot when we came into work this morning," he said.

I'm not sure if he said this for effect (I don't think so) or if there really was a crocodile in the handicap spot that morning, but it was clear that, as tourism industry jobs go, his gig was slightly different than checking tickets at Pirates of the Caribbean at Walt Disney World.

With eyes peeled, off the bus we went, walking briskly toward the edge of the parking lot as instructed. The "cage of death" was actually a metal walkway elevated about two feet above the water that led from the parking lot to the boat dock. On either side were railings, and leaning on those railings were propped-up sections of seven-foot-tall

Croc-protected walkway at the Yellow Water Billabong, Kakadu National Park

chain-link fence designed to keep people from becoming lunch. Thick vegetation covered much of the water, and the inability to see what might be in said water offered an eerie feeling as we walked the seventy or so meters from one end of the platform to the other. Upon reaching the dock, the view opened up to reveal the open water of the billabong. It was a giant wetland that seemed like a river, but it wasn't flowing in any discernible direction.

There are four major river systems in Kakadu—the East, West, and South Alligator rivers and the Wildman River—and all have large populations of the extremely territorial saltwater crocodile. Yellow Water is Kakadu's most famous wetland, made up of river channels, flood plains, and swamplands. It sits at the end of a tributary of the South Alligator River named Jim Jim Creek. There used to be three Jims, but one was eaten by a crocodile. Not really, but that would be a believable story here. The South Alligator River, by the way, is home to a grand total of zero alligators. It was given the name by an early Australian explorer who thought the crocodiles were alligators. He used to walk around saying, "See you later, crocodile!" and "After a while, alligator," until someone corrected him. I'll see myself out now.

As we boarded the boat, a few rays of sun poked through and a passing sunshower cooled us ever so slightly. The fifty-foot, flat-bottomed boat was a weathered, tin-ish craft that looked to me like something you might see in an old Vietnam War movie. As long as it floated for the next ninety minutes, I didn't care.

"The light rain is perfect timing for you guys," our boat captain said. "We should see a few crocs today because the rain brings them up to the surface."

So does an arm dangling over the edge of the boat, as he made crystal clear during a casual safety seminar as we pulled away from the dock and headed down the billabong. (A billabong is a pond-type body of water left behind by a flood.) The first safety tip was to keep our hands inside the boat at all times because crocs can jump two-thirds of their body length, which was both a frightening and handy bit of information. He also told us where to find the life jackets should anything go wrong with the boat. Then, in what had to be the least reassuring promise ever made, he added, "You won't need them, but just in case."

Within a couple of minutes, we spotted a fourteen-foot female croc cruising across the middle of the billabong.

"On average, there is one croc every ten meters in this river," he told us as he pulled the boat up alongside her for a closer look.

"Just out of curiosity," I asked, "what exactly is the lifejacket going to do for us? Delay the inevitable?"

"Yep, pretty much," he replied with a hearty chuckle. "That life jacket would not do a thing. It might keep you afloat while the crocs came to get you a couple of seconds later. I just told you that because there are regulations that say I have to tell you where they are. If I were you, and I wound up in the water, I'd take of my life jacket, throw it one direction, and swim as fast as I could the other way."

"That's what I figured," I said. And then we all shared one of the more nervous laughs of our lives.

"Yeah, you wouldn't want to fall in here," he added casually. "So, let me tell you about some of the bird life…"

Local wildlife blending in at the Yellow Water Billabong

There were plenty of birds, but the estuarine saltwater crocodile of Australia is the largest reptile in the world, so that was the star of the show. Growing up to seventeen feet in length, it makes the American alligator seem like a docile house pet. I'm not saying you would want to put an alligator on a leash and carry a plastic shit bag around behind it in the park; I'm just saying that saltwater crocodiles are really mean and infinitely more hungry in comparison. If they think they can eat you, they will.

There are actually two types of crocodiles in Australia, saltwater (called salties) and freshwater (called freshies). Freshies cannot be found anywhere else in the world outside of the northern part of Australia. They have a narrow snout, grow to about nine feet in length, and, although they can deliver a painful bite if harassed, they have a much more agreeable personality than salties, which is why they get less publicity. As their name suggests, they live mostly in freshwater areas and rarely in tidal rivers, though they can survive in saltwater.

Saltie is an overly affable sounding nickname for the other kind of crocodile, which is essentially a Tyrannosaurus Rex that swims. They live mostly in tidal areas of rivers and can also be found in wetlands like swamps and lagoons. They can sometimes even make their way toward beaches and swim miles out to sea, like to the Great Barrier Reef, which is another comforting fact about them. Though they are extremely aggressive, salties eat what they can and, being somewhat lazy in nature, only attack when they are certain they will get what they're after. They don't seem to swing and miss a lot, mostly because they are perfectly designed killing machines.

Growing up to twenty feet in length and living for up to seventy years, saltwater crocodiles have powerful tales that allow them to leap nearly the full length of their body out of the water. Once they do that, the force of their bite is the strongest of any creature measured on earth at 3,700 pounds per square inch. Though they don't hunt on land much, big salties can also move somewhere in the range of 20 mph in short bursts. I don't know what kind of 100-meter dash time that equates to, but Usain Bolt has been clocked at 27 mph and he's at least twice as fast as you. That means if a croc decides to attack you, bend over, put your head between your legs, and kiss your ass goodbye.

On the bright side, you don't have to be the fastest guy on the riverbank; you just need to be standing a bit farther away from the water than your mate. The general consensus seems to be that if a crocodile attacks you, you won't know it until they have you in their jaws. But don't worry; while saltwater crocodiles have grabbed the occasional wild pig, horse, and cow, they mostly dine on small reptiles, turtles, and birds. Oh, and people. Sometimes they eat people. If you fall in, a croc eats you before you even have time to wish you were being attacked by a shark. If you stand on the bank and play with your fishing road, it might eat you there, too. If you stand on your boat fishing for barramundi in the river, it might eat the barramundi off your line and then snatch you off your boat and eat you later. Bottom line: Don't stand on the riverbank or put your arm over the side of the boat on the crocodile boat tour. I'm not rambling on about crocodiles because I was nervous watching crocodiles swim by the boat, but I did look to make sure we weren't taking on water once or twice.

A few minutes and several crocodile sightings after we set off from the dock, we came across the large male croc who "owns" Yellow Water. One male crocodile, we were told, exists every few kilometers and mates with all of the females in the area, which sounds like a rough existence. He owns that section of water until he dies, or until another, bigger crocodile comes into his area and fights him for it. To the victor goes the spoils.

Our boat captain, who lived on the East Alligator River in a village of 100 people, was the son of an Aboriginal woman and a white New Zealander. He was easily six feet with broad shoulders, a snazzy blue captain's hat of some kind, and mirrored sunglasses that would have made him the world's coolest sheriff if he wasn't busy driving around as the world's coolest looking crocodile tour boat captain. He also knew an absurd amount about the ecosystem of Yellow Water. It was a huge benefit that he was a local who could give us the real story of the place. He told us that "60 percent of my people's food comes from the land," and that the water rises nine meters during the wet season.

He pointed out small Jacan birds, described how they raise their offspring, and explained that they are called Jesus Birds because they appear to walk on water across leaves, which is exactly what I was hoping to do if the boat had any trouble floating. He showed us endangered birds that will earn you something in the neighborhood of a $50,000 fine if you shoot one. You could shoot Big Bird, a bald eagle or a fellow human in the US and get off with a lesser penalty. He even told us, quite candidly, that some of his people are irresponsible when they hunt for food, often hunting far more than they will ever use.

He was also a comedian.

"See that bird there? We hunt those birds," he pointed out. "Ten minutes on the barbie, then flip it for ten more minutes. Bird in one hand, and some salt in the other. Nothing better. Mmmm!"

"So, in the old days, where did the Aboriginal people get the salt to store their food?" asked one of the guys in our group.

"Hmm, that's a good question," he said, pausing, as if he were going to answer it with some profound story about Aboriginal elders and food storage. "I don't know. I get my salt at Coles supermarket."

Later, he told us about how the Aboriginal women often hunt for File snakes in the water near the banks of the river. I was busy staring at the lush green surroundings and only heard something to the effect of "...they go in the water up to their knees and hunt for the snakes."

Croc on Land

"I'm sorry, did you just say you go in the water hunting for snakes?" I asked. "With crocodiles in the water?"

"Hell, no, mate," he said, as if I was crazy to ask. "The women do. I sit on the bank behind them with a 303 (rifle)."

He laughed a big belly laugh, adjusted his sunglasses, and peered off into the distance.

The sun came out as we made our way back to the dock and more crocodiles did, too. We saw them resting on the bank under trees, floating lazily by the boat, or just blending in with the tall grasses along the sides of the waterway. Eventually, with the help of our eagle-eyed captain, we even saw them where our untrained eyes never would have. They were everywhere.

Despite that, people still get complacent about the dangers in the area. Upon entering Kakadu, a sign warns you: "It's Not Worth the Risk" to swim in areas that are not cleared as safe to do so by park rangers. Just three months prior to my visit, a fifteen-year-old Aboriginal boy was taken by a crocodile while swimming with his friends in a billabong just off the road we drove in on. The croc first grabbed another boy by his arms and pulled him into the water. When the eventual victim jumped in to help his mate, the croc let go of the first boy and grabbed the hero. Days later, half his body was found upstream and the other half was found downstream. When we visited, the boy's "sorry business" or "sorry time"—the Aboriginal terminology for a sort of funeral—was set to take place the next week.

In my two days in Kakadu, I saw hundreds of signs warning people not to enter the water or even stand near the riverbank. This could explain why, on average, there are only about two crocodile fatalities per year in Australia. (It's not because the crocs aren't hungry.) Usually attacks happen when the victim has made an extraordinarily curious decision to do something (like swim) someplace where they should have known not to. In a clear disservice to tourists who will visit after them, some people even steal the warning signs and take them home as mementos. Brilliant.

As we crossed over a small bridge during our drive into the park earlier that morning, I had noticed a guy fishing in the middle of a stream just beyond two signs urging people to stay out of the water. I mentioned it to the boat captain during our cruise, and he simply shook his head and said, "Not smart." The most startling story was that of a twenty-six-year-old Darwin man and his friend who decided to swim across the 280-foot wide, croc-infested Mary River during a birthday party at a nearby outback tourist retreat months earlier.

"The Mary River is known worldwide to have the largest saturation of saltwater crocodiles in the world," one police sergeant said in a newspaper article I read about the incident. "You don't swim *in* the Mary River."

Actually, as the victim learned the hard way, you can swim in the Mary River. You just aren't likely to swim out of it. As a dozen other partygoers looked on, the man was grabbed by a crocodile who then swam up the river with him in its mouth. His remains were found several days later after authorities killed three crocs in the area, including the culprit. Several weeks after my visit to Darwin, a sixty-two-year-old man was "taken" (as they say in these parts) by a crocodile when it leapt from the water and grabbed him off his small boat. There was a splash, the newspaper story said, and when his fishing partner turned around, the man was gone.

For a moment, I thought I might witness something similar when one of my boat mates, an amateur photographer from Sydney, dropped his hands over the side of the boat almost to the water line to get the perfect upward-angled photo he was after. Noticing this, and concerned he might get a close-up photo of the exact moment his arms were removed from his body at the shoulders, I yelled to him quickly, "Man, your hands! You might lose them." He quickly pulled his arms and camera back up over the railing and into the boat.

"Thanks. I forgot," he said to me, wearing fear and relief on his face.

Old mate in the captain's hat has just gone on for an hour about the swimming dinosaurs that can jump out of the river and eat a horse, and you forgot they were there? Tourists.

Following the cruise we headed next door to our lodging for the evening, the Gagudju Lodge Cooinda. A somewhat rundown-looking piece of property under a canopy of trees, it had newly refurbished rooms and strong air conditioning. I headed to the pool immediately after check-in and found it was rimmed by an iron fence to keep any man-eaters from crawling in for a dip. Imagine the irony and overall shit luck it would take to be eaten by a crocodile in the hotel pool immediately following a cruise to look at crocodiles in the wild.

The temperature cooled enough for us to have a moderately sweaty meal outside under a large canopy after sunset. Adhering once again to my karma-based rule of not eating anything that can eat me, I turned down the crocodile dish and had a gamey, but mostly edible kangaroo steak. The Skippy Special—again, my name for it, not theirs—I had chosen was thin and reminded me of a flank steak, but not quite as good. After a full day "sweating like a gypsy with a mortgage" (to quote former Australian rugby player Nick Cummins), my air-conditioned hotel room beckoned. Given the wild kingdom I was currently inhabiting, I'd be lying if I said I didn't walk back a little more briskly than normal, eyes scanning the darkened landscape for anything deadly.

Hiking in Kakadu National Park

Chapter 11: More Adventures in Kakadu

The next morning we were back on the bus and headed for another outdoor excursion led by Jack, who was now dishing out his verbal diarrhea in more digestible quantities, if that can be said of diarrhea. I had come to appreciate that he was a motivating tour guide, making the most of our time in the park. He also seemed happy that our group was on the younger side and capable of activities that required a bit of stamina. On today's agenda was an eight-kilometer bush walk (hike) to and from the Gubara Pools, which he told us he "only does with more capable groups." The busload of folks I rode around Litchfield with earlier in the week would not have loved (or survived) this same jaunt.

At 9 a.m., we arrived at a small parking area along a dirt road, lathered ourselves up with sunscreen, and set out walking. The first kilometer took us along a dirt path through savanna woodlands, and the trail was washed out in spots by heavy rain that had fallen overnight. This offered a few mildly exciting challenges of crossing smallish streams without getting our feet soaked, not that they wouldn't have dried out within ten minutes in the 90-degree heat of the morning. Above the trail was a sandstone cliff that we would eventually wind our way past and around. Jack told us that the "rock escarpment" was an area we were not allowed to visit because it is a special place to the native people. And maybe because they sell dairy products there. Who knows.

A little while into the hike, we came upon a river that flowed through the forest. Recent rainfall had flooded out the path alongside the river where we intended to walk, so we traipsed through the woods over brown leaves until we reached the small pools at the end of the walk. I dunked my hat and head in the water to cool off and we hung around in the shade a bit to rest. At every small creek were short bridges with signs next to them that read "Beware of Crocodile." In this area, the only danger seemed to be freshies, but the overall edginess you hike with in the bushland of the Northern Territory is ratcheted up from anywhere else I have ever hiked.

It's no secret that Australia isn't exactly short on reptiles, animals, and insects that can kill you so it wasn't a total surprise when, as we strolled through the forest alongside the overflowing river, Jack told us to be alert for snakes. In particular, he warned us about Death Adders. The thing you want to know about Death Adders is that they can kill you in one bite. Even more disappointing to hear from Jack was that their manner of ambush-style hunting makes them considerably more of a threat to the occasional passing human. And wouldn't you know it, it turns out they are particularly dangerous to humans walking in the kind of brush we were sauntering through at that very moment.

"What makes them dangerous is that they don't scare away like most snakes when they sense you walking in their direction," Jack told us. "They lie in wait for birds or small mammals to pass, and then strike."

"So, what would happen if someone were to get bit by a Death Adder?" I asked Jack.

"We apply tourniquets and I run to the truck and call for help on the satellite phone," he said.

"You don't have the satellite phone with you, Jack?" I asked him, because I was a journalist at one time and this seemed to be the next obvious point to raise.

"No, it's in the truck," he said matter-of-factly.

"And why would you leave the satellite phone in the truck, Jack?" is what I wanted to say next. "At the very least it would give you another reason to talk when we all die out here."

Instead, I minded my manners and listened to him continue to scare the shit out of all of us.

"I actually know of a guy who was bit by one," said the guy who left the satellite phone in the truck four kilometers away. "He stayed in the woods for two days and then walked out okay. He was a land surveyor. He got very, very sick, passed out a few times, drank enough water to flush out the poison from his system, and stayed very still so it would not travel through his body."

As he finished his story, I subtly slotted myself squarely in the middle of our seven-person conga line, believing that the first person either gets bitten by the snake or alerts said snake to person No. 2. The remainder of the walk was less enjoyable than when we were all oblivious to the dangers potentially lurking among the leaves.

As we neared the end of the overflowing river five minutes into our return trip to the truck, the same guy who tried to feed his hands and his camera to the crocodiles the day before alerted us that he had left his expensive and evidently hugely important sunglasses on a rock at the turnaround point.

"I'm going to head back up and look for them quickly," he said, sounding like a guy in a horror movie who is about to get eaten by a crocodile.

"Can you just wait for me here for a few minutes?" he asked, as if he was auditioning for the part in the horror movie where the character's last words are: "Can you just wait for me here for a few minutes?"

"Okay, try not to get eaten," Jack said.

Really, that's what he said to him.

Since this book isn't titled *The Day I Heard a Man Get Eaten by Crocodile*, you can probably gather that he returned safe and sound. Sadly, without his precious sunglasses.

We ate our boxed lunches outside and then went on one final short

Nourlangie rock art, Kakadu National Park

bush walk with our loyal leader, this time to a piece of rock art called Nourlangie, with movie-screen-size galleries that depict how Aboriginal life has changed through the centuries. Our guide was in his glory here and his knowledge was impressive, unless he was completely full of shit. If so, I'm even more impressed.

After exiting the park borders, we made one last stop at the self-proclaimed "World Famous" Humpty Doo Hotel along the Arnhem Highway. The Humpty Doo is a watering hole in the middle of nowhere with a very friendly staff, especially considering the amount of tourists they must greet daily. After a strictly enforced fifteen-minute stop during which we all bought ice cream and cottage cheese (not really), the drive continued directly into a spectacular orange sunset that seemed to be landing on the road ahead of us. The pavement stretched on forever. I thought about the last two days and a quote I saw posted on a wall at one of the visitor centers we had poked our head into. It was from an Aboriginal woman named Mandy Muir, a Kakadu native who runs a cultural tourism company from her family's land near Jabiru.

"Without culture," she said, "you don't really feel that you have a place of belonging. We have our culture. Our land is our life."

Then I faded off to sleep.

When I woke up, we were cruising into Darwin and making plans to rendezvous two hours later at the local night markets that Jack had recommended. There is nothing in Darwin that will give you a sense of its multiculturalism more than the Mindil Beach Sunset Market, an outdoor collection of 300-plus food and craft stalls that set up shop above Mindil Beach every Thursday and Sunday evening from the last Thursday in April to the final Thursday in October.

Thursday is the big night, and that was evident by the huge crowd strolling the grounds. The idea is to come and enjoy the sunset on the beach, then cruise the market for a tasty bite or whatever else strikes the eye. The market does not serve alcohol, but the FAQ page on the mindil.com.au website "encourages people to bring their own with them to enjoy whilst watching perhaps the best sunset in the world and enjoying a diverse range of food offerings." And if a message of encouragement from the official website of a pop-up market to BYOB doesn't sound Australian, I don't know what does.

I met up with a few members of the tour group after sunset and we took one last stroll together, this time without our tour guide. It was a quieter, but less informative experience, I must admit. The smell of food was intoxicating. There was barbecue chicken, crocodile, steak, pizza, Greek dishes, and all kinds of Asian specialties I couldn't even begin to list. After much deliberation, I settled on a delicious plate of Thai food and then went back for a plate of roast beef and potatoes, partly because I could and partly because potatoes sounded like they might help prevent the homemade Thai food from imprisoning me in the airplane lieu the next afternoon.

In the "crafts" section of the markets, you could even get a Thai massage. I snuck a peek, which was easy because the tent was wide open. Inside, a sizable Thai women was lying face-down on a man's back. "Is he paying for that?" I wondered aloud. After a couple moments, it was clear that this was indeed a legit operation, and by that I mean I don't think he could have been arrested for paying her to do what she was doing to him. Given the stature of the masseuse, a happy ending must mean being able to stand at the end. The "massage table" was a New York Yankees beach towel that had been laid over blankets on the ground. Seeing no evidence of running water with which she might wash her hands between clients, I decided that my oft-troublesome lower lumbar region felt just fine.

I used my final day in Darwin to visit the Defense of Darwin Military Museum as well as the Museum and Art Gallery of the Northern Territory, each about ten minutes from town by taxi. Again, I'm not much of a museum guy, but I'd run out of sweaty outdoor things to do in Darwin...like walk and breathe. An air-conditioned museum sounded peachy, so you can imagine my delight when I learned that the Defense of Darwin Museum was made up of outdoor paths from one military exhibit to another. At the Northern Territory Museum was an exhibit that offered visitors the opportunity to feel what it was like to experience Cyclone Tracy back in 1974. Inside a dark sound studio was a recording of the howling wind from that night. The sound alone is scary enough to be thankful you weren't there watching crocodiles and poisonous snakes fly through the window and into your kitchen.

My five days in the Top End of the Northern Territory confirmed that it consists largely of vast areas of very harsh, but breathtaking country. If you visit, there can be moments when you wonder what you came all this way to see. The wet season sounds daunting and the dry season sounds oppressive. Still, outside of tourist destinations like the Sydney Opera House or Harbor Bridge, this is the Australia I had envisioned before ever stepping foot on Aussie soil. Though it was rare to meet Aussies in my day-to-day life down south who had been to Kakadu or even the Top End, all of them spoke of it with pride, referencing the natural beauty and the local peoples' spiritual connection to the land. If you go to a place like Kakadu, you will feel it firsthand. It's difficult to explain how or why, but when you leave, you feel a little different inside.

If nothing kills you.

UNSOLICITED ADVICE: THE TOP END

MUST DO:

In Darwin, the **sunset at Cullen Bay Marina** was well worth a short cab ride, and the **Darwin waterfront** is a nice way to spend your first afternoon… I highly recommend a visit to Darwin's **Mindil Beach Market** if it's in season… In Kakadu, do the touristy stuff like the **Yellow Water cruise** and talk to locals like my boat captain. Experiencing how Aboriginal people live in a place like Kakadu is so far removed from anything you can do, wherever you're from, that it should not be missed… Having an energetic tour guide and a group of active tourists seemed to make a difference in the Kakadu experience, so if you use a tour operator, ask what you can expect and tell them what you'd like to do… And keep your hands inside the boat.

UP TO YOU:

The big tour bus into **Litchfield National Park** makes it easy and comfortable to see the park. However, depending on your thirst for adventure, a car would give you much more flexibility and shorten the day. You just won't get the pearls of wisdom from a guy like Warren behind the wheel, and driving in that sun would be tiring if you've traveled a long way to get there… If you get to Litchfield, **find a plunge pool** beneath a waterfall, check with officials to be sure it has no crocodiles, and jump in. A tour of Litchfield is well-suited for those who don't need to do a ton of walking… To me, **Kakadu** was the pearl of the two, but it is better experienced with a little walking and hiking. The **museums of Darwin** were interesting as well, but as I'm not a museum guy; my favorite "exhibit" was their air-conditioning.

NEXT TIME:

If I had it to do over again, I would have spent just a couple of days seeing Darwin itself, and spent **more time in Kakadu** trying to interact with the locals. While Darwin serves as a nice jumping-off point for all the real adventure the region has to offer, you shouldn't go there expecting Sydney or Melbourne. That's not a negative; it's just a word of warning if you dig city life. I don't think you need four full days to see Darwin itself unless you want to walk all the halls of all of its various museums or plan to spend a day recovering from a night on Mitchell Street.

PART V:
WESTERN AUSTRALIA

State War Memorial overlooking Perth atop Kings Park and Botanic Gardens escarpment

Chapter 12: Perth

The ocean waters off Perth are rich in sailing lore. It was here that American skipper Dennis Connor won back the America's Cup from Australia in 1987 by captaining *Stars and Stripes 87* to victory. The America's Cup had not been held outside the US in 132 years, so the spectacle of it coming to Western Australian (WA) waters did much to put this area on the map internationally. In advance of the world's visit, millions of dollars were spent to develop a boatload—yep, I said it—of infrastructure. A railroad line was built from Perth to Fremantle, along with new marinas like Challenger Boat Harbor in Fremantle and Hillary's Boat Harbor, about twenty-five minutes north of Perth.

Hillary's is where I found myself two days after arriving in Perth, witnessing a display of nautical navigational skills that I can confidently state fell well below the lofty bar set by Connor and his crew more than a quarter-century earlier. While it may not be a twelve-meter sailing yacht on the open sea, it seems there is an art to piloting a fifty-two-foot motor yacht. I'm not speaking from experience, but the longer I stood uncomfortably at the stern of the one I was aboard, the more obvious that became. I'd met the skipper, a lovely chap with whom I shared a mutual friend, only minutes earlier. He seemed to be a confident fellow, and I presume most people are confident as they show you to their fifty-two-foot yacht, but that confidence eroded visibly after we shoved off. This seemed a shame to me considering that one of the main purposes of owning a yacht is to derive pleasure by moving from one place to another across bodies of water.

The captain—we'll call him "Brian" because that may or may not have been his name—had just purchased this spectacular new vessel, an upgrade on his previous forty-footer, and was still getting used to its formidable size. Today, he was preparing to take it out the following day on its maiden voyage. To get his feet wet—metaphorically speaking, I assumed—the plan was to cruise across the marina about 500 meters and fill 'er up with petrol for their big overnight trip the next day. As luck would have it, it was Christmas week, the height of the Aussie summer holidays, so it was rush hour on the high seas. And when I say "high seas" I mean in the marina...next to his boat slip...where there were no waves.

To be clear, I'm not saying piloting a fifty-two-foot yacht would be easy. In my mid-twenties, my childhood friend Chris Davidson had done well enough in the financial world to own a forty-foot yacht by the ripe, old age of thirty-three. I probably don't need to explain that this was an accomplishment that was highly treasured by his friends. He kept it docked in a fancy marina in Boston and drove it around like he was Rodney Dangerfield in Caddyshack yelling things like, "Hey, you scratched my anchor!" After a few close calls, Davidson got himself some lessons so he didn't sink his $130,000 "investment," though I don't think that term applies to boats. Brian had also had a few lessons driving his new toy and those sessions had gone well, we were told. The boat was still floating, after all.

Now, after fifteen minutes of waiting for the perfect opportunity to head for the fuel pump, we carefully plotted a course across the waterway, the distance of which we could swim with a reasonable amount of effort.

"Whoah, whoah, whoah! Easy!" I yell from the stern, where I've been positioned to help, though I'm not sure how to do that except by yelling, "Whoah, whoah, whoah! Easy!" The port side of the stern moves slowly, but with great force, toward the wood pylon on the fueling jetty and collides with it. (Though, to be fair to the dock, only one of us was moving, so "collides" seems a bit harsh on the dock.) At any rate, the impact cracks the boat's plastic swimming platform. *Crrr-runch!* Onlookers turn and gaze judgmentally. Brian—and I have to give him credit here—seems unfazed. He readjusts our position and she fits like a glove. After pouring in several million dollars worth of fuel, we begin the treacherous 300-meter voyage back across the marina to his slip. Disaster is averted.

The next day, Brian, along with my friend Eric Watterson and some of their mates, will head out into the open ocean to nearby Rottnest Island for a few days of R&R. I will be doing something much safer. Like maybe base jumping.

Eric is known to everyone in these parts as Watto. And it's not because he's the most qualified first mate in Perth. When I say everyone knows Watto, I don't mean he can't walk down the street like Bono, Oprah, or Tiger. Watto enjoys what I would say is the perfect level of regional fame, though he would say fame is the wrong word because he is a most modest fellow. After growing up in these parts, Watto played professional basketball for the Perth Wildcats in the late 1980s and early 1990s for Australasia's National Basketball League (NBL). The league was at its peak in popularity and the Wildcats were the team to beat. The NBL rode the wave of basketball hysteria that enveloped Australia during the era of the Michael Jordan-led

Chicago Bulls. The Wildcats were kind of the Bulls of the NBL, often playing in front of sell-out crowds of 8,000 in Watto's day. Sort of like a Tampa Bay Rays baseball game.

Over his decade-long career, Watto played 306 games for the Wildcats in his trademark blue-collar style. Some of them he played with a highly questionable blond mullet, which may be part of the reason folks in Perth still remember him wearing uniform No. 4. He is also a splendid guy without a hint of ego and, like many Aussies, has no problem at all poking fun of himself.

That last character trait has come in handy over the years because Watto was part of something called the Wildcats Rap, a promotional video (to put it kindly) that hit the airwaves in 1988. A brainchild of the team's marketing director, the cheesiness of the Wildcats Rap is difficult to overstate. You can still find it on YouTube and I would encourage you to do so. If you have seen Michael Jackson's "Thriller" video, it's nothing at all like that.

If you're launching a rap career, Watto is probably not your guy, but if you need to diagram a pick-and-roll or take a tour of Perth for a few days, there is no one better. When his playing career ended he found his way to his current job as a sales rep for Callaway Golf in WA. To say Watto knows the ins and outs of the area is an understatement. Even better, he has pride in his hometown, so he was enthusiastic about making sure my visit was a positive experience. He insisted I stay at his home, brought me along to Christmas dinner with his mom and daughters, and finished it off by taking me to a Boxing Day gathering at a friend's house. If you delete the near-*Lusitania* experience he roped me into at Hillary's, Watto was batting 1.000. For a few days I got the locals' experience from one of Perth's favorite sons, and his friends were just as welcoming.

When you visit Perth as a foreigner, you get the feeling from locals that they appreciate the effort you've made to journey across from the East Coast to their seaside slice of heaven. For most visitors to Australia, adding a stop in Western Australia just doesn't fit into the itinerary, and that's understandable. It's a long way from Melbourne or Sydney and they are a long way from anywhere else. So, while the locals might not want more people moving to their little piece of paradise at the end of the earth, they all seemed pretty pleased I made the effort to go and see it. If you can take a local sports legend along on your sightseeing tours, that probably helps raise the level of warmth with which you will be received.

The "loneliest city on earth" has a million reasons to be the most popular kid on the island. The capital of the enormous state of Western Australia, Perth boasts perfect weather most of the year, some of the best beaches you'll ever plop down upon, and a shiny and quite modern CBD (central business district). The women are pretty, too, as long as I'm sharing observations. It's also just a few hours' drive from one of the planet's most pleasant and productive wine regions and is the home base for the country's booming mining industry, which carried Australia's economy straight on through the global financial crisis of the 2000s and headfirst into the immediate future. Some people say Perth is what San Diego was forty years earlier—a few less people, a lot less coastal development, and maybe a few less surfboards in the water, though just as many sharks. More, actually.

It was founded in 1829 and is named after Perth, Scotland, which looks decidedly unlike Perth, Australia, because you can see the sun here. The "loneliest city" moniker stems from the fact that Perth is awfully damn far from anyplace else. You can say that about a lot of places in Australia, but Perth takes it to another level. I'm sure there are cities and villages that are more remote in the Amazon, Alaska, or Siberia, but no city this size—about 2 million as of 2021—is as far from another major city. From where it sits on Australia's southwest coast, Perth's closest neighbor is Adelaide, which is 1,324 miles away. That's the distance from New York to North Dakota. Darwin and Melbourne are 1,600 miles away and Sydney is 2,000 miles away. East Timor (1,700 miles) and Jakarta, Indonesia (1,865 miles) are closer to Perth than Sydney. To the west, the next stop is South Africa, 5,000 miles across the Indian Ocean and a ten-plus hour flight. You get the point.

Still, this is the twenty-first century; it's not like you have to walk or take a covered wagon to get there, and thank God for that because you'd never survive. It's hotter than hell in the area between here and everyplace else. Perth, with its coastal desert climate, is much more welcoming. The average year-round temperature is in the upper 70s F. In the summer months (November through March), it sits in the mid-80s and lower 90s. Winters are moderate, usually in the 60s. When I landed in Perth on Christmas Day, it was just as the brochures advertise: 80 degrees F and no clouds.

Watto was busy on the morning I arrived, but as luck would have it a former colleague with whom I shared a cubicle wall for three years in San Diego was also in Perth for the Christmas break. Jeff, a Los Angeles native, was a "webmaster" back when we worked together, and these days he was heading up the digital operations of an ad agency in Sydney. He is a gifted dude when it comes to all things nerdy digital, like coding and building entire company websites. When we worked together he often communicated with me via instant messenger or text when he could have just looked up and spoke to me over our shared cubicle wall. During the flip phone days, when everyone first started walking around taking photos with their RAZR phones, Jeff built a website that allowed people to upload their mobile phone photos. About five or six years later, an app called Instagram came along. Sometimes it's bad luck being too soon. Hundreds of millions worth of bad luck, in this case.

The day's plan was to spend the afternoon at a place where friends of Jeff's roommates lived in Scarborough, one of Perth's prime beach communities northwest of the city. Jeff's Sydney roommates happened to be two fun, gorgeous sisters from England. We spent the mid-day hours lounging on the beach watching as helicopters kept an aerial patrol for sharks (seriously) and were told that one had been spotted that morning. This is not uncommon in these parts. Over a seven-month stretch in 2017, forty sharks a week were reported off popular Perth and South West beaches. There have been numerous attacks in the area, many of them by great whites, which are known as white pointers in these parts. In Australia, you may even hear someone refer to a shark sighting as someone seeing "the man in

Cottesloe Beach

155

the gray suit" because saying, "I saw a shark" is too straightforward for Aussies. You can imagine two surfers bobbing in the ocean, one saying to the other, matter-of-factly, "Hey, mate, will you have a look at that? It's the man in the gray su...." and before he can finish his sentence, his mate has lost a leg.

Despite the morning shark sighting, the water was too inviting and it was too hot outside not to take a dip. From the beach, the ocean water at Scarborough and most of this coastal area is a spectacular turquoise hue. It's so clear that you might even see the man in the gray suit approaching. When we returned to the apartment up the hill, half of England had congregated there. It was like a Liverpool/Man City soccer match had broken out, and Oasis was the halftime show. Scouse and Mancunian accents filled the air and only escalated as the drinking ramped up. By evening, Jeff and I were looking for sub-titles. When I found myself crammed into a plastic kiddy pool in the yard with the temperature dropping, it was time to *pull up stumps*. Watto was swinging by to get me, and I could only be so many beers deep to attend a Christmas night family dinner cooked by his mother.

An hour later I was enjoying a delicious meal with the Watterson family, during which the group shared more about Perth and Mom-ma Watterson told me proudly about her sons, who were now living around the globe. The next day, known as Boxing Day in Australia and other countries that were part of the British Empire, started with the overly exciting intra-marina boat tour aboard the fifty-two-foot-er, and continued with a drive around Perth to see some sites. Watto and his two teenage daughters served as my guides. We stopped off at the stunning Cottesloe Beach for a swim, then walked across the road to the open-air Cottesloe Hotel bar for lunch and a cold pint.

From there, Watto and the girls took me to Perth's Kings Park and Botanic Garden. Resting on a cliff, with a panoramic view of the city, the park has a moving memorial that honors the service of men and women who participated in the conflicts and wars that Australia has taken part in. "Let silent contemplation be your offering," the me-morial states. Below, the Caning and Swan rivers cut through town and empty into the sea.

After a brief snack and a cold drink at a café in the park, we drove through the Perth CBD, a shiny metropolis of abundant construction. Cranes dotted the skyline, evidence of the healthy WA economy. On the surface, everything in the city looked shiny and new, with things being erected everywhere you looked. (Get your mind out of the gutter.) At the time, the new football stadium that is now shared by the AFL's West Coast Eagles and Fremantle Dockers was in the works.

Much of the building in Perth in the last decade or two was driven by the fact that the city is the business center for Australia's mining industry, which kept the country from feeling the effects of the global financial crisis of the late 2000s. It's far more complicated than I'm going to get into (or have knowledge of), but the basics are this: the Aussie mining business kept booming while banks and housing markets around the world plummeted because, during all that chaos, China kept right on building. That demand for iron ore from China had a very positive financial effect on a number of young Aussies who found work in the mines, and the mining job market became highly competitive due to the healthy salaries on offer.

In 2011, the *Wall Street Journal* published a story titled "The $200,000-a-Year Mine Worker," which offered a glimpse at how high school dropouts were making serious salaries "running drills in underground mines to extract gold and other materials." Indeed, in Australia, it's not uncommon to hear stories of people earning $100,000 salaries to push a broom around a mining site. As *The Journal* story detailed, there was high demand for individuals willing to work twelve-hour days, often in dangerous conditions where most people would not want to live for weeks on end.

The salaries are high because the sacrifices are plentiful. Often, employees work odd shifts that might last eight or more consecutive days, and sometimes a month. Many work two weeks on and then have one week off. The mining sites—which resemble small cities and are scattered across the interior of Western Australia—have sleeping quarters, cooked meals, cleaning services, and even sports facilities like a gym, pool, or athletic field. On the downside, workdays are long (usually twelve hours), life is monotonous, and the sites are in very remote, very warm places.

Perth is the nearest access point for these mining industry employees. For example, a nurse working on a mining site might fly from Perth to the site on a charter flight, work eight days in the camp, then fly out and have six days off, before returning again. Like it often is for lottery winners and first round draft picks, unaccustomed wealth can be difficult to manage. In Australia, the multitude of wealthy young mining employees has given rise to an entire populous of high-salaried young people with no clue how to save their riches, what Aussies call "cashed-up bogans." (The closest equivalent to the term "bogan" in American-speak would be "trailer trash," I suppose.) I heard anecdotal stories of twenty-five-year-old mining workers who have earned hundreds of thousands of dollars in their short careers, but had no savings to speak of and who lived, well, nowhere. A twenty-five-year-old on $150,000 AUD might finish a two-week shift at a mining site, fly back to Perth on the charter flight, then take another flight to Bali, Indonesia for his off-week. While there, he'd live like a king, pissing away his earnings on wine, women, and song, then fly back to Perth and on to the mining site for his next two-week shift. One hundred and fifty grand goes a long way in Bali.

Mining work seems to be the type of job a lot of people say they'll do for only a year or two to save some money, before moving along to something with a more "normal" schedule. But if you're making $200,000 a year as a twenty-five-year-old with a high school diploma—as opposed to, say, the letters MD after your name—and you grow accustomed to making that kind of scratch, it's awfully hard to be happy with whatever you might do next. I guess. I wouldn't know. At twenty-five, I was working as a magazine editor trying to save enough money to take my then-girlfriend on an occasional dinner date and drink beer three nights a week. Unfortunately for visitors to Perth like me, the exorbitant salaries of the mining industry is one reason a pub in Perth can charge $10 AUD for a pint of beer…a lot of people there can afford to pay it.

Later that afternoon, Watto took me along to his mate's house for an afternoon barbecue with a group of his friends and their families. They were all tanned and friendly, and the house had been designed to take full advantage of the perfect Perth climate. Large doors opened to an open-air patio with a roof over it, giving you the feeling that you were still inside, except you weren't. Most of the outdoor area was occupied by a table-tennis setup, where spirited matches were waged all afternoon. Teenagers battled each other and their dads, the trash-talking over points won and lost amusing the audience. It was great fun. There was cold beer, good wine, and good Aussie banter. It was a perfect snapshot of an Aussie Boxing Day barbecue. After an hour, I felt like I was one of them and that's a good feeling when you are the lone outsider in a group of fifteen. It says something about the Aussies that I could feel this way in a matter of hours.

The star of the day was Watto's mate, Puee (that was his nickname), who had come upon the primary dish of the barbecue by extraordinary luck. Two days earlier, as he sat outside a local shop, a delivery truck sped by and bounced over a pothole. Out fell—and I'm not making this up—an $80 slab of pork belly that settled at his feet. Unable to decipher who owned the truck and reasoning (correctly, I would hope) that whatever store the roast belonged to would not be selling a hunk of pork that had fallen onto the road, he looked down and picked up the pork belly from the pavement. After waiting ten minutes to see if the delivery man would return, he tossed it into his car, and later his fridge. It was in a package by the way, not covered in road debris. On Boxing Day morning, he brought the gift to his good mate Palmey's house and Palmey's wife did the *hard yards* from there. She and the pork belly did not disappoint. The food was delicious, and its circuitous route to our plates led to a lively discussion at the table. Even the roadkill in Perth is top-notch. After dinner, we drank more red wine from the nearby Margaret River region and played more table tennis until evening. WA was feeling like my kind of place.

Fremantle Boat Harbour

Chapter 13: Freo

Watto had cleared the rest of the day for a bit more sightseeing, and it was another *cracking* day for that. The sky was bright blue as we drove south to Fremantle, forty-five minutes from Watto's place and twenty minutes southwest of Perth's CBD. Freo, as it's known, is a blend of old and new. Sitting at the mouth of the Swan River, it serves as the port of Perth and is known for well-preserved architecture from the 1800s. The Whadjuk people are the traditional owners of the greater Fremantle/Walyalup area and their cultural beliefs are still important to the Indigenous people of southwest Australia today. Walyalup was the country on both banks of the Derbal Yerrigan (Swan River). According to legend, the mouth of the Swan is where the Wagyl fought the Crocodile spirit and used the crocodile's tail to separate the fresh water from saltwater.

During World War II, Fremantle was home to the largest base in the southern hemisphere for allied submarines, hosting up to 150 subs with US, British, and Dutch flags. Still, it wasn't until 1987, during those America's Cup races, that the small city gained worldwide notoriety. At that time, Freo was home to about 25,000 people. It's not much bigger these days (32,000 according to the 2021 census estimates) because as Perth boomed beginning in the early 2000s due to the riches of the mining industry, Freo was left on the outside looking in. A 2015 report titled "Fremantle as a Re-Connected City" looked at the area's history from an economic, social, demographic, and political standpoint. It concluded that, like most places, it had experienced its fair share of "ups and downs" over the years, but that it had recently experienced retail decline and a gap in the housing market and was generally losing its importance in the region. Basically, it said that Freo had peaked in 1987 when the America's Cup came to town. Given the magnitude of that event, it's easy to see how that might be the case. Personally, I loved the place.

When you visit Fremantle today, you don't go with preconceived notions of what it was, what it could be, or where it should be economically. It's just a charming place to stroll around. Watto and I started near Fremantle Oval, an old football ground in the center of town that is home to the South Fremantle Bulldogs of the Western Australia Football League (WAFL for short, an acronym that always makes me hungry for a Belgian waffle, in case you were wondering). Opened in 1895, the oval is wedged between Fremantle Hospital, the

Fremantle Markets, and the now-closed Fremantle Prison, meaning it has nearby locations to take players, fans, and referees, respectively. Western Australia, South Australia, Tasmania, and Victoria are all dotted with charming old football grounds like this, many of which started as cricket grounds and are still used for both sports.

The oval was quiet today, and we continued along for a peek at the prison, which sits on fifteen acres and is surrounded by fifteen-foot-high walls, as prisons often are. Opened in 1855 and closed in 1991, Fremantle Prison was originally used to house convicts sent from Britain, but began housing local lawbreakers in 1886. Watto and I strolled in for a quick look at what has now become a tourist attraction. I've toured a few old prisons and jails and they are generally creepy places to go for a wander. The Cork Jail in Ireland was such a place. I found Alcatraz to be equal parts fascinating and haunting. In fact, I remember a feeling of relief washing over me when it was time to board the boat and head back across the bay to San Francisco. The Fremantle Prison felt more like a museum because it seemed like something from the distant past, not a facility that was used until 1991.

Watto led us over the road to the Fremantle Markets, which has more than 150 shops and is housed inside an old Victorian building that opened in 1898. The main hall had everything from "bush foods" to Aboriginal arts to T-shirts to candles and jewelry. The Bush Food Café advertised 'Roo & Croc dogs and something called the "Sampler" dish of roo, croc, and emu. Each would set you back $6.50. We had recently eaten and 'roo is a bit too gamy for my liking. The Bush Food Café menu board had concise descriptions of the more exotic dishes. They were undoubtedly written for tourists:

• Roo is 98% fat free and rich in protein, omega-3 and iron and tastes similar to filet mignon. (I would argue that last point vehemently, but not to the owners of the Bush Food Café.)

• Crocodile is clean white meat, rich in flavor and low in fat. The flavor is similar to crab meat.

• Emu is virtually fat free and tastes more like the tastiest prime steak you have ever eaten. (Color me suspicious.)

The market also has a pretty steady lineup of *buskers* who sing there, and its website even has a comprehensive busking schedule with artist profiles. I was reminded again that my tour guide was a local celebrity when one charismatic vendor recognized him as we walked past.

"Wattoooooo!" a tall man yelled, extending a large, friendly hand to greet Watto. "Ladies and gentlemen, we are in the presence of greatness. This is Mr. Eric Watterson. Legend of the Perth Wildcats. How ya going, Watto?"

Watto smiled, laughed, and turned red in the face as the man attempted to bring attention in Watto's direction.

"Do you know him?" I asked.

"No, mate," Watto said. "Seen him here a few times through the years. I guess he's a big fan of the basketball. He always gives me that greeting."

After covering the football oval, the market, and the prison in just an hour, we were well on our way to *taking the chocolates* for Most Aussie Tourist Day. A stop at the pub would just about lock things up. Wouldn't you know it, Fremantle has a few.

South Terrace, Fremantle

163

From the market, we strolled down South Terrace, which the worldwide interweb tells me is known as Freo's Cappuccino Strip for its multitude of coffee shops and restaurants. The road parallels the coast for maybe a mile and a half, turning into Market Street to the north and Ocean Road to the south. The part we walked had a number of heritage buildings, pubs, cafés, and various tourist traps. It was a pleasant place for a stroll and offered some protection from the sun under the overhangs of the old hotels. We poked our heads into a T-shirt shop, where I laid eyes on the greatest tourist item I had ever seen—a black T-shirt with a drawing of a cowboy riding a kangaroo on the steps of the Sydney Opera house and a caption that read: "Americans Will Believe Anything." Needless to say, I was $15 lighter when we continued the tour, which eventually wound its way to a pub, as all locally guided Aussie tours seem to do. It was late afternoon and the Norfolk Hotel was buzzing.

Set on the corner of South Terrace and Norfolk Street, the Norfolk has been a Freo social staple in some form since 1887. Originally it was called the Oddfellows Hotel, but was renamed because normal people started going there. Actually, it reopened nearly a century later in advance of—you guessed it—the defense of the America's Cup. The entrance was through an old stone archway that former Fremantle Dockers ruckman Aaron Sandilands would have a difficult time fitting his six-foot-eleven-inch frame underneath. Beyond the entrance was a huge indoor/outdoor area that was canopied by trees. One thing the Aussies know how to do is beer gardens, and the Norfolk's was top-notch. Watto and I found a table in the open-air and settled in for a refreshing pint of one of the exotic Aussie IPAs on tap. A band was setting up to play later that afternoon for a crowd of mostly locals.

We rested our feet and rehydrated for a pint or two before extricating ourselves from what was a relaxing spot—and what would have been for several more hours—because we needed to move the car. Is this not one of the more annoying things in life, by the way…being settled in a location (like a beer garden in Fremantle, Western Australia on a perfectly sunny afternoon) and having to get up to do something trivial (like move your car eight feet to avoid a hefty fine)? That's a rhetorical question. I know the answer. You bet your ass it is.

We decided to move the car a whole half-mile to a parking lot near the Royal Perth Yacht Club. This would bring us closer to things like the Western Australia Shipwrecks Museum, the Western Australia Maritime Museum, and a historic nineteenth-century prison called The Roundhouse. We planned to visit none of those, but I'm sure you can get tours of each of them and it will make for a lovely day for you and yours. Locals don't take you to places like that, so Watto and I kept right on walking, engrossed in a rather in-depth conversation about all things basketball—his 300-plus games as a pro, my short collegiate career, and the 1980s Boston Celtics—all the way to Little Creatures Brewing Company, which was just across the water.

From the car park the walk around the Fremantle Fishing Harbor took us past a statue of the late AC/DC front man Bon Scott, who grew up in Fremantle after his family emigrated from Scotland in the 1950s. He eventually joined AC/DC as the band's lead singer for six albums, including *Highway to Hell*, which came out in 1979. With Akka Dakka, as Aussies refer to the band, on the cusp of becoming international superstars in 1980, Scott died after a night out on the booze in London. His ashes were interred at Fremantle Cemetery, a short distance away, and it is said to be the most visited gravesite in the country. The statue here at the Freo Fishing Boat Harbor was unveiled in 2008 and shows him crooning atop a Marshall amplifier.

The fishing harbor was a lively but quaint-looking place filled with (surprise) fishing boats that had just returned from a day's work. Most of the noise in the area was coming from the Little Creatures Brewery, which is housed in an enormous building that was originally constructed to house the yachts that would race off against each other for the right to represent the Royal Perth Yacht Club in Australia's defense of the America's Cup. In the end, it was *Kookaburra III*, sailed by Iain Murray, that won the right to face *Stars and Stripes 87.*

Following the America's Cup, the building became a crocodile farm. Little Creatures Brewing opened its doors here in 2000. If dining on tasty pub food and sampling a few good malt beverages amidst a lively atmosphere in a quaint harbor-side setting is your thing—and why wouldn't it be?—Little Creatures is your spot. But only if you like perfect weather, too. The Great Hall, as it's called, is a cavernous facility with brew tanks, an open kitchen, and wood-fire pizza ovens. The place was heaving and it felt like walking into an old airport hangar. Balcony-type seating ringed the edge of the second story and looked down on the patrons below. An outdoor dining area offered views of the small harbor. The Brewhouse, located right next door, pumps in fresh pale ales.

Watto and I ordered beers from the large bar area, then managed to grab an outdoor table. There were a multitude of accents in the air and it wasn't easy to find a place to sit, but the atmosphere was top-notch. As a perfect summer afternoon turned into evening, I couldn't think of a place I'd rather be. That seemed to be happening a lot in WA.

Gnarabup Beach, Western Australia

Chapter 14: Margaret River

The next morning, Watto shipped off to Rottnest Island with Captain Brian and lent me his car for a couple of days. I said goodbye and told him I really hoped to see him again. I headed south toward the Margaret River region, about a three-hour jaunt down the Kwinana Freeway, which eventually turns into the Forrest Highway. If you know where you are on the map—of the earth, I mean—driving away from Perth feels a bit like heading to the edge of the world. The last big city for a long while is in your rearview mirror, and the highway stretches through sections of farmland and forest, with views of the ocean popping up off to the right every so often. The Indian and Southern oceans meet where the "Margs" region (local slang) juts out into the water. If you feel the need, or your bladder forces you, you can make stops along the way in the seaside towns of Bunbury and Busselton. I had just two days to explore, so I made a beeline for Margaret River.

If you are a wine lover, you have surely sampled a grape or two from this corner of the world, and I was eager to do the same. My Aussie mate Nick Coulthard, a Melburnian who worked in the family vineyard on Victoria's Mornington Peninsula for the better part of two decades, armed me with a thorough list of Margaret River vineyards to pop my head into over the next couple of days. I accepted his challenge and arrived in the picturesque town of Margaret River just after lunchtime. I parked along the main road that leads into town and promptly found a pub where I could demolish a small steak, veggies, and chips to line the belly for the afternoon vineyard crawl.

There are more than 200 wineries in the Margaret River region today, but the first vineyards were not planted here until the 1960s, so it's a relative baby compared to major winemaking regions of the world. Over lunch, I peered at the map and crafted a strategy to hit Nick's recommendations. I'd start with the one that was farthest afield and work my way back toward town in the direction of where I expected I might sleep that night, though that was not confirmed. Jeff, my American buddy, was intermittently texting me about potentially meeting him and his new Liverpudlian/Macurian mates and staying with them in one of the towns I had just driven through on my way down. Seven years of California living taught me that you never quite know if a Californian is committed to something or waiting for a better offer, but I decided to trust that he would come through and focused on the other important considerations surrounding an afternoon of wine tasting.

As most wine tasting sessions are for me, this one would be a bit of a race against the clock. Whether you are in Napa, Sonoma, Bordeaux or Bourgogne, most wineries close at 5 p.m., while others are more than happy to entertain the last-call crowd that wants one more taste before 6 p.m. So a little strategery, as former President George Bush liked to say, goes a long way. In the Paso Robles area of California's Central Coast, for instance, the 5-6 p.m. crowd is the most entertaining group of the day, desperate to sneak in one or two final Zinfandels or Cabernet Sauvignons before swerving back to their hotel. In looking at the wineries of Margaret River, however, I couldn't find many that stayed open past 5 p.m. Suddenly, time was of the essence.

The first stop would be Leeuwin Estate Winery, one of the five founding vineyards of the region, a few minutes south of Margaret River. To get there, I continued on the Bussell Highway out of town, took a right onto Gnarawary Road and a left down Stevens Road, past a fence holding back a massive, ornery ostrich.

At the Leeuwin Estate Winery sign, I turned down a dirt road that wound through a forest and arrived at a perfectly manicured complex. The main building was set at the end of a long and lush green lawn that would have made even my father, the Duke of Lawn Care, jealous. On the second story of the winery was a deck that overlooked the property. A number of people were sitting comfortably up there in the mid-day sun drinking wine and enjoying a late lunch. Across the way, at one end of the lawn, was a decent-sized stage for concerts. It looked like a place where people have a lot of fun and, if you search online for photos of Leeuwin Estate concerts, you may well wish you were there right now. There is also an art gallery and a restaurant onsite if you are more cultured than I was on this particular day, or any day really. I explored the grounds a bit, tasted some great wines, chatted with the employees, and left with a bottle or two that would be thank you gifts for Watto unless I got thirsty before then. Nick's tips were looking *the goods* already.

From there, I headed back toward town and found my way to Caves Road, a rolling country route that runs parallel to the main road I had taken into Margaret River. Aptly named, Caves Road ran through a thickly forested area past a number of vineyards and tasting rooms. It seemed to be the nerve center for wine tasting around here. After ten or fifteen minutes I arrived at the next of Nick's Picks, a place called Vasse Felix. Considered one of the must-do vineyards in the region, it is another one of the founding wineries of Margaret River, getting its start in 1967.

A large glass and stone building with an ample balcony overlooked an impeccably landscaped property. A small lake ran up the left side of the entrance walkway, and the vines crept to within a stone's throw of the building. It seemed like a rough place to go to work each day. The tasting room was sleek and elegant and the wines were, too. That's what you say when you like the wines, know they are good, but don't know enough to pretend you are a sommelier and don't want to take shit from people who think they are. It was creeping closer to 4 p.m. now and that meant it was time for halftime adjustments to my original game plan. While tasting a couple of drops at Vasse Felix, I looked at Nick's Pick's, consulted with the nice lady pouring my wine, and devised a plan...which went to shit ten minutes later.

The next stop on my list was not the Cheeky Monkey Brewery & Cidery. However, for some reason, the idea of a brewery that is smack-dab in the middle of a wine-tasting region blew my mind. It was as if some guy whose Mrs. dragged him around tasting wine all day had the balls and the money to say, "You know what? Some people just want to have a beer in the middle of an afternoon of wine tasting." I'm sure this is not what happened, but this imaginary person needed to be rewarded with my patronage. Also, the sign said it was a restaurant, too, and I was a wee bit *peckish*. PECKISH and WINE TASTING is not a good combination, especially when coupled with DRIVING A CAR YOU BORROWED FROM A FRIEND.

Believe it or not, all of these thoughts flashed through my mind in a matter of moments as I saw the entrance sign to the Cheeky Monkey. With the skill of a race car driver pulling in for a pit stop, I checked the rearview mirror for a potential tailgater, firmly stepped on the breaks of Watto's SUV, and turned, with one or two wheels off the ground, into the driveway. (Sorry, Watto. It was a company car anyway.) Bo and Luke Duke would have been proud and Daisy would have winked at me. The place was humming with people scattered across a lawn and children playing in the kids play area. This, by the way, is a simple stroke of brilliant marketing: build a children's play area at a brewery so parents can sit and imbibe while their kids tire themselves out. Cheaper than daycare and feels better, too. Someday I'm opening up Swing Sets and Suds, the first weekend brewery/daycare center.

Cheeky Monkey sat on the edge of another small lake that Ty Webb from *Caddyshack* might more fairly refer to as a pond. ("We've got a pool...and a pond...the pond would be good for you.") I found a spot on the covered patio and ordered a pizza and a small glass of their Australian lager. It seemed rude not to. The building's large floor-to-ceiling glass doors were flung open toward the lawn, where picnic tables under umbrellas offered shade to relaxing, thirsty visitors. A warm summer breeze blew over me and into the brewery's big, open room. Cold lager in hand, I came to grips with the fact that today's remaining wine tasting plans were going slightly sideways, but at least it was for a good cause. There was no reason to hold myself to a schedule. I had tomorrow and this was good living. With the clock ticking toward 5 p.m.—aka winery closing time—I threw down two glasses of water, strolled to the car, turned back on to Cave Road, and carried north—or was it west?—driving parallel to the coastline.

By this time, Jeff had informed that me he had an extra bed for me in the cabin his group had rented near Busselton, about forty-five minutes north of where I was. After twenty or thirty minutes, I had two choices. Turn right to stay the course on Caves Road and potentially piss my pants or go left, presumably toward the ocean, for what I hoped was a nice view and a tree that looked like a urinal. With sunset looming, I darted left and followed something called Yallingup Beach Road for two minutes. Best as I could tell, I was within the confines of something called the Leeuwin-Naturaliste National Park, which makes up 190 square kilometers of the coastal area here. As is often the case on a road trip, a little curiosity was rewarded. The-road-whose-name-is-hard-to-say deposited me at the ocean's edge, where I would bear witness to one of the more spectacular sunsets I've laid eyes on. Also spectacular was the fact that the area was somewhat secluded and there were bushes around that would allow me to take a *slash* and empty my bladder, which I did immediately after parking.

The last hour of daylight is my favorite time of day and this was a magnificent place to spend the end of this one. I parked in a small lot where a few other people had assembled, grabbed my hoodie from the back seat, and, now that I could walk comfortably, strolled down a short dirt path to the rocks near the water's edge and found a comfy place to wedge myself for the next little while. The coastline here was rocky and red. Small waves crashed quietly in front of me as the sun dipped in the distance. Off to my right, a small bay let the waves run their course past me all the way to shore. As the sun fell lower on the horizon, it gave the rocks a red-clay tint, the color contrasting sharply against the deep blue of the ocean. Somewhere out there—way out there—was Africa. I pondered the fullness of the day and the moments that had put me here: a friend's borrowed car, the drive south, lunch in Margaret River, the angry ostrich, visits to vineyards, a surprise brewery stop, and, finally, a little curiosity to turn left. I was in no rush to leave.

Eventually, as darkness began to set in, I drove down a different road through a crowd of vacationers walking across to a small music venue. They were dressed in light sweatshirts and shorts, the attire you wear on a cool summer night when the temperature has changed just enough from daytime to night to require another layer. I was sure they had spent the day at the beach, gone home to barbecue, then headed back out for a couple more hours of summer vibes and live tunes. It reminded me of an August night in New England as a kid and it struck me how the rituals were the same a world away.

Consulting Google Maps, I decided to take the more country road to Busselton. Now, with the last speck of daylight gone begging, the winding, unlit road was stretching on just long enough for me to wonder if I was going in the right direction. My headlights revealed

Leeuwin-Naturaliste National Park, Western Australia

a few animal eyes in the dark of the woods to the left and right. That, coupled with just the slightest bit of uncertainty of where I was and when I'd arrive, was exciting. Twenty-five minutes later, my enthusiasm dimmed when I arrived at the cabin and RV park where Jeff and his friends were staying and saw the bed I'd be sleeping in.

The cabin was small and my top bunk was made for someone approximately seven inches shorter than me. It also had been slept in the night before and certainly not laundered. Still, after four or five total hours of driving and drinking—it doesn't sound as bad when you put the words in that order—I wasn't going to be fussy. I cleaned up in a shower made for hobbits and we headed into Busselton for a pub meal at a slightly American-looking bar and restaurant. A burger and a couple more beers ensured that the degree of difficulty climbing to the top bunk an hour later would be as high as possible. Like a size 12 foot in a size 9 shoe, I crammed myself into the top bunk, tossed and turned a bit until I found a comfy position, and promptly fell asleep.

Early the next morning, five of us hopped in two cars and back-tracked along Caves Road for nearly an hour. Somewhere around the town of Margaret River, someone knew to take a right onto Wall-cliffe Road, which took us to Gnarabup Beach. At the end of the parking lot was the White Elephant Café, a jam-packed restaurant with an enormous outside dining area and an ocean view. I ordered a delicious plate of scrambled eggs on sourdough and added a side of bacon and hash browns so I'd look my bloated best in my *bathers* minutes later. While my fellow diners raved about the coffee, I sipped on a piping hot English breakfast tea. This was living.

The location could not have been better. To the right, looking north, the beach faded into the distance. To the left, the sand ended 100 yards away where it became a rocky point. Other than the White Elephant Café, the place was mostly unspoiled by structures and buildings. Small wooden steps descended from the café to the sand a few feet below and, just to the right, a well-worn jetty extended about sixty feet into the ocean. It was the type of experience that forces you to look around and admit that Aussies know what it means to live well. In Australia, these moments pop up more frequently than they do elsewhere. And in WA, they were popping up all the time.

When my food arrived, so did the flies. We all stuffed our faces for the next twenty minutes and simultaneously swatted at flies like Mr. Miyagi, but without chopsticks. After *brekkie*, we walked down the beach and carved out a comfy nest in the sand. The beach was steep and shallow and the water was crystal clear for the first few hundred meters offshore. It was difficult to find a cloud. Jeff and I spotted a few standup paddleboarders drifting around the calm, more protected area of the bay just below the café and went for a stroll to the board rental shop, which was a blanket in the sand.

The proprietor, a fit, bikini-clad woman in no rush to stand up from the blanket she was sitting on, was immersed in deep conversation with friends about nothing important at all. We stood and waited for what seemed like two minutes for her to acknowledge our presence. Eventually, she extricated herself long enough to perform the chores of her business, which was renting people standup paddleboards whenever she felt like it. Boards in tow, Jeff and I set off into the shallows of the pools in front of the restaurant for a short while, attempting to knock each other off our boards and generally acting like teenagers. When playing grab-ass got old, we decided we were ready to leave these more gentile waters and go for a paddle up the beach. We passed the small dock and cruised comfortably a few hundred yards in the direction of where our group was gathered on the sand.

"This is easy," I said to Jeff.

"Yeah, no problem. We're professionals," he said.

"Might as well be Laird Hamilton," I replied, knowing that a Californian would get my obscure reference to standup paddleboarding royalty.

The difference between the two of us and Laird Hamilton, or anyone else with half a brain, is that Laird would have understood that the current was aiding our efforts paddling north. When we turned to paddle back from whence we came, it felt like I was on a paddleboard treadmill. Effort was in abundance; progress was not. Envision two ducks, looking smooth and unhurried on the surface but moving with great efficiency beneath the water. Now picture the opposite.

We laughed at our predicament for a few minutes and then considered our options. Neither of us was going to paddle into shore and carry the board down the beach. Not with people watching. Male pride would have set us on a course for Cape Town before that happened. Eventually, we both dropped to our knees for more leverage and upped our stroke rate. As an Aussie might say, it was time to *get on your bike, son.* (In other words, get moving!)

"Here we go!" I yelled. "Now, we're making progress."

And, for that fleeting moment, we were. After approximately one minute, however, it became quite clear that the current had more endurance than we did. I rested my arms for ten seconds and was back where we had turned around, then checked the paddle to make sure it didn't have a hole in it. Negative. It brought to mind a former Finnish colleague of mine who, when I encountered technical issues with my computer, used to say, "Sweeney, I think your computer problem is sitting between the chair and the screen." Pretty funny for a Finn, even if he was usually correct. In this case, the issue was that there was no chair and, more crucially, no tech support. Or so I thought.

"We could be out here all day," I said to Jeff before calling myself several names and jumping off the board to cool off, both physically and temperamentally.

When I climbed back on the board, tech support was approaching from the south in the form of blanket lady. The SUP vendor was apparently concerned enough with losing her boards to the ocean that she pressed pause on her important conversation with her mates and set off to save us. Within a minute, she was within earshot. And, yes, if it occurs to you that I have now been rescued/retrieved twice from the ocean waters off Australia, well, I can't argue with you there. Thanks for noticing.

"Come closer to shore," she barked. "The current is stronger out where you are."

"Right. We're just enjoying the day," I lied. "It's beautiful out here."

"Yeah, you seem to be having a little trouble," she said, seeing through my bullshit.

She lingered a couple of minutes to make sure we followed her advice and then sped off against the same current we'd been battling for fifteen minutes and was back on the beach in what seemed like thirty seconds. With our tails between our legs, Jeff and I paddled sixty or so meters closer to shore and then followed her lead back toward the Elephant Café. It was certainly easier closer to shore, but not nearly as easy and she made it look. As with most water sports, technique is paramount. That's my story, anyway. Ten minutes later we were back among the shallow tide pools resting our shoulders.

That same afternoon, about four and a half hours to the southeast, a seventeen-year-old boy was "taken" by a great white shark while spearfishing with his friend, who defended himself by firing his spear gun into the mouth of *the man in the gray suit*. I wouldn't say we narrowly escaped danger by any means, but I was a little more thankful for the rescue when I heard that news bulletin come over the radio on my drive back to Perth that evening.

With standup paddleboarding in the Indian Ocean reasonably conquered and the rest of the group heading back for a nap in their hobbit beds, I persuaded Jeff to join me for more wine tasting on Caves Road.

Our first stop was a place called Saracen Estate, which had a remarkable glass-fronted tasting room and deck overlooking what seemed to be a man-made pond. The entrance garden was marvelous and included a boardwalk type thing that ran over a koi fish pond sort of thing. I can't recall if there were actually koi fish in the koi fish pond sort of thing, but I've never understood the reason for those things anyway. On the grounds of the Saracen winery was the Duckstein Brewery, makers of fine German-style beers. We were looking at another two-for-one prospect here and, wouldn't you know it, we took advantage. We ordered lunch, tasted some wine and beer, and spoke about how much better this was than accidentally floating out to sea on a standup paddleboard.

So you don't go looking for the Saracen/Duckstein sign, you should know that since our visit, Saracen and Duckstein have closed shop. The good news is both businesses have been replaced by what appears to be a similar offering, plus gin! As of the time of this writing, if you visit the same location you will find something called the Caves Road Collective, which the internet tells me is home to Black Brewing Company, Dune Distilling, Ground to Cloud wines, and a restaurant. So, basically, take a brewer/winery/restaurant operation and add a gin distillery. Fun for the whole family. Actually, it is fun for the whole family because there is a playground here as well. I knew the daycare/brewery thing was a good idea.

After lunch, we adjourned to Watto's SUV and drove it a whopping two kilometers up the road to Driftwood Estates, a boutique winery that opened its doors in 1989. Driftwood has a bit more rustic feel than the other places I visited, and the folks inside were down-to-earth and jovial. That could have been because we were also jovial after spending ninety minutes sampling the goods at the winery/brewery/now distillery up the street, or it could be that they are just nice people. Let's say it was B. We ended up staying until closing time because the sweet ladies kept on pouring.

"This is a special blend. We don't usually offer this one at tastings, but I'll give you guys a splash," is the line they always seem to use when they know they have the hook in your mouth.

"Don't mind if I do. Thank you."

The ladies seemed genuinely interested in where we were from, what had brought us there, and what we thought of the area. I believe they call this the Soft Sell. It worked. They were so sweet that I magically purchased two more bottles of wine without a hint of thought about how I'd get them home. I'm not normally a sucker for sales jobs like this, but I seem to fall prey to it much more frequently when I go wine tasting.

"You say I can get this bottle and this one for $40, and you will throw in the reserve for $30 and wave the $10 tasting fee? You know what, let's do it. Sure. Why not? How often will I be in Margaret River tasting wine?"

We shoved off when they finally kicked us out a few minutes after five, then made our way back to the cabin/dollhouse, where I dropped off Jeff and continued on my merry way back to Perth. I was quite content with what I'd experienced during my thirty-six-hour stay in the Margaret River region, and it was a perfect evening for a drive. The summer air blew in through the open windows as the sun set over the ocean to the West, as it tends to do.

I arrived at Watto's place north of Perth later that evening and packed for my return trip to Melbourne. I was a little sad to leave. I thought maybe it was because this place is so far away that you don't know when or if you'll ever come back, so I decided right then that someday I would. It might be years from now and the place might be bigger and even shinier. A pint may cost $20 by then, and it would still be a million miles from anyplace, but to me that was part of the draw—there was mystery in a place so drastically off on its own. Before I left, I swaddled a few bottles of wine in my dirty T-shirts like a savvy travel veteran to prevent them from breaking inside my luggage. I left a couple more on Watto's counter with a thank you note:

#4,
Well, if you're reading this, I suppose you've survived the boat trip. What a relief. Thanks for the hospitality, playing tour guide and for the use of your wheels. I had a great time. What a place this is! A couple bottles of vino here to say thanks. Save them for a special occasion or drink it all now to celebrate the fact that you are still alive.
—Sweens

UNSOLICITED ADVICE: PERTH AND WA

MUST DO:

It's not a trip to Perth if you don't spend time on **the beach**, and there are some good ones nearby. **Scarborough** and **Cottesloe** are two of the more popular spots... I really loved strolling the Victorian streets of **Fremantle** and spending the afternoon at **Little Creatures**. The brewery was extremely crowded and they didn't take *resos* (reservations), but the crowd made for a fun session. Work up an appetite on foot, then stop for a pub meal, a pint, or a touristy T-shirt of a cowboy riding a kangaroo on the steps of the Sydney Opera House, then land at Little Creatures when things are livening up... The **Margaret River region** was a special place. If you're going to go all the way to Perth, spend a couple days down there. Do your homework on the vineyards and plan the visits. You could easily spend several days, especially if you like wine... The **White Elephant Beach Café** on the beach was a good way to start the day, but the main street in Margaret River itself has plenty of shops, pubs, and restaurants... I loved the brief time at sunset that I spent along the coast near **Leeuwin-Naturaliste National Park**, too. It looked like a nice neck off the woods to post up for the night. Instead, I drove 30 more minutes to sleep in a shoebox.

UP TO YOU:

As you go **farther north of Perth**, there is less and less industry along the coast. I didn't have a chance to explore much in that direction, saving time for a couple of days in Margaret River instead, but it's an area that people rave about... If quieter, more secluded coastlines are your thing, you can also **keep going past Margaret River**, where the natural coastline seemingly goes on forever in the direction, eventually, of Adelaide... I didn't spend a ton of time in the **city of Perth** itself. To me, the draw here is the coastal areas, so I listened to my tour guide in that respect... I also didn't get to **Rottnest Island**, which is a tourist favorite about twenty kilometers off the coast of Perth. It can be accessed by ferries from Fremantle (a twenty-five-minute journey), the Barrack Street Jetty in Perth (forty-five minutes), or Hillary's Harbour (ninety minutes), the place where we smashed into the petrol station jetty. Rottnest is home to a nature reserve, gorgeous beaches, and Aussie wildlife, including the famous quokka, a fury creature about the size of a cat that looks like a little kangaroo. A bike is the best way to get around on Rottnest.

NEXT TIME:

Plan your trip to Perth and WA as you like, of course, but I would spend **more time in the Margaret River region** if I did it all again. The wineries were only part of the fun. The parts of the coastline that I saw were magnificent, sometimes rugged and charming. There is more of that farther south of Margaret River that I plan to explore next time... I'd also visit the places between Perth and Margaret River, near **Busselton and Bunbury**... It wasn't Aussie Rules Football season, but if you visit Perth when the season is on, see the **West Coast Eagles** or **Fremantle Dockers** at the new stadium. The atmosphere is said to be top-notch... With an endless amount of time, I'd rent a van, point it north, and just keep on exploring for days up the **WA coast**.

PART VI:
TO THE ACT

Hyams Beach on the shores of Jervis Bay

Chapter 15: On the Road to the Capital

The roadside sign welcoming drivers to the Australian Capital Territory was written in old-school black stenciled letters, like something you'd see promoting a nine-year-old's lemonade stand at the end of a suburban driveway. The highway department, or whoever was responsible, spared some expense in creating it. It's nice to see tax dollars not being wasted unnecessarily. The welcome sign was a sight for sore eyes after nearly seven hours behind the wheel.

I had spent the last couple of days in Sydney catching up with my good buddy Richard Ennis, a transplant from Northern Ireland whom I met within a few weeks of moving to Melbourne years earlier. Since then, Rich moved from Melbourne to Sydney for an English girl, the lovely Dee, who is now his wife. They live with their young son in the spectacularly unrealistic beach hamlet of Double Bay, a Sydney suburb, where we had spent two days doing the types of things you can do in Sydney a few minutes from your front door. The day before, we kayaked to a small island and had beers on a tiny beach, then took a ten-minute ferry ride to a sunset dinner with a view of the Sydney skyline and Harbour Bridge.

Around mid-day, I left that idyllic life behind for the Australian capital city of Canberra, which is three hours away from Sydney if you take the most direct route, and even farther away if you measure it metaphorically. I'm adventurous, so I chose to take the longer coastal route. All right, fine, there is no coastal route to Canberra. I just wanted to drive as much of the coast as I could, following the Prince's Highway south from Sydney through pretty towns with some of the most unspoiled and sparsely populated—at least on a Monday afternoon—beaches you'll find this close to four or five million people. The road wound past busy schoolyards with kids in Steve Irwin safari hats (really), then into an agricultural region and rolling hillsides dotted with vineyards. I was in no real rush, stopping here and there to stretch the legs at scenic overlooks as the road played peek-a-boo with the sea.

The highlight of the drive was a stop-and-stroll on a small, deserted piece of sand called Chinamans Beach, which I stumbled upon accidentally while looking for the more popular Hyams Beach, five minutes away by foot. They say that these are the "whitest white sand beaches in Australia" and, whoever "they" are, they aren't lying. The sand was awfully white, and the sea was clear. Chinamans and Hyams beaches sit on Jervis Bay, which evidently is a fantastic place to snorkel due to the bounty of sea life, including whales during their migrating seasons. I accessed the sand down a short path that disappeared beyond a small sign for "Chinamans Beach" and spent thirty minutes listening to the sand squeak beneath my feet. A dozen or so people relaxed on the sand. None of them appeared to be Chinamen, if you can even say that word anymore. Someone will let me know, I'm sure.

Ninety minutes of driving later, I arrived in Bateman's Bay, took a quick spin through a McDonald's drive-thru, then headed inland on the King's Highway toward Canberra. While munching on the last of my fries, I came to the realization that my unhurried drive had left me three more hours of driving and two more hours of daylight. I don't mind driving at night, but fatigue was setting in. It wasn't long before the King's Highway began climbing rather steeply through a thick forest around tight curves and past runaway truck ramps toward the 2,562-foot summit of Clyde's Mountain. The roadside was littered with kangaroo carcasses. Roos are a real danger on country roads in Australia, and I was on high alert hoping Skippy wouldn't dart out of the woods in front of me and join me in the passenger seat by way of the windshield. To keep myself awake and alert, I began counting dead 'roos and reading the entertaining road signs along the way. They were for nondescript places that I'm *tipping* only a handful of people each year (or never) go in search of. I passed over Cabbage Tree Creek, flew by Tomboy Road and Misty Mountain Road, and cruised around Government Bend and over Doughboy Creek, which I can only assume was named for a portly local fellow who once fell into the river.

At the top of the climb, the road flattened out and continued through open farmland. Horses, sheep, and cattle dotted the roadside fields that stretched to the horizon. About an hour from Canberra, the sun was setting on the road ahead of me and my eyes were closing. By luck, I happened upon a rest area and pulled over to walk around a bit. It was a dirt parking lot, about 300 meters from end to end. Across the lot, under a few big trees, were two camper vans. It felt like the ideal place to murder an American tourist sleeping in his car for a few minutes. Naturally, I reclined the driver's side seat, set my phone alarm for twenty-five minutes later, and zonked out as the last sunlight set behind the trees of a nearby farm. I woke up startled by a dream that two farmers with long beards and overalls were dragging me across the parking lot into the back of their horse trailer as banjo music began to play, but was nevertheless quite refreshed.

In the annals of power naps, this one was an all-timer. I was refreshed and back on the road a few minutes later when, seemingly out of nowhere, the town of Braidwood appeared. Braidwood is a Heritage-listed slice of rural paradise that dates back to the 1800s and serves as the local capital city for the small communities nearby. The next hot spot ahead was Bungendore, where several homes looked to be for sale. I wondered who lived out here. Not a creature was a stirring on a Monday night at 7 p.m., and I noticed a number of houses with For Sale signs. I found myself imagining what it might be like to simply up and move to a place like this. How would they receive me? What the hell would I do with myself? Do they have a good *brekkie* spot? Would I die of a snakebite in my backyard while chasing my pet koala?

Evidently, people do this more and more these days—the moving part; I can't speak to the koala chasing. A 2017 *Canberra Times* story explained how places like Bungendore are growing because Canberra residents want to move there and folks from Sydney come in search of a quieter life than the one they've left. They also get more bang for their buck, especially compared to Sydney. On the other hand, studies by none other than the United Nations say that by the year 2050 nearly 70 percent of the world's population will live in urban areas. Maybe Braidmore and Bungendore will *be* urban places by then. I sure hope not. What they do today in places like this, I have no idea. I guess some people build giant meth labs underneath their home, as two Adelaide transplants did. An online newspaper article I uncovered later said that authorities discovered this little operation thirty kilometers from Braidmore in January 2020. The *coppers* said the goods on hand had a street value of $34 million. So, if you're on the lookout for a fixer-upper with a checkered past outside Braidwood, get cracking. (Get it? Never mind.)

The last clever sign between Braidmore and Canberra was authored by a guy selling chunks of grass (not that kind), who asked passers-by to "put their trust in sod" and finished it off by borrowing from Fleetwood Mac. "You can grow your own way" the rest of this brilliant ad writing read. I thought about the brands I've worked for who've paid millions to agencies full of "creatives" who would have dismissed that gem of a tagline with a laugh. And mistakenly, I might add.

Now, six-plus hours after departing Sydney, with darkness setting in, still in the middle of nowhere, I was chuckling to myself at the "Welcome to the ACT" sign in black stenciling. The one I told you about back at the beginning of this chapter. The simplicity of the sign was hardly surprising. Everything I had ever heard, read, or was told about Canberra involved someone making fun of it. The most common:

"There's not much there, except government stuff, mate."

"It's just a big country town, mate."

"Don't bother going, mate."

To be fair, I was only visiting Canberra because I thought that if one decided to write a book about his or her travels in Australia, he or she ought to include a visit to its capital city.

I arrived in Canberra a little after 8 p.m., in the dark, so as I approached the town I missed out on seeing...nothing. Absolutely nothing. In fact, there was not much warning at all that I was in Canberra. I saw no bright lights or big buildings shining in the distance. There were no highly engineered on-ramps or highways built to handle massive amounts of traffic. I didn't even see suburbs. There were farmlands and then, a few minutes later, I was in the nation's capital. Kind of cool if you think about it. Less cool if you're looking for a good time.

I had booked my hotel room on my phone a few hours earlier while waiting for a burger, fries, and monster ice tea in Bateman's Bay. For the price of a modest room, I wound up in a beauty of a suite that could have slept six, which coincidentally was the number of people I could have eaten for at the time. I was famished. Unfortunately, Canberra isn't exactly Times Square or Shibuya Crossing in Tokyo when it comes to late-night dining options. And when I say "late night" in Canberra, I mean 9 p.m.

After the hotel front desk people tried to sell me on their own restaurant by telling me there would be nothing open, I walked all over town attempting to prove them wrong. I don't know why. The hotel was in a newish area of town called Braddon, which had a fair number of modern-looking eateries and bars, all of which were not serving food. On the bright side, the half-mile loop I walked seemed like it had some potential for liveliness, if not nourishment. There were modern cafés, bars, and a few restaurants ranging from Indian to English pubs to Asian fusion.

190

There was even a spot for live music. It was all positively dead tonight, but it was promising for tomorrow. Finally, after fifteen minutes, I saw a place that seemed to have people inside raising what looked like food from a plate to their mouths. It was an Asian fusion restaurant with sushi, various teriyaki plates, and noodles, and they were kind enough to serve me. There were fifteen or so people in the place and all of them were under thirty, which backed up the rumors I'd heard about Canberra increasingly becoming a young person's place, both because of the government jobs and because of the national university there. I ordered half the menu, ate half the menu, wandered back to my room, opened the Canberra section of my guidebook, and promptly fell asleep with it on my chest.

The view from atop the Australian Parliament House

Chapter 16: Canberra

If you do a quick internet search for things to do in Canberra, you'll uncover a litany of mean-spirited articles with titles like "7 Reasons Canberra doesn't suck. Really." I'm *tipping* that sort of thing doesn't excite the Canberra tourism board, but if they needed a more tantalizing ad slogan, surely they would have turned to the poetic sod guy just out of town. As it turns out, Canberra is not completely unspectacular. You wouldn't necessarily go there and say, "Gee, this place really sucks." You just wouldn't necessarily go there. There's a lake to run around, a lot of hilly trails to walk up, a bevy of parkland, and a bunch of free and unique tourist attractions that would offer a pretty nice way to spend an afternoon if you are not from there, or even if you were.

For whatever it's worth, Canberra must be one of the most approachable national capitals on earth. It just doesn't seem to make sense as the capital city of such a cool nation. Partly because it is a purpose-built city and partly because of its lack of proximity to any place of note. It feels nothing like going to London, Washington, DC...or, I don't know, Reykjavík. Placing Canberra on your must-see list would be like saying: "I really need to see Harrisburg because it's the capital of Pennsylvania." Exactly—no one ever says that. (My apologies to Harrisburg, where I've never actually been.)

Smartasses such as me like to poke fun at the location of Canberra, but it was chosen as the site of Australia's national capital precisely because of where it is, which is just east of the middle of nowhere. Canberra is a compromise. After Australia decided to become a nation in 1901, the people in charge had to choose a capital. Government being government, it took only seven short years for everyone to come to an agreement. A rivalry between Sydney and Melbourne, which was serving as the capital in the interim, was the main cause of the holdup.

Australia's new constitution said that the capital city would be in New South Wales, but that it had to be at least 100 miles from Sydney in order to keep the Melbournians happy. A number of towns raised their hands, but the area then known as Limestone Plains was chosen in 1908. The region around Canberra became the Australian Capital Territory (abbreviated ACT) in 1911, when the 975-square-mile piece of land was handed over to the Commonwealth by New South Wales. In 1913, Canberra was officially named the capital of Australia. It was partially in order to be safe from a potential coastal attack that the Aussies put their capital up here, but it is amusing that a nation that thrives on coastal living has a capital that is two hours from the ocean surrounded by mountains at an elevation of 2,000 feet where it sometimes snows.

White writers of that time period referred to the local Aboriginal people as Kamberra, Kgambury, Nganbra, and Gnabra, which the nca.gov website says means "meeting place for people not invited to the important meetings in the big city." Actually, it just means "meeting place." The word Canberra evidently grew from those terms. The city/town was master-planned by a Chicago landscape architect named Walter Burley Griffin and construction began in 1913 on his plans for a city that extended out from Parliament with a man-made lake at its center. Although World War I slowed things and Griffin stepped away from the project in 1920, his vision is mostly what you see today when you visit Canberra. Scrivener Dam was built on the Molonglo River in order to create the man-made Lake Burley Griffin, which sits at the center of the city surrounded by ample green space and pathways for people to run, walk, and bike on.

After picking up my guidebook from the floor beside the bed and crafting a plan my first full day in Canberra, I went in search of *brekkie*. On the street behind the hotel, a modern and spacious café called Rye served up a delectable offering of tea, scrambled eggs on sourdough with bacon, and potatoes for the low, low price of twenty-something Australian dollars. No, that did not include a shampoo, a haircut, and an oil change.

Lonsdale Street, the main drag in front of the hotel, had a modern train/light rail type thing that ran down the middle of the roadway between the car lanes, rather than among them like in Melbourne. A mid-morning crowd waited on concrete islands for the next train, and traffic seemed minimal after whatever passes for "rush hour" in Canberra. A small street sign in front of the Marvie & Wolfe café pointed right for "food and coffee" and left, in the direction of the government buildings, for "real life." I don't know how many governments are truly connected with real life these days, but I turned left because I was full.

Mistakenly, I thought the walk toward the Parliament building would be just a few minutes. It was more like forty, presenting me with the perfect opportunity to work off the bacon. As I walked down Commonwealth Avenue and over a bridge that spanned part of Lake Burley Griffin, a strong wind battered me on what was an otherwise ideal day. It's hard to do stuff in wind, unless you are a sailor, and there is no real defense against it. Wind sucks.

Soon enough (but not really) I was on the other side of the lake and entering the Parliamentary Zone, according to a red sign. At first, I thought it said Paramilitary Zone, which would have made Canberra infinitely more exciting, but less touristy. The Parliamentary Zone is a well-marked area full of national and government buildings where the master-planned element of the city becomes evident. There is a vast amount of open space between buildings and hectares of parkland along the lake. It was all very dry—the land, not the lake—on account of something like a three-year drought. I arrived first in an area occupied by the National Library, Magna Carta Place, the National Rose Garden, and the Treasury Building, which was flying both the Australian national flag and the black, yellow, and red colors of the Aboriginal flag above it. You don't have to be in Canberra long to notice that the government seems intent on letting visitors know that it is trying to right some of the wrongs that have been done to the Aboriginal people. Or at least play the public relations game well. As the day went on, I'd learn plenty more on that topic.

Up ahead, on a big patch of grass near the National Rose Garden, twenty or so middle-age men were using their lunch break to play a brand of soccer that will not send shivers down the spine of the Brazilian national team should they somehow encounter each other. The makeshift mini goals at each end had no netting, so on the off chance they strung together enough passes to score—and that seemed a fantasy from what I saw—someone had to run another forty meters past the goal to retrieve the ball. Surely, they could pilfer some random government coffers, call it "team building," and invest in a couple of nets. Overall, Canberra seemed quite active, much like every other Aussie city. A number of folks were running along the lake or out for a lunchtime bicycle ride. I'm sure the runners and cyclists would have preferred to play soccer, but there was that issue of no nets.

My first stop was the Old Parliament House, a structure that opened in 1927 and was the meeting place for Parliament until 1988. Parliament had met in the Victorian Parliament House in Melbourne from 1901 until 1927, in case you were wondering. The sprawling, white three-story building was known as the Provisional Parliament House during its day and was intended to be used for fifty years, which seems like a long time for something to be provisional. It became obsolete in the 1980s when 300 people worked inside, and the government operations moved into the current Parliament House up the road.

Today, the Old Parliament House is a museum that cost me a whopping $2 to visit. As tourist attractions go, it offers a high return on your investment. It was worth at least twice that. In also seriousness, there was a lot to take in and learn if learning is your thing. There are several exhibit rooms, a room that profiles past prime ministers, and an area where one can tour through the former government offices, which was the highlight for me. Just downstairs from the entrance was a temporary exhibit of the year's best political cartoons. Only in Australia would they promote the cartoons making fun of politicians in the former Parliament building.

A stroll through the old Prime Minister's Suite and the suite of the president of the Senate is particularly fun if you are a child of the '80s because the offices have been recreated to look like they did in 1983, when then-Prime Minister Bob Hawke and his team occupied the place before they moved into the shiny, new digs up the hill five years later. Old typewriters, filing cabinets, rotary telephones, and '80s-era TVs make it feel like you are on the set of *The West Wing – Australia*...in 1983. In the Prime Minister's Suite, you even get to see where he sat on the throne. That is, you get to see the bathroom area where Hawke and PMs before him prepped for TV interviews.

Just down the hallway was the Cabinet Room. Across the hall was a public toilet where I found the most Australian thing in the entire Old Parliament House—a urinal trough where three men could stand shoulder-to-shoulder and take a piss. Yep, the men's room where Australia was governed had a step-up, chest-high urinal trough that you'd find in just about any grimy pub across the land or in an old American ballpark. This was perfectly Aussie to me, and I could have left town then, completely satisfied with my Canberra experience. Alas, I felt a bit like an intellect at this point, so on I learned.

In the center of the Old Parliament House is a grand foyer called the King's Hall, and on either side of that were the House of Representatives Chamber and the Senate Chamber. This is where each group would gather to govern back when governments governed and debated instead of screwing around and not talking to each other like they do today. In the House of Reps Chamber, I struck up a conversation with an older gentleman working as a security guard, whom I guess was there to make sure no one stole the seat cushions.

"Canberra is still a town where you can walk down the street and run into someone you haven't seen in a couple weeks," the *old codger* said to me. "Today, we have a lot of young people coming to work here in the public sector. Unfortunately, housing prices are going up, too. Not to Sydney's levels, of course, but things like fuel costs are high."

Conversation turned to the building in which we were standing and he mentioned that many of Australia's oldest buildings have been knocked down and rebuilt, leaving "very few buildings in the country that are more than 150 years old," which is astounding when you think about how long people have been on this land.

Across the hall was an exhibit on the country's prime ministers. Australia is governed by what is called the Westminster system, based on the British parliamentary system. The big difference from the US presidential system is that the prime minister is not put in office by a national election. The lawmakers are elected by voters and then the largest party gets to make its leader the prime minister and form the government. However, and here's where it gets amusing, the ruling party can choose a new leader without it ever going to a vote by the citizens. In Australia, they seem to like doing this.

Since 2007, when John Howard ended his nearly 12-year run as Australian Prime Minister, the country has treated its PMs like you ought to treat your socks and underwear—they change them frequently and don't use them for long. In 2022, the country had its eighth prime minister since 2007 (though one of them had two stints) when Anthony Albanese took the reigns as the first Labor party PM in nine years. Before that, it was Scott Morrison for nearly four years. He took over when lawmakers forced out Malcolm Turnbull, even though Morrison and Turnbull were from the same party, the Liberal Party—what Americans would call the conservative (Republican) party in America.

In Australia, the prime minister can be challenged to an election (called a "spill") by someone in his or her own party if they feel you're not doing the job and are ripe for a takeover. It's a bit like being backstabbed, but not in the back. Imagine that happening at your company—one of the VPs risking it all to ask the people in the company to vote between him/her and the current boss.

As I walked around the room of prime minister profiles, the stories of the men and one woman who have held the office were strangely entertaining. The shortest-serving PM was Francis Michael Forde, who took over after wartime PM John Curtin died in office at the age of 60 in 1945. Forde immediately lost a leadership battle and was out after what must have been a highly impactful run of eight days. Eight!

He barely had time to place photos of his wife and kids on his desk.

Strangely enough, Curtin was not the only PM to die in office. The first was Harold Holt, who is presumed to have drowned while swimming off the coast of Mornington Peninsula in Victoria in 1967. I say "presumed" because he was never found. Holt went for a dip in rough conditions at a place called Cheviot Beach and was never seen again. It seems like it should be pretty hard to lose a prime minister. This is not your car keys we're talking about. Is there no security with him? Does an advisor not say, "Gee, sir, the sea looks a bit rough today, and I'd prefer not to have 'the guy who lost the prime minister on my LinkedIn profile.' Maybe we go to the pool instead?"

Julia Gillard, who served as the prime minister from June 2010 through June 2013, is the only woman prime minister in the country's history. She was replaced by the same guy who was prime minister before her, Kevin Rudd. Then, Mr. Rudd was replaced two and a half years later by Tony Abbott, who was replaced two years later by Turnbull, who was replaced three years later by Morrison in 2018, who lost the election to Albanese in 2022. Before I finish typing this page, Albanese may be out and someone else may be in.

As I walked around the room, it seemed as though half of the prime ministers were direct descendants of convicts. At least in Australia, being a criminal is in their blood. In America, they are politicians and THEN they become criminals.

A few steps beyond the Great Hall was another exhibition on the history of the Indigenous people of Australia. To say that history is complicated would be a laughable understatement. As the exhibit explained, the Indigenous people of Australia have been on the land since the beginning of time. DNA studies done by anthropologists have confirmed that Aboriginals of Australia likely left Africa somewhere in the neighborhood of 75,000 years ago. I'm no anthropologist—and I would imagine that is fairly evident if you got this far—but from what I've read, that means they may be the oldest living culture on earth. The exhibit inside the Old Parliament House centered mostly on the rights of the Indigenous people through the last century, probably because they had none prior to that. Unless you want to count all the time before white people arrived, when rights were not much of a problem. Also, 75,000 years would be a lot to cover in one room.

In 1939, the Australian government adopted a policy of assimilation, essentially saying that Aboriginal people should assimilate into the white community. If that sounds to you like something that would be easier said than done, congratulations. You're smarter than whoever came up with the idea. To achieve this, the federal and state government agencies, as well as church missions, removed mixed-race children of Aboriginal and Torres Strait Islander descent from their families and attempted to indoctrinate them into white Australian families and white culture. This had been going on since the turn of the century to some degree, but ramped up in the 1940s and continued right up until the 1970s. A national inquiry called the Bringing Them Home Report of 1997 said that at least 100,000 children were taken, with many forced to live in orphanages run by church missions or raised by foster parents. This generation of Aboriginal children came to be known as the Stolen Generation.

In the late 1950s an organization that was then called the Federal Council for the Advancement of Aborigines launched an effort to end the Australian constitution's discrimination against Indigenous people. Twelve years later, in 1962, Indigenous people were given the right to vote in federal and state elections. Then, in 1967, the council's efforts came full circle, when Australians voted on a referendum that would count Indigenous people in the official census. The results were overwhelming: 90.7 percent of the population voted to count Indigenous people in the population. They would be seen as citizens for the first time. Words on the wall in the exhibit summed up what the referendum meant:

"The 1967 Referendum is a moment in history that asked all Australians to contribute to our shared national identity. It asked the questions of who we are, and who we want to be. When Australians went to the polls 50 years ago, the majority 'yes' vote demonstrated a deep sense of fairness and justice lay in the hearts of Australians, as well as a belief that we are stronger when we stand together."

Approaching the Old Parliament House an hour earlier, I'd seen something called the Aboriginal Embassy on the grass across the street, and not thought much of it. Made up of a few tents, some trailers, and another small structure that looked like a shed you'd find in someone's backyard, it was basically a makeshift campsite with a large "SOVEREIGNTY" sign next to it. I figured it was some sort of temporary Aboriginal protest, and I figured wrong. As I learned inside the Old Parliament House exhibition, the Aboriginal Tent Embassy had been established there in 1972 to draw attention to Aboriginal land rights. In the decades since, the Tent Embassy has grown to become a symbolic center of all protests for Indigenous groups. In

1995, it was added to the Australian register of the National Estate.

There have been other recognitions through the years, including a High Court decision in the 1992 Mabo Case. To follow that one, you have to go all the way back to the seventeenth-century doctrine of *terra nullius*, a Latin term that essentially means land that belongs to no one. The early European settlers in Australia relied on this doctrine to claim possession of the place by saying that Indigenous people had no settled law governing occupation and use of the land, which was incorrect. In 1992, the Australian High Court ruled that the lands of Australia were not *terra nullius* when European settlement had occurred.

"The High Court recognised the fact that Indigenous peoples had lived in Australia for thousands of years and enjoyed rights to their land according to their own laws and customs," reads a passage on the website of the Australian Institute of Aboriginal and Torres Strait Islander Studies. "They had been dispossessed of their lands piece by piece as the colony grew and that very dispossession underwrote the development of Australia as a nation."

The website goes on to explain that the High Court decision altered the foundation of land law in Australia. The very next year, in 1993, the Native Title Act 1993 (Cth) was passed in the Australian Parliament, which opened the way for claims by Aboriginal and Torres Strait Islander peoples to their traditional rights to land and compensation.

See what I mean? Complex.

In 2008, then-Prime Minister Kevin Rudd offered an apology to the Indigenous people of Australia and particularly the Stolen Generation, calling it a blemished chapter in the country's history. "We apologize for the laws and policies of successive Parliaments and governments that have inflicted profound grief, suffering and loss on these, our fellow Australians," Rudd said. "We apologize especially for the removal of Aboriginal and Torres Strait Islander children from their families, their communities and their country. For the pain, suffering and hurt of these Stolen Generations, their descendants and for their families left behind, we say sorry."

These steps are considered landmark moments in the country's history, especially for those of Indigenous descent. What the exhibits and the monuments in Canberra didn't delve into quite as much is the challenges that still exist today for the Indigenous people of Australia. Many live in poverty in rural areas, with limited educational opportunities. Addiction to alcohol is rampant. The 2016 Australian Census reported that there were more than 150 Australian Indigenous languages spoken at home by people of Aboriginal and Torres Strait Islander descent. Most of those people speak English as well, but on the point of language alone, you can imagine the challenges of rightfully wanting to preserve your own ancient culture and somehow meshing with a modern one. It would be another book to cover and I'm going to leave that to someone smarter than me, but if you visit Australia and travel beyond the biggest cities or most splendid beaches, the struggles of its native people are evident. In the days I spent in the Northern Territory, it was particularly obvious.

When I finished my longer-than-expected visit to Old Parliament House, I wandered briefly through the originally named Old Parliament House Gardens, then up a slight incline a few hundred meters along a lawn called the Federation Mall. It ended at the current Parliament House on Capital Hill. At the entrance was a massive mosaic on the ground done by an Aboriginal artist. Towering above the shiny, ultra-modern building was a large Australian flag that snapped in the sturdy wind of the day.

I grabbed a quick lunch in the cafeteria, which is called the Queen's Terrace Café so that they can charge you more money for a salad, and wondered if any of the suits dining beside me were important people. No one seemed at all bothered by their presence so I assumed not. They were probably busy plotting how to switch prime ministers again. After lunch, I signed up for what old folks in the US would refer to as the "nickel tour" given by one of the guys who works at the front desk. It was free.

For thirty or so minutes an official-looking gentleman in his sixties and dressed a bit like mall security walked a group of us around the building, pointing out the important symbolic designs of the place as well as some of the odd stories that I can't remember and didn't bother to write down. A large reflection pool made of Australian granite is the centerpiece of the Members' Hall, which is the centerpiece of the building. So the pool is the centerpiece of the centerpiece, if you're keeping score. Its flowing water creates a white noise that is intended to prevent people from overhearing important things that might be said by the members. You might say that is an artistic way to keep things private, or you might say the government built a pool so that the people who put them in office can't hear what they are doing even if they come to check up on them, and then told them exactly that. There is also a Great Hall, which is basically a giant function room

Parliament House, Canberra

that any regular bloke or sheila can rent out for as low as $6,000. Our guide told us there have been wedding receptions there as well, which will set you back $70,000. This seemed to me a strange thing—to be able to rent out the hall in the Parliament House for your wedding. It also seems like a fascinating way for a government to make a little extra cash on the side, as if it's the local country club or a function room at your local football club. The hall has even hosted table tennis championships. No word on if the Beer-Pong Championships will be coming to the Great Hall next.

After the short tour, I took the opportunity to spend a few minutes listening to Parliament members, who happened to be in session today. It didn't take much to get into the room. I gave my small backpack, including my phone, to a security desk and then passed through a security check you might find at an airport in a small American town where airport security still doesn't require a rubber glove and a moment of anal intrusion.

While sitting there observing, I wondered if it's possible to watch

Congress in America…you know, just *rock up* to the place and grab a seat in the balcony like I did here. Turns out, in D.C., you need to obtain a pass through your local congressional representative or apply for a pass in advance if you are not a US citizen. Because wouldn't that be an exciting way to spend a Tuesday? After a few minutes of Aussie Parliamentary proceedings, the novelty wore off and I was pondering a little *kip*. (Again, if they were paramilitary proceedings, different story.) Though I'm sure one or two Parliament members were also asleep, I didn't know how they'd take to visitors doing the same, so I slipped out.

The highlight of a trip to the Australian Parliament House—unless you are married there or crowned a table tennis champion, I presume—is the roof. An elevator to the top floor delivers you to a well-maintained lawn that sits above the top of the building. Towering above all that is the 101-meter-tall flag mast. Outside of a hike up a local mountain, the roof of the Parliamentary building boasts the best view of Canberra. Across the street from the front entrance, the tree-lined Federation Mall stretches away to the Old Parliament House. In the distance, across Lake Burley Griffin at the end of what is called ANZAC Parade, is the Australian War Memorial. Behind it, at 834 meters tall, Mount Ainsley towers above it all. Perfectly master-planned.

With an hour before the National Portrait Gallery closed, I hustled down the road to take a look inside for thirty or so minutes because I had read that it was a fascinating place, and it was free. A fan of art—or anyone with an ounce of knowledge about the subject—could spend hours in the place. While I have always respected the talent and expression of painters and the like, I must admit to having no idea what I'm looking at when I walk into an art gallery, especially when it comes to paintings or drawings or sculptures. With limited time, I gravitated to the room full of modern-day portrait photographs of some of Australia's noted characters. There were paintings and photos of Indigenous legends, politicians, sports icons like Cathy Freeman and cricketer Shane Warne, and musical greats like INXS lead singer Michael Hutchence. There was one particularly eye-catching painting of the Aussie band Midnight Oil. I'm not sure if it was an oil painting, but that would have been clever. I was just getting into it all when the security guy looked at me with an evil eye and gave the *Onya bike, son!* look.

Because it wasn't too far away, I made a quick detour from my planned route home to check out the Australian National Library. Aside from being slightly surprised to see that university students still use libraries to do research rather than their phone, I was quickly satisfied that I had seen all the library offered... books, mostly, in case you're wondering. The walk back to the hotel didn't look too long, so I decided to take a slightly longer path that would return me to my hotel via the King's Avenue Bridge and through the parkland surrounding the lake. Forty minutes later, I was still walking/dodging afternoon joggers and cyclists along a lakeside path and the wind was blowing so hard that I felt like one of those morons they interview on CNN who says he is going to stay and protect his house when a Category 5 hurricane is bearing down on Florida. By the time I found my way out of Commonwealth Park and back toward my hotel, it was approaching 8 p.m. As ascertained the previous evening, Canberra is not exactly the city that never sleeps when it comes to dining options after 9, so, after a quick shower, I ventured out for a bite.

I tried for the BentSpoke Brewery, but no tables seemed available. All of the sudden, Canberra was Cancun during spring break. Where the hell did all these people come from? Next door was the Greasy Monkey, which was just what it sounds like, only better. The Monkey had burgers of all kinds, greasy pizza, and even coleslaw. I had some slaw with my chicken burger, which came with a free beer because it was Tuesday. Suddenly, the Canberra nightlife was on the upswing. At a table on the outdoor patio across from me were four guys who were as hungry as I was. I deduced this because I watched them chatting quite happily among themselves for twenty minutes until their food arrived. From the moment the waitress dropped their plates in front of them until fifteen minutes later, when they were finished, they uttered not a single word to one other. This is how you know men are hungry. Food begets silence.

The chicken burger settled in my belly like a lead balloon, I headed next door to the aforementioned BentSpoke Brewing Company, a brewpub that opened in 2014 and became an instant hit, if you are to believe the reviews I had read online. I ordered a Canberra pale ale called the Barley Griffin at the ground floor bar, then headed upstairs for a bird's-eye view of the brewing tanks and to see if I could find a place to sit down. From a spot by the bar that overlooked the street, I struck up a conversation with a couple of the women who worked there. A few minutes later, one of them offered me a free gin and tonic that was the size of my head, which I did not need but happily accepted and stationed next to my half-full beer. "This guy called Bobby a dick, and I'm the only one who's allowed to call Bobby a dick," she told me. "So we told him to leave, but he had just ordered these three gin and tonics. So, it's all yours."

I didn't ask about the other two.

"Bobby seems cool to me," I said, while wondering who Bobby was and appreciating that, somehow, Bobby's feelings being hurt had indirectly lifted mine. After a few minutes of chatter, the ladies shared that they figured I was some sort of American military intelligence person.

"Is this because I exude intelligence?" I asked.

"No, you have an American accent and there is some sort of place here in town where American military people come all the time," she said.

Ahh, right, so not the intelligence thing. I didn't know what military-related location she was referring to, but there is also the possibility that some American tourist told them he was American military intelligence because he thought it would get him sex. At any rate, I guess they figured there was no other reason for an American to come to Canberra. Clearly, they have not seen the rotary telephones in the replica prime minister's office in the Old Parliament building. Probably because they wouldn't know what a rotary telephone is…or was.

The bartender told me she wasn't really sure why Canberra was growing, but guessed that perhaps the prices in Sydney had driven young people this way. "Although prices here are getting crazy, too," she added.

Before someone else could call Bobby a dick and leave me staggering shit-faced through the wild streets of Canberra on a Tuesday, I thanked them for my extra beverage and headed for my hotel, which tonight was in a new location more downtown, the only place I could find availability now that Parliament was back in session.

As I neared the hotel, I saw a sign for a massage parlor and thought about treating my aching feet the next morning. On the window was a sign listing the prices and treatments on offer, which in hindsight seemed to be plentiful. When I was three feet from the window, a motion detector opened the door and I noticed that the sign above said OPEN. It was at least 11 p.m. Hmmmm. A few seconds later a Chinese woman in her thirties or forties appeared from behind a wall and smiled at me through the glass, which had now closed, then waved for me to come in. She was wearing only a towel, as if she had just come out of the shower, or wanted to go take one. Sadly, I was without my loofah brush or any bail bonds, so I waved her off with a smile and turned away, surprised by what Canberra seemed to have on offer. It wasn't easy, mind you. My feet were sore.

Country road sign somewhere in country Victoria

Chapter 17: Canberra to Victoria

I awoke the next morning with sore feet, but I hadn't been arrested for soliciting a happy ending, so things were better than they could have been. With a little effort, I found another café for a hearty breakfast while thumbing through the newspaper. Hearty breakfasts will be the death of me, but it will be a more pleasurable way to go than a kangaroo through the windshield. Both *The Australian* and the *Sydney Morning Herald* had photos of the increasingly catastrophic bushfires on their respective front pages. The images were so intense that it felt like holding the newspaper might burn my hand.

In the days, weeks, and even months to follow, the bushfires of December 2019 and January 2020 would rage to levels this country had not seen. Enormous areas of New South Wales, the Australian Capital Territory, Victoria, and South Australia would burn. Thousands of Australians lost their homes, huge populations of wildlife were wiped out, and ranchers lost massive amounts of livestock. Australia will feel the effects of it for years to come. You can help by going to visit them, spending a little dough, and having a good time, which is an easier way to help people than clearing charred ruins from their land or laying bricks to help them rebuild their home, which is what many of them needed to do.

If you go to Canberra—and let's be honest, I probably haven't convinced you—I would recommend a visit to the Australian National War Museum after a hearty breakfast. It's one of those rare places that would be fun for the whole family, or even just a solo-traveling, middle-aged male feeling slightly *dusty* on a spring morning after chasing a few strong pale ales with a gin and tonic the size of a basketball. (Bobby pours a stiff G&T. Turns out, he was indeed a bit of a dick, after all.) Anyway, the Australian National War Museum in Canberra looks nice enough from the outside, with its freshly mown lawns, flowerbeds, and military artifacts dotting the entrance, but the treasures inside were more than I expected. With what very well could have been their last words on this earth, the immensely welcoming and immensely life-experienced staff advised me what to spend my time on if, like them, I had a limited amount of it. Using their guidance, I briefly poked around the oldest displays just after the entrance, then headed for the more recent war exhibits.

The Anzac Hall, which the young whippersnappers at the front desk told me not to miss, was incredible. It was the size of ten gymnasiums. Full airplanes hung from the ceilings, submarines sat out on the floor, and huge video screens played short films from wars gone by. It felt like I walked onto the set of a History Channel re-enactment. If you have any interest in history at all, you'd love it, and your kids would, too. Anzac Hall and Aircraft Hall, with a collection of classic war planes, could be its own museum. Just fantastic. From there, I wandered back toward the entrance and through the Hall of Valour, which the museum says "recognizes the deeds of ordinary Australians under the extraordinary conditions of war." Knowing that my mate Leighton's great-grandfather was a decorated serviceman, I took a quick look around for his name. It was easy to find. The plaque for Lance Corporal Albert Jacka detailed what a legend the man was and why he was the first Australian to be awarded the Victoria Cross in World War I at Galipoli.

The plaque said that during a heavy Turkish attack, Jacka and four others were holding a portion of a trench. When the others with him were killed or wounded, he single-handily attacked and killed seven Turks to keep the trench from being overrun. He was honored twice more for additional instances of bravery. After serving his time, he returned home and embarked on a business career before dying of poor health in 1932 at just thirty-nine years of age. Leighton is quite proud of this family lineage and, based on the plaque, he ought to be.

Outside, just above the Pool of Reflection, a military veteran in his late sixties or seventies sat in a chair and held court with a class of schoolchildren who looked to be about twelve. He was dressed in formal military attire, a host of medals hanging from his chest. Beside him, a woman, possibly the class teacher, stood holding a picture of him as a young man. Periodically, she would ask questions of the kids to encourage their participation. As an American traveler, I've heard plenty of jokes from foreigners about how we tend to play up the US military at sporting events and go out of our way to honor service men and women. I'm patriotic, and it's one of the things I love about my country, so I've never paid much attention to the comments. Australians honor their veterans often as well, and they do it with great sincerity, often through the simplicity of silence. As I watched the group of school kids listen to the stories of sacrifice from a man who could be their grandfather, it was clear that this legacy of honor will continue. As I left the Australian War Memorial, it made me smile.

Australian National War Museum, Canberra

With a couple hours to spare before a long drive down the coast toward Melbourne, I decided to lighten the mood of the day with a quick campus tour at the Australian Institute of Sport, a few miles away. It's Canberra; everything is just a few miles away. The Institute of Sport is a bit like a university campus for people who are so good at sports that they don't have to go to school...much. My tour guide was a strength and conditioning coach for the women's basketball program. The place is home to facilities for track and field, basketball and netball, gymnastics, combat sports, volleyball, soccer, tennis, and a huge strength and conditioning gym.

The aquatic center, a state-of-the-art facility with two fifty-meter pools and a twenty-five-meter pool, is the crown jewel of the place. It has cameras stationed below the water that capture the data of swimmers. Our tour guide told us something about American swimming legend Michael Phelps coming to train here leading up to one of his Olympics because the pool is so high-tech. The Aussies agreed to let Phelps use the pool, but only if they could keep his data, which I presume they then used to help make their own swimmers faster. Or perhaps they just sold his data to a call center in Mumbai that will badger him relentlessly with robocalls offering great credit card deals. Data is the future, they say.

The start of the tour offered the opportunity to try a few of the sports on simulators. The other person getting the tour was an Indian man in his sixties. It felt strange as the two of us put up jump shots on the mini basketball court and tried our hands at the skeleton simulator while the thirty-something tour guide stood there and watched us like a parent at the playground. Still, for the $30 entry fee, you're crazy if you think this former college hoopster was not missing a chance to throw up a few jumpers. The whole tour lasted ninety minutes, and that was plenty. The place was actually rather quiet. The only people in the gym were staffers, who apparently use it during lunch breaks.

In February 2020, *The Australian* published a story that detailed the highly questionable "spending priorities" of the Australian Institute of Sport (AIS) and quoted one official as saying that the organization was "a shell of its former greatness." The article explained how, after the London Olympics of 2012, funding cuts caused the loss of top coaches, sports science, and technical talent. Former officials who managed the operations in the glory days of the 1980s and '90s said the current administration cared more about the management than the athletes. There were tales of executives living basically anywhere but Canberra, raking in huge salaries and hardly ever setting foot on the sports campus. Some sources even said the place was a "ghost town."

My afternoon plan was to drive from Canberra to a place called Lakes Entrance, along the coast, more than five hours away. That would leave me with a comfortable four hours back to Melbourne the next day and maybe time for a stop I had in mind. I gassed up on my way out of town and ran into a cheery, talkative fellow who, I imagine, decided that he was going to liven up his days behind the cashier stand by just being friendly to people. What a novel approach to life. *Good on him.*

"Busy day for ya?" he asked.

"Not particularly," I said, realizing it felt good to say this. "I'm on holiday."

"Enjoy it," he said. "Great day for it."

"Yeah, it is," I said. "Hey, I've got a long drive ahead of me and looking for a quick lunch. Any place around?"

"Yeah, the guy across the road there makes sandwiches. Just *rippahs.*"

I thanked him and drove to the small shopping center across the street, picked up a roast beef sandwich and a bag of chips, and headed on. The sandwich was edible, but hardly a rippah. A rippah (ripper) is generally something extraordinary. It can be a ripping day, or a gorgeous woman can be a rippah, or your mate can be a *ripping bloke.* This sandwich was just a sandwich. Sandwiches in Australia are just okay. You won't find much like the sub shops that dot the American landscape, where they actually do make ripping steak and cheese subs. In Australia, my colleagues thought Subway subs were rippahs. I'll stop there to avoid a lawsuit.

Canberra disappeared in the rearview mirror behind me as quickly as it had appeared on the darkening landscape two nights earlier. After only a few bites of my average sandwich I was on a one-lane highway rolling through excessively dry farmland under a cloudless sky. The landscape reminded me of what you see in Colorado or other high desert environments, except more parched. Along the side of the road, the kangaroo roadkill count was climbing rapidly. Still, it wasn't the dead animals that worried me; it was the live ones. At various points along the Monaro Highway, cattle grazed just off the highway between the fence that I presume was there to keep them off the road and the road itself. The only things keeping them from walking in front of the cars going 100 kilometers per hour was their good sense or the fact that there was no grass to eat growing from the pavement.

After an hour, I cruised through a deserted-looking town called Bredbo. There was a pancake and crepe place for sale and a healing center that was shut down, its landscaping overgrown. Bredbo looked like the type of secluded place where Charles Manson might have hidden out with his crew.

Two hours into the drive, I happened upon a tiny place called Nimmitabel, New South Wales, home to 300 people. For whatever it's worth, the internet says Nimmitabel is thirty-seven kilometers south of Cooma and seventy-five kilometers west of Bega. I would have a hard time finding either of those on a map and would venture to guess people from Nimmitabel might as well. Nimmitabel actually has its own website, which is as charming as the village itself. It looks like it was designed in a high school computer class in 1996. The website, not the town. The village of Nimmitabel sits in an area that has been one of the top wool-growing regions of New South Wales for more than 100 years. The name of the place is based on an Aboriginal word that means "the dividing waters." The moniker stems not from the fact that Moses once lived here—though that might make it busier—but rather because it is from here that the southern waters flow into the Snowy River and the northern waters flow into the Murrumbidgee River. Full credit to the Nimmitabel High School website design class of 1996 for both of those handy bits of info.

I believe the website because a sign on the road somewhere had told me that I was in the Great Dividing Range, which scared me at first. The idea of happening upon a place where everyone is good at long division was hardly appealing after all the math I had done adding up roadside kangaroo carcasses for the last two hours. Alas, the Great Dividing Range is not a place for mathematics experts at all, but the name for the mountains that run the length of the entire east coast of Australia. It's not the Alps or the Himalayas, mind you, but what it lacks in height, it makes up for in girth. I mean length. The Dividing Range stretches more than 3,500 kilometers (2,175 miles). I read somewhere in my travels—I can't remember where—that it is the fifth longest mountain range in the world.

Nimmitabel looked a little sleepy, as you might expect of a place thirty-seven long kilometers south of a teeming hot spot like Cooma and seventy-five kilometers west of a booming metropolis like Bega. On the main street, which was joined by the highway

I drove in on, many of the businesses looked like they had been shut down for months. I parked in front of the Nimmitabel Bakery and told myself I was stretching my legs, though I knew I was going inside to eat something bad for me. From across the street, a man with a long, bushy beard eyed me for a second before nodding at me in the way you nod at another person if you are the only two people within a hundred miles. The exterior of the bakery looked like it belonged in just such a place. It had an old and worn rock exterior and four pillars that propped up an overhanging roof, which offered shady seating on the sidewalk out front that no one was using.

Inside was everything you could hope for in a roadside stop. A friendly, smiling woman stood behind the counter, and in front of her beneath the glass was an assortment of delicious pies, muffins, and even donuts. If I had dreamed up the type of the place I would come across in the middle of a five-hour drive, this was it. I ordered a sugar-coated donut, a chocolate chip muffin, and a tea for the road. If you think it didn't take every ounce of my being not to add a pie to that order, we don't know each other very well. While the woman fixed my order, we chatted briefly about the town and the weather.

"It's not normally THIS dry," she said, ominously. I asked why so many shops seemed closed down. "People not spending any money, I guess," was her answer, which makes perfect sense if you're not looking for much in the way of an explanation.

Five minutes later I was off again, doing my best not to transfer the melting chocolate from the muffin to my hand to the steering wheel while passing through places with highly original names. I crossed over Hopping Joe Creek and pictured a guy with one leg who didn't mind the occasional swim. Maybe the locals felt bad for him and named the creek after him instead of calling him One-legged Joe. There were numerous others, but the road was just too dangerous to try to jot them down. Somewhere near Coopracambra National Park, a roo darted out of the woods and decided to hop alongside my car. I slowed quickly before it headed back to the woods from whence it came, foiling my effort to add to the roo carcass count.

A few minutes later the road narrowed to the width of only one car due to a *land slip* (Aussie speak for a landslide), where a large gap in the pavement needed to be rebuilt. Between the wildlife and the winding road with missing sections of pavement, this was turning into the sketchiest drive ever done under ideal weather conditions. At some point the dry, high desert landscape turned green as I de-

215

scended in elevation toward the coast. Before long I was cruising through rolling green farmland and had crossed into the state of Victoria. The varied landscape of Australia was unfolding before my eyes on one afternoon drive, from the arid plateau of the agriculture region outside Canberra to the thick forests and the tropical-looking coast.

Finally, after five-plus hours, I arrived in Lakes Entrance, a fishing village and vacation spot for Melbournians in the heart of what they call Gippsland. I had never been to the area before, which is surprising for someone who lived in Melbourne for three years. I vaguely recall the man who looked after my apartment complex telling me that the last person to die from a tiger snake bite was in Gippsland, so maybe that's why I never went. It wouldn't be long before the sun disappeared, so I checked in quickly to the Bellevue on the Lakes Hotel and used the last hour of daylight to stroll along the waterfront.

Fishing boats and a few small cruising yachts filled the docks across the road, and Aussie flags whipped violently in a gusting breeze. After being stuck in the car all afternoon, the whipping onshore wind felt good, until it started to feel cold. I sauntered along—I like to saunter when I can—up the road a ways and snapped a few photos of a lone small boat moored to the shore against a colorful evening sky. The town was quiet, but seemed like the type of place that might come alive on weekends when city slickers like myself roll in. Because I'm me, it wasn't long before I was hungry. Pasta night at the restaurant inside the Bellevue on the Lakes seemed like a solid option, and that turned out to be the case. Plus, from the looks of things, finding a place to eat after 7:30 p.m. seemed as though it could become an ordeal on the level of finding sustenance in Canberra on a Monday.

I had planned on having a beer next door at the local RSL (sort of like an American Legion Club or Elks Club in the US) after dinner, but a giant bowl of pasta, a local Pinot Noir, five hours of windshield time, and the LeBron James impersonation I put on that morning at the Aussie Institute of Sports left me nearly face-down in my carbonara at 8:30 p.m. As I imbibed the last drop of wine in my glass, I accepted that it was time for bed.

I woke up early to one of those chilly, blustery coastal days that doesn't stay chilly for long. The sky was cloudless once again. The Princes Highway carried me along with views of the coast for the first few minutes before turning inland in the direction of Melbourne. Despite living in the area for a few years, I'd never ventured this far out of town to see how folks lived in the rural areas I'd often heard mentioned on the news. There wasn't much out here, but being here still made me feel like I should have come sooner.

Scattered along the roadside were koala/kangaroo/wombat crossing signs, giving the impression that they all gather together at certain points at wildlife crosswalks. According to more signage, the East Gippsland Rail Trail for bikes, horses, and walkers was somewhere nearby. The trail travels nearly 100 kilometers across this area and it's not uncommon for folks to tackle it over the course of a couple of days to explore the region. Farther up ahead, a sign for an Honor System Egg Sale was posted above a large basket of eggs by the side of the road, where people were expected to actually put in money and take only what they paid for. I came across this once on my first trip to Australia years earlier at a golf course in the country, which had no employees and only an honor system greens fee box. The first fairway had sixty kangaroos on it, so the money wasn't going toward keeping them from shitting all over the greens, I can assure you. Still, you know you're in the country when the honor system can be relied upon to pay the bills, and that is comforting in this day and age.

Roadside signs everywhere seemed to give the impression that I would see koalas the entire way, but still…nothing. I scanned the trees over the roadway more than I should have, but saw no signs of the elusive gray, fury beast. In three years of living in Australia and a number of other visits, I'd never seen a koala in the wild. It was becoming a mission of sorts. After a few minutes, it occurred to me that it would be strangely ironic—not to mention extremely stupid—to crash into a kangaroo while scanning the trees above for koalas. After nearly two hours, I turned off at a place called Rosedale and headed for a deserted mining town called Wallhalla. It was a bit out of the way, but I had time, and the photos I'd seen on the internet made the place look cool in the way that Denny's uses pictures on their menu to make their Moons Over My Hammy look delectable at 3 a.m.

From Rosedale, the road cut through a couple of small towns and then into a thick forest as the road began to climb. For some reason, my mind gravitated to the image of Tom Hanks in *Castaway.* In the final scene, Hanks stands beside his car on a deserted Texas road with a map laid out on the hood. Out of nowhere, an attractive redheaded woman in a pickup truck pulls up to help him with directions. That was me, but there was no redhead. Maybe in Wallhalla.

Ahh, negative, mate. Big negative there.

Wallhalla, Victoria

When I eventually reached Wallhalla after driving along a ridiculously winding and windy road, with tree debris strewn across the pavement, it was difficult to count the number of people in town. Not because there were so many of them, but because I couldn't find any. When they say it's a deserted mining town, I hadn't realized they meant today as well. Right before town, a high bridge spanning a river took me past an old train line and train depot, then around a corner and up into a small *car park*. (That's a park for cars, I guess, which looks a lot like a parking lot.) I had walked three steps before two flies the size of bats landed on my arm.

There was a time when Wallhalla was one of the most wealthy towns in Victoria. About 4,000 people lived in this tiny place searching for—and finding—a fair bit of gold after it was discovered around 1850. The mining boom took place through the latter half of the 1800s, when I presume there were just as many flies. Just twenty or so people live here now, according to the information I could find online, and the place is frozen in time. It's been a small tourist trap since the 1970s. There was a small corner store, a raised gazebo for brass bands (I guess) to play from, and an old fire station built in 1901 for 155 pounds, the sign said. A small stream trickled past below one side of the road. Up ahead, the Wallhalla Star Hotel stood quietly, having labored dutifully to earn all one of those stars.

I saw a sign for a trail that promised to take me to a mining area 500 meters away and started walking. It climbed up a fair hill and then continued along a dirt path that overlooked the town. From above, I could see a few small houses that looked to be inhabited, and thought, *Holy shit! People live here?* After a couple of minutes, the trail opened to a small clearing where old, rusted mining equipment was scattered across the grass. There were mining buckets designed to run on a small train track and, I guess, ferry gold from inside the mountain. It all looked like a scene from an Indiana Jones film.

A sign, which was written in a font that you might expect in an Old West mining town, hung above a tunnel that was closed off with an iron gate and a padlock. "Long Tunnel Extended Gold Mine," it said. On the gate another sign said this was the Long Tunnel Extended Tourist Gold Mine, but warned that no one was to enter without an authorized person. To the left was a small building, from which I presume the tours start when there are people present. The whole thing seemed a bit touristy to me and, to be honest, I didn't see anyone around who would seem to be giving a tour, or giving a shit about me being there at all, really.

I strolled down the other side of the hill back toward town and came upon a house. A wooden, makeshift sign that looked to have been constructed sixty years ago hung above the entranceway. "Tisdall," it said. The site was once the schoolhouse for the children in town, and the headmaster, Henry Tisdall, lived here. I found some information online saying that the Tisdall house now offers accommodations for visitors to Wallhalla, though most of those websites made the Nimmitabel website look like CNN.com. Farther down the street, a man mowed a lush green lawn at a small bed and breakfast along the stream.

A sign by the road said there was a cricket ground forty-five minutes up another path through the woods. Cricket grounds are boring enough when they are filled with people playing cricket. I didn't need to see an empty one on a Thursday morning. In the main part of town was a café that was open, which made it something of a novelty in Wallhalla today. A forty-ish man inside kindly made me a tea and fixed me a meat pie, which I was excited to ingest because I had skipped *brekkie*. The only individuals more enthusiastic about the pie were the flies inside the café, who attacked from all angles.

The man at the café told me that the town is often filled with schoolchildren and that's when it dawned on me: Wallhalla is the sort of place you visit as a kid in school and never have any reason at all to come back to again. They get you once with the touristy bits and, for some reason, no one ever tells their friends that it's not really worth the two-hour drive to eat a meat pie while being attacked by the Aussie national bird when you could have had the same experience playing golf.

Also, there were no koalas.

UNSOLICITED ADVICE: CANBERRA

MUST DO:

The Canberra "hot spots" that stood out to me were the **Old Parliament House**, the **National Portrait Gallery**, and the **Australian National War Memorial**... I liked the streets of Braddon for eating and drinking... Give yourself ample time to do the **Old Parliament House**, and then maybe half that time to do the current **Parliament House**... A visit to the **Australian War Memorial** will stick in your memory, and even the kids will dig it because of the real-life planes and submarines. All of those places are either a couple bucks to enter or completely free, so the price is right.

UP TO YOU:

If you have unlimited time in Australia, and government and museums are your thing, Canberra might be worth the effort. But let's be real: unless you have to drive through it, there's no way you're going there instead of Sydney, Melbourne, the Reef, the West Coast, or Adelaide... The **Australian Institute of Sports** visit was okay. The kids will probably find it cool for a little while, but at $30 a pop, it's expensive... I hear the **Australian National Museum** is nice, too, but how many museums can you do in a couple of days?... Skip the library; it's just books... The late-night massage parlor is your call.

NEXT TIME:

If I had extra time, I would have explored some of the **national parks** not far from Canberra in the ACT, Victoria, and New South Wales. I had planned for my journey to Melbourne to take me on a more scenic route to visit a mate in Jindabyne, in the heart of the **Snowy Mountains**. Unfortunately, he was called away on business... I had planned on strolling up **Mount Ainslie** as well for the bird's-eye view, but the historical stuff seemed more prevalent to the story here... If you like to stay active on your travels, you won't be alone **jogging around Lake Burley Griffin**.

PART VII:
MELBOURNE

Yarra River, Melbourne from Morell Pedestrian Bridge

Chapter 18: "Fishing in an Aquarium"

The dapperly attired young man in the *queue* ahead of me is in a sparring match with the ticket vending machine that I am waiting to use here at Flinders Street Station in Melbourne. I'm not sure what the problem is. I've bought my train tickets here before and it never felt like I needed an algorithm to solve it. But old mate looks to be a few beers deep, despite the fact that it's 11:30 a.m., and that could be the source of the holdup. To the right, a group of his mates are good-naturedly urging him to get his shit together. I know this because they are yelling things like, "Get your shit together, mate!" All, except one, are dressed in suits that fit just a bit too tight, as is the custom in Australia. The odd man out is wearing a dress, a woman's wig, and lipstick. Either he didn't get the memo or he's the lucky bloke getting married and this is his *bucks* day. Across the way, a flock of twenty-something women are dressed to the nines in high heels, fancy hats, and dresses you might see at a summer wedding.

Today is the first Saturday in November and that means it's Victoria Derby Day, which will kick off Melbourne's Spring Carnival of thoroughbred racing at Flemington racecourse, six kilometers northeast of the Melbourne CBD. The Melbourne Spring Racing Carnival carries on throughout the spring, as the name might imply to those of you familiar with the seasons of the year, and people come from across the land, and many faraway lands, to experience it. It's also a shit show, as the brunch-time scene at the train station might have foreshadowed.

The Melbourne Cup, which will happen on the coming Tuesday, is billed as The Race that Stops a Nation because it actually does bring Australia to a halt. In the state of Victoria, Cup Day is a public holiday. People have the day off from work because a group of equine quadrupeds partake in a three-minute race. Across the country, people stop what they're doing—even schoolchildren, I'm told—to watch and *have a punt* (wager) on the race when it goes off at 3 p.m. The Melbourne Cup draws somewhere around 100,000 people to Flemington, even in the rain. Two days later, Oaks Day (on Thursday) draws another 70,000-plus and is the traditional Ladies' Day at Flemington, though it has jokingly become known as Blokes Day because if it's ladies' day, well, yeah, the men of Melbourne are no dummies. Each of these big days on the calendar—Derby Day, Cup Day, and Oaks Day—feature myriad fashion shows and judged competitions for best-dressed attendees, none of which were likely to include the bachelor from the train station.

Five years earlier I spent my very first weekend in Melbourne attending Derby Day with Leighton and some of his mates in a biblical rainstorm that left my shiny black shoes as caked in mud as those on the horses. Despite the rain, the day was a blast, and so was the night that followed. It was a hell of a way to be introduced to Melbourne. Leading up to that first Derby Day experience, Leighton had described the Spring Carnival as "fishing in an aquarium" for single people, and if a more Australian thing has ever been said, I'd like to hear it. Shakespearean prose there from the man who likes to call himself The Wiz.

As I marched into Flemington on that rainy day with 80,000 other well-appointed and reasonably well-behaved (for now) individuals, I remember thinking that I was about to attend the biggest party of my life...all day long...and well into the night, if I could manage. And this proved to be the case. In horse racing parlance, it's good to be a *stayer* on days like this. Thankfully, this is one of my talents.

Today, on a partly cloudy but perfectly acceptable Melbourne spring day, we are doing it again—me for the fifth time; Leighton for the umpteenth. As wily veterans of the Carnival, the scene at Flinders Station hardly raised an eyebrow as we boarded the train to Flemington dressed in the traditional Derby Day black and white.

There are a number of ways to enjoy a big racing day at Flemington, and I have been fortunate enough to try most of them. You can get a pass to one of the exclusive branded "marquees" in an area called the Birdcage, where you will drink free alcohol, nibble on fancy *canapés* (hors d'oeuvres), and watch the beautiful and famous people move about these temporary daytime nightclubs. Or you can get a highly sought-after ticket to sit in the grandstand and watch like a real horse racing fan who studied the racing form the night before. Or you can watch the ponies along the rails until some of the people around you are using the rails to keep themselves vertical. Or you can do what we are doing today: buy a ticket that gets you into a giant grass car park where you will watch the racing on video screens with the masses. This assumes you have a mate who is kind and dedicated enough to leave home at some absurd morning hour to drive to Flemington and park in his or her reserved spot, thereby hauling all of the food, booze, and whatever else you might want for the day. It turns out, our colleague Matt Sullivan is just such a mate.

Heading into the day, the car park tailgating plan sounded like going to a football game in the US and never going into the stadium or attending a concert and then watching the show on a video screen completely out of view of the stage. As it turns out, spending Derby Day tailgating in a suit and tie while watching horse racing on a video screen a few hundred meters from the track itself is surprisingly fantastic. And even if it's not, don't worry; the first time you go to the Spring Carnival, you aren't likely to remember all of it anyway.

The car park has just about everything you need: food, copious amounts of alcohol, somewhat clean toilets in close proximity (the importance and abundance of which cannot be overstated during such a day), and, of course, lots of betting windows, which are important for two reasons. First, you are at the horse races and this is why they run around the track. Second, Aussies gamble like they have an endless supply of money coming from some mysterious source whose location was never divulged to me.

When we arrived at his car park, Sully had a pink boa draped around his neck, which clashed with his dark suit, checkered shirt, and dark tie, but paired quite well with the pink pony on a stick that he was holding between his legs and pretending to ride. You may find this image surprising, but then again, you don't know Sully. A born salesman with a sharp wit and a knack for telling lengthy and mildly amusing stories, Sully is a native New Zealander who makes his living selling golf clubs and has been in Melbourne since he married a local girl named Sophie twenty or so years earlier. He also has an affection for a drink or two, which, as the night wears on, he rests comfortably on his slightly protruding belly while slouching into whatever chair he might eventually fall asleep in. Somehow, he never spills a drop. He's what they call in Australia *good value*, which is to say: you want him around at a session such as this. Or anytime really.

We spent the day meandering to (for refills) and from the home base that Sully and Sophie set up, hobnobbing with people we know who parked a few minutes away, bumping into friends and placing bets on horses and jockeys we knew little about. The guy whose horse finished last in each race was forced to carry the pink horse on a stick and wear the pink boa until the next race finished, at which time someone else hopefully took the loser's mantle for the next half-hour. Late in the day, Leighton and I split a wager on the Victoria Derby, the seventh race of the day, and won $400 between us. I recall being happy because I told myself these winnings would cover my alcohol expenses for the day and some of the night, though deep down I knew this to be false.

Melbourne CBD above the Yarra River

When the day crawled to a close following the last race in the five o'clock hour, women who left the house looking like supermodels were carrying their high-priced, high-heel shoes because their feet hurt or they could no longer keep their balance. Others kept them on and were stumbling around like baby giraffes. Not to be outdone, many men were staggering to and fro with a *skinful* of liquid courage attempting to talk to the giraffes. Leighton might say they were casting a line into the fish tank. Around 6 p.m., the goal was to get ourselves back in the direction from which we came. The options: find a taxi (good luck!), meet your reserved group limousine (a smarter option), or head back to the train platform and wait for a lift back to the city with 50,000 other people.

Eventually, Leighton and I made our way to the train and began the journey back to the city. Halfway to Flinders Station, a group of guys in our cart erupted into a rousing singalong of "Waltzing Matilda," a traditional folk song written by Aussie poet Banjo Paterson (because that name sounds real) in 1895. The tune was made famous by the immortal folk singer Slim Dusty, who looked like a cross between Mick Dundee and Willie Nelson, and actually sang it at the closing ceremony of the Sydney Olympics. As "Waltzing Matilda" gained steam and the entire crowd joined in, I caught a glimpse of Leighton grinning ear to ear between lyrics. The whole train was smiling, too.

"You got the full Aussie experience today, mate," he said through the crowd.

"Great day," I confirmed, thinking of the $200 burning a hole in my pocket. "So where should we go next?"

...

"Melbourne is the place you want to live. Sydney is the place you want to visit."

That's the phrase many proud Melburnians are fond of uttering to international visitors who will listen. And as I was a resident of this fine city for about three years, I can understand where they're coming from while also admitting to their bias. Let's be clear: Sydney is one of the most scenic, heavenly cities I have ever been to. You'd be a little crazy to say it's not a place you'd like to live in, insane cost of living aside…and that's a big aside. What slightly irks the good folks of Melbourne is that their city probably doesn't get the notoriety it deserves worldwide alongside its neighbor 450 miles to the northeast. And also, no one pronounces it correctly. It's Mel-bin, not Mel-born.

Over the last decade or so, though, that has begun to change. The notoriety, I mean, not the mispronunciation. From 2011 to 2017, this city perched at the northern point of Port Phillip Bay was named the world's most livable city by no less of an authority on livability than *The Economist*. In 2018 and 2019, it was No. 2 behind Vienna, Austria in the same poll. The boys choir was the tiebreaker, I guess. Although if *The Economist* heard the "Waltzing Matilda" singalong on the train, maybe that would have changed their opinion. Despite these lofty rankings, it seems that among regular folks around the world, Melbourne is a bit of an unknown unless they've been there. If you ask travelers who have been to Australia about Melbourne, they will tell you one of two things: they loved Sydney and the East coast, but never made it to Melbourne, or they visited Melbourne and absolutely loved it, often to their surprise.

The second-fiddle complex seems to have left the folks of Melbourne with a healthy little chip on their shoulders, mostly because they know that a fair few people from Sydney look down their noses at them. There is also a feeling that not everyone knows just how good they have it. Being from the Boston area, where people carry a similar chip because of the city's proximity to New York (and also just because they like to), this mentality made me feel quite at home rather quickly. I like the chip. A business meeting with a woman in Sydney shortly after I arrived at my job in Melbourne cemented things for me. When I shared my excitement over recently arriving in Australia, she met my enthusiasm with what can only be described as, well, snobbery.

"It's just too bad you have to live in Melbourne," she said. "It's not a nice city and the weather is terrible. You want to be in Sydney."

I learned two things at that moment. First, she sucked and I wasn't going to do business with her. Second, she is the reason Melburnians say ridiculous things like, "Sydney is a city with no soul, man," which is probably a mild exaggeration. Well-traveled Aussies from both cities will tell you to think of Sydney as Los Angeles and Melbourne as San Francisco. And, if you are an ounce more open-minded than the woman I met with—which isn't asking a hell of a lot—you understand that both places are great for different reasons. And that's ideal because you can fly from one to the other in an hour, and why would you want to fly to the same place you came from?

It's true that Melbourne doesn't have a funky-looking opera house or an absurdly picturesque harbor, and there are no beaches on the level of Bondi, Coogee, or Manly within shouting distance of Melbourne's

Central Business District (CBD) to draw you in on first glance. But it does have just about everything else—plenty of industry and jobs, a gluttony of cultural happenings and events, an absurd amount of sports and entertainment, cultural diversity, and plenty of day-trip options within ninety minutes. It also feels more like a proper city, with neighborhoods that offer their own distinct vibe.

Australia's second largest city (population: 5 million to Sydney's 5.2 as of 2021) also has plenty of happy people, if the folks at something called The Time Out City Life Index survey (whatever that is) are to be trusted. Their research found that 89 percent of Melburnians enjoyed living in the city and nine out of ten felt happy in the previous twenty-four hours. The poll evidently surveyed 15,000 people from thirty-two cities and looked at anonymous data across seven categories: food and drink, culture, relationships and community, neighborhoods, affordability, happiness, and livability. (For context, the same survey determined that Parisians were the most sleep-deprived and had the most sex, and one could argue that there is a direct correlation between those statistics.) If you're one of those people that likes to do more than walk around bleary-eyed due to too much sex (or you just don't like croissants, cheese, and cigarettes), but you like being happy, maybe Melbourne is the place for you. You won't be alone. Projections say Melbourne will likely overtake Sydney as the biggest city in the country before 2030.

What I loved most about living in Melbourne, in addition to the people, is that it has a social calendar that is absolutely *chock-a-block* (full). In January, the capital city of the state of Victoria hosts the Australian Open, the first grand slam tennis tournament of the season. In March, the Australian Formula 1 Grand Prix takes over Albert Park. From there, you get into summer cricket, and then the Australian rules football (AFL) season runs from late March through September, with ten of the eighteen AFL teams based in the state of Victoria. When the footy ends, the aforementioned Spring Carnival with the ponies starts up. There are also two pro rugby teams and two pro soccer teams. At the risk of sounding sexist, I understand if the above list sounds like a decidedly male-oriented list of happenings, though I would posit that the female population of Melbourne is quite sports-minded. That's because Melbourne is absolutely sports mad, mostly about Aussie rules football.

If sport spectating isn't your jam, don't fret. There are plenty of cultural events of the non-sporting variety around that you might want to schedule to visit. There's the Melbourne Comedy Festival in

March and April, a Fringe Festival, a fashion week, a writers festival, concerts at the Sidney (*not* Sydney) Myer Music Bowl, and on and on it goes. As a resident, there is always something happening. On the off chance there isn't, Melbourne also has plenty of pubs, beer gardens, live music venues, and museums. If you want to break away, there are day-trip options, too. In one direction are the beaches, wineries, and golf courses of the up-market Mornington Peninsula less than ninety minutes away, where they specialize in Pinot Noirs, Shiraz, and Chardonnay. Eighty minutes in the other direction, the spectacular Great Ocean Road begins from Torquay and the famed Bells Beach and continues for 243 spectacular kilometers along the Victorian coast. Forty-five minutes to the Northwest of the city are the wineries of the Yarra Valley, where Chardonnay and Pinot Noir are the dominating grapes. Farther afield are a multitude of nature preserves and mountainous areas to get your outdoor fix.

Sprinkled in just the right places throughout the city are a number of charming tree-lined parks and gardens. There are also splendid outdoor recreation areas along the Yarra River, which cuts through town and is dotted with rowers and lined with runners and bikers most of the year. On weekends, the city's giant markets—Queen Victoria (opened in 1878), South Melbourne (1876), and Prahran (1891)—are where locals come to shop, meet, and just amble around with a coffee in hand while colorful characters hawk fresh produce, meats, and various arts and crafts.

The CBD is Melbourne's financial center, with its gridded street map and iconic laneways. The key landmark of the area is Flinders Station, the city's main transportation hub. Though it's more lively Monday through Friday, the CBD has more than enough quality restaurants, quaint cafés, and lively rooftop bars that are perfect for a few afternoon drinks in the shadow of the city's high-rise office buildings. Along the banks of the Yarra River, a few steps from Flinders Station, are a bevy of outdoor restaurants and bars, as well as the Crown Casino.

All that said, to get to know Melbourne you need to leave the CBD and venture into its surrounding neighborhoods, each with its own distinct and visible identity. If you live there, this variety makes leaving your neighborhood a sort of mini adventure. Richmond, within a stone's throw of the sports precinct, has an endless choice of English-style pubs. Collingwood has dive bars, music halls, and coffee shops. Fitzroy and Brunswick have a hipster vibe and live music venues.

A Melbourne tram passes by Flinders Station

In Carlton you can cruise Lygon Street and its endless Italian restaurants. Just across the Yarra River from Richmond is South Yarra, with its leafy streets, and the beautiful Botanical Gardens. Prahran and Windsor have the fashionable shops and nightlife of Chapel Street. St. Kilda has the beach along Port Phillip Bay, drunken backpackers, and loads of twenty-somethings from Ireland. Farther down the beach are trendy enclaves like Elwood and Brighton. There are Vietnamese neighborhoods and restaurants, Thai eateries, Michelin-level fine dining, and theaters that get worldwide plays and musicals. I could go on, but you get the point and this isn't *Lonely Planet*.

Oh, and if you like coffee, your only challenge in Melbourne will be choosing where to get your morning fix. Someone somewhere told me that there are more cafés per capita here than in any city in the world. The residents wear their discerning coffee palettes as a badge of honor, and travelers who love a cappuccino or latte (and I don't know the difference) say it is here that you will find some of the best cups in the world. Australians in general are so uppity about their flat whites and skinny whatevers that after Starbucks opened eighty-four coffee shops across the East Coast in the early 2000s, sixty of them were forced to close within seven years and the company had lost more than $105 million on them. This is mostly because many Australians—especially Melburnians—believe that, in the words of an Aussie friend, "Starbucks coffee is shite, mate." It's also because Melburnians love to visit their local coffee shop, sit down with their beverage in hand, and have a conversation with a mate.

While I don't do coffee, the Tim Sweeney City Livability Scale is heavily tied to whether or not it is possible to find good *brekkie*, and Melbourne and I were quite compatible in this way because the first meal of the day here is a bit of an event. I have never been to a city where so many business meetings took place at 8:30 a.m. over breakfast at a local café rather than the office boardroom or over lunch. I loved that it was perfectly acceptable to meet someone for eggs, toast, and a coffee or tea. Oh, and avocado. People here worship avocado.

Aesthetically speaking, this is Australia's most European (British) feeling city, and not just because of the architecture or because it's in a state named after the former queen of England. The weather can be decidedly British as well. Melbourne's cool, drizzly winters are one of the real knocks on the place, and even the locals are fond of saying that they can have "four seasons in a day." Again, being from Massachusetts, bad weather is a relative term. It never snows in Melbourne and the streets never freeze over with black ice that can leave you with a cracked skull on your walk to work, so I never understood how you could claim to have four seasons in day. Summers, on the other hand, are dry and subject to the occasional heatwave, which always seems to strike in January during the Australian Open, where players have reported hallucinating when temperatures on court stretched to 40 degrees C (more than 100 degrees F).

I would guess that one of the challenges for the folks at the local tourism office is that Melbourne, like an interesting person, is a place where you need to peel back the layers. While a weekend visit to Sydney is likely to leave you wowed because you saw all you expected to see, Melbourne is a place you need to get to know. If you don't have time for that, a local tour guide makes a big difference. Just beware: If you spend a week or you know where to go during a long weekend, you might end up persuading yourself to move here, which is what happened to me.

The AFL Grand Final at the Melbourne Cricket Ground

Chapter 19: The Footy at The G

Sitting on a couch in suburban Boston is about as far from an Australian rules football oval as one could possibly be, yet this is where I had my first experience with what Aussies call "the footy." Most Sunday mornings in the 1980s, after being dragged to church by our parents, my brother and I would each take our three donuts into the living room and turn on ESPN. The donuts, it should be noted, were the reward for good behavior at church. With chocolate glaze on our faces and tall glasses of milk in front of us, Chris and I would camp in front of the TV for an hour or two and watch tape-delayed Aussie Rules Football matches. Our favorite part was when the goal umpires—who back then dressed in white suit coats, white top hats, black ties, and black pants—would give their two-finger salute after each goal.

The game seemed crazy, like someone could die at any moment, and the announcers, with their wild accents and obscure terminology, fascinated us. Later, we would go into the backyard and kick our American footballs through the wooden goalposts dad had built for us out of two-by-fours. With every kick that sailed through the uprights, we'd substitute the NFL field goal signal for the two-pointed-fingers-at-the-waist from Aussie Rules. I could never have imagined that some twenty-five years later I would have the opportunity to watch the Grand Final (their Super Bowl) in person with 100,000 people while eating Four 'N Twenty meat pies in the upper reaches of the Melbourne Cricket Ground.

As a resident of Melbourne, I watched an unhealthy amount of Australian Football League (AFL) games on TV and attended ten or so every season for three years. Doing this will endear you to the locals, who are fond of asking (and answering) the question: "So what do you think of our footy? Great game, huh?" Once, on a flight back into Melbourne, I found myself in a lengthy and in-depth discussion about "the footy" with the man seated to my right. We debated the chances of certain teams, which players were performing well, and even in-game strategy. I was dropping the names of somewhat obscure players and referencing results from the early part of the season when he finally stopped me.

"Jesus, man!" he said, dumbfounded. "You're American. How much footy do you actually watch?"

"Yeah, a lot," I said. "I live in Melbourne. I don't have a choice."

During my first day of work in Melbourne, I was asked repeatedly by coworkers if I had picked a footy team yet. When I told them that Leighton had lured me into being a Geelong Cats supporter before I ever set foot in Australia and that I had watched them win the Grand Final while living in the US, my new colleagues called me a front-runner and spent the next month attempting to switch my allegiance so that I would *barrack* for their club. (Side note: They don't say "root" for a team; they say "barrack." *Rooting* means having sex. You're welcome.)

Office conversation on a Monday in Melbourne is about the footy played over the previous weekend, and office conversation from Tuesday through Friday is about which teams the boys at the office will be wagering on the next weekend. As is the case with anything they can bet on, everyone fancies themselves an expert. Without a hint of doubt, they will proclaim from week to week which team is a "good side," who "is shit," who will make "the eight" (the finals, as they call the playoffs), and who will win the flag (the championship). The following week the same conversations occur, except with completely different proclamations. The truth is, until about the fifteenth week of the twenty-two-game season, no one knows a damn thing. I've never been a gambler, especially on sports I don't fully understand, and I didn't know anyone who was making money *on the punt*, but they all seemed to claim that they were. That's what gamblers do, you see.

If you've seen it, but not studied it—and why would you?—Aussie rules football can be a difficult (or impossible) game to follow, which is probably what non-North Americans think when they watch the NFL (American football). As is the case with the NFL, no one else on earth really plays Aussie Rules except Aussies, so unless you attend a game, go searching for it on YouTube, or found it broadcasted to your country during a global pandemic, you're not likely to ever see it. The first game of Aussie Rules Football in a format that resembled its current look is said to have been played in Melbourne in 1858 between two local colleges (high schools). One year later, an official book of rules was put in place by members of the Melbourne Football Club. Today the Melbourne Demons, also known as the Dees, are still a team in the sport's top league, the eighteen-team Australian Football League (AFL). In fact, many of today's biggest clubs date back to this period. The game itself takes a little bit from a number of sports that were played in the UK, Ireland, and Australia prior to the mid-1800s.

In winter, life in Melbourne revolves around the footy. From April through September, there are at least three matches in the two big stadiums—the Melbourne Cricket Ground (MCG) or Docklands

Stadium downtown—from Friday night through Sunday afternoon. If you want to drive anywhere in Melbourne on a weekend, you should know the footy schedule because if two big local clubs square off, there could be 80,000 people trying to get to the MCG. The footy is also on every TV in every pub and, with nine of the eighteen AFL teams in Melbourne, there is always an interested fan base in the bar and supporters of the other teams there to give them shit.

The players often make up a large part of the newspaper gossip pages for what should not be news at all. While Sydney seems to focus its attention on actors and reality TV types, Melbourne's gossip pages cover footy players, footy coaches, footy announcers, and the wives and girlfriends of footy players, footy coaches, and footy announcers. Of course, with twenty-two players to a side (and more in reserve) and nine teams in the city, that means there are a couple hundred professional athletes doing normal life things around town every day. They are at your grocery store, in your pub, or at the table on the other side of the restaurant. It's different from, say, being one of twenty-six New York Yankees in a city of eight million.

Across the country, the AFL has grown in leaps and bounds over the last two decades. At one time, the game was only a focus of the residents of Victoria, South Australia, Western Australia, and the Northern Territory, but that has changed. Today, there are also professional teams with loyal followings in Queensland (Brisbane and the Gold Coast) and New South Wales (Sydney and Western Sydney), states that have traditionally been owned by rugby league and rugby union. Rugby is still the No. 1 draw in those places, but the ultra-professional, NFL-like marketing strength of the AFL has made inroads in those states. It has the most spectators and highest TV viewership of any Australian sport, and the AFL Grand Final, held every September at the MCG, is the highest attended club championship match in the world, drawing 100,000 people. There is no doubt that the AFL is, as the league proudly boasts, the national game.

If you're curious, these are the facts: An AFL oval is 165 meters long by 135 meters wide, but that can vary. You could play it in a city park... like the entire park. An American football field or soccer pitch can fit inside an AFL oval easily. Each team has eighteen players on the field at one time, with four interchange players (substitutes) on the bench, but the team can only make ninety total interchanges in a match. That means you run your ass off. Imagine the NFL with a field that is one-third bigger, then take away the whistles and pads and turn it into hockey without skates, sticks, and ice. I'm glad that made things clear.

Players can move the footy (the oval-shaped ball, which is also known as a Sherrin) by running with it, kicking it, or hand-balling it, which is sort of like punching it with a couple of knuckles on one hand while holding it in the other. Throwing it is not allowed. When they run with it, players must bounce it to themselves (like a dribble in basketball) every fifteen meters, though the actual distance seems up to the umpire's judgment. Any ball played off the ground means the player who takes possession can be tackled. If a player on either team catches a kicked ball out of the air (called taking a *mark*) that goes fifteen meters, there is a quick whistle and the player has a few seconds to make a free kick in the direction of a teammate or the goal. If a completed kick to a teammate goes less than fifteen meters in the air, the umpire rules the player to "play on," which means he can be tackled and no free kick is given. Anytime the ball hits the ground, it's considered live for anyone to gather up and run with.

Easy, right? Yeah, you really have to watch it (for a month) to understand.

There are four vertical goalposts at either end of the ground. If a team kicks the ball between the two big goalposts in the middle, they get six points, called a *goal*. If they miss the middle space and it goes inside the smaller posts to the right or left side, they get one point, which is called a *behind*. On average, teams score anywhere from sixty points to 140, which would be quite high.

If you were to attend a game of AFL football today, you could pick up some rules quite quickly. Others are more difficult to understand because they seem slightly open to the umpire's interpretation on a week-to-week basis. Even the most ardent fans of the game would agree with that assessment. Watching the footy on TV doesn't make it any easier. The announcers have a fantastic ability to build drama, but they interject so much local lingo that you feel like you're learning a new dialect.

As I still follow the Cats since departing the fine shores of Australia, I tune in regularly to watch the footy. I do this partly because it reconnects me to the country I've come to love, but mostly because it's a magnificent game to watch and listen to. When I sat down to loosely transcribe a passage of play (with some poetic license), I was struck by how many catchphrases might be used in two minutes. It sounds something like this:

Now-retired commentator Bruce McAvaney: *Lindsay wins the boundary throw-in cleanly. Rugers comes away with it and kicks a loooong ball into the pawket (pocket). Palmer takes the mark in a one-on-one contest with Lorde. Lorde goes down, so Palmer will* *play on. Palmer aroooound the corner in the direction of Pollock. Pollock's mark will live longer than memory, I reckon. About ten minutes ago. Flint handballs to O'Meara. Shows some candy to Wokulski and keeps on going. Handballs to Graham. Another disposal for him. Lovely bit of play. Gee, this is a good game of footy, isn't it? (This is a rhetorical question.) Graham back to Rugers. The Eagles have got a taste for it. Collingwood under the pump at the moment. Rugers lowers his eyes and kicks for Sherman, and Sherman will play on and kick the goal and the roof is lifted off the G (which has no roof, by the way). Massive goal in a big moment. Just a rippah before quarter time! Doesn't he love a big moment? HE. IS. A. WEAPON.*

Color analyst: *He's a star, Bruce. Reminds you a bit of Dusty, doesn't he?*

Bruce again: *Been a big quarter of footy. Magic scene here at the MCG.*

If you are not Aussie, or have never watched a game of Australian rules football, you're forgiven for not having the first clue what the hell might be going on there. But trust me; there, in those 200 or so words, is the essence of the footy: the over-the-top language, the slang, the scene being dramatically painted, and the first-name reference of a player whose team is not involved in the game but who you are expected to know anyway. In big moments the announcer might even throw in an overly dramatic line like: "Cometh the hour, cometh the man" and you'll think you're watching a World War II documentary about Winston Churchill.

...

The Melbourne Cricket Ground (MCG) was built in 1853, twenty-one years before Sir Winston was even born. Today, it is the home of Aussie rules football and Australian cricket, as well as the centerpiece of Melbourne's Sports Precinct. This part of town includes the training grounds for three Aussie rules football teams (Collingwood, Richmond, and Melbourne); a 30,000-seat rectangular stadium used by two rugby teams and two professional soccer teams; the multi-purpose Melbourne Arena (now called John Cain Arena), which is home to a professional basketball team and also used for the Australian Open; and of course the National Tennis Center, which is home to the 15,000-seat Rod Laver Arena. All of these sports venues are less than a ten-minute walk from one another and many host concerts and other events as well. Additionally, there is a 50,000-seat, retractable-roofed stadium built for Aussie rules football across town in an area called The Docklands. So, yeah, sports are about as important as fresh air in these parts.

The Melbourne Cricket Ground with a full house for the footy

My first experience at the MCG came during my first visit to Melbourne, when I embarked on a self-guided city stroll and stopped in for the stadium tour. Visiting an empty stadium is not something I would normally do. Sports venues are about atmosphere, and that means people, nerves, noise, competition, emotion, food, and (often) libations. At the best ones, it's about the tension and excitement that spills from the stadium into the streets, neighborhoods, and parking lots nearby. The anticipation of the experience plays almost as much a role as the game itself. Attending a sporting event that is important to a place's inhabitants is a unique way to learn about the fabric of the culture. I have felt that at some of the most legendary soccer (football) stadiums in Europe, at a baseball game in Japan, ski races in the Austrian Alps, and at multiple stadiums and arenas across America. If you love sports for the sake of sports, you know what I mean.

I took the tour of the empty MCG that random weekday afternoon because I kind of stumbled into it, because I wasn't sure I'd ever be back, and because it's a famous sports stadium and I love sports. I left with the understanding that the MCG is to Melbourne what the Opera House is to Sydney, the Eiffel Tower is to Paris, or the Statue of Liberty is to New York City. And, when it comes to the quantity of meat pies and beer consumed inside, it's got those other three covered by a furlong or two.

My tour guide was a senior citizen with a serious limp and disconcerting stamina issues considering the toasty temperature of the day. Still, between heavy breaths, she managed to exhale a few interesting facts about the place.

"Known as the MCG, or simply The G, the Melbourne Cricket Ground has the tenth largest seating capacity of all the stadiums on earth with room for 100,024," she said, and then gasped for air. "The G was established in 1853 (gasp), only eighteen years after the city was founded."

Excuse me, ma'am. Are you okay?

"Since 1859 (struggling for more air), the Melbourne Cricket Ground has been the home of football (breath), and it was the home stadium for the 1956 Melbourne Olympic Games (big sigh)."

"The security camera system here is monitored twenty-four hours per day, seven days a week, 365 days per year."

Umm, yes, but is there a hospital on the premises? With a ventilator?

246

"The biggest crowd in the history of the MCG was 130,000 for an appearance by evangelist Billy Graham."

I think we may need a priest here soon.

The G is the second largest cricket ground on earth behind some monstrosity in India. Every Boxing Day (December 26) since 1950 the Australian cricket side has begun a five-day test match at the MCG against whatever international squad is touring the country that summer. The Boxing Day Test can draw 90,000 people. In countries that are passionate about cricket—England, India, the West Indies, Pakistan, South Africa, Sri Lanka—attending a match at The G is a bucket list item, a sort of pilgrimage to one of the sport's grand theaters. Personally, I think that's a long way to go to watch grass grow for five days, but who am I to judge? In 2015, I attended a one-day Cricket World Cup match at The G between South Africa and India and I must admit it was wild. Half of India was there.

"It's gonna be impossible to catch a cab in Melbourne tonight," is how Sully summed things up, alluding to the notion that nearly every taxi driver in Melbourne (many of whom are Indian) was currently inside The G *barracking* for India. That was his joke, not mine.

In addition to the stadium tour and the potential opportunity to save the life of an out-of-breath tour guide, a visit to the MCG on a non-event day also means a chance to wander through the Australian National Sports Museum, which is located right there inside *the ground* (stadium). Sports are important to Aussies. They take particular pride in their sporting accomplishments, often quoting a statistic about the number of Olympic medals they win in relation to the population of the country, as if all of the residents are competing in the Olympics, rather than just the best athletes. To be fair, they have an incredible record of athletic achievement for a country that has 14 million less people than California.

I don't hide my lack of adoration for museum touring while traveling, but the heat of the day made an air-conditioned space filled with sports artifacts quite appealing, so, after the tour ended, I spent an hour wandering the sports museum. It was time well spent, offering everything from educational tips on cricket and Aussie rules football to mementos from Australian Olympic glory and horse racing. The highlight was a video simulator that let visitors attempt to kick a goal with an AFL footy. In another area, I fielded ground balls (which is probably not what they are called) in a cricket simulator and then threw the ball at the wicket. I was having a blast until a group of nine-year-old punks sauntered up looking to play and eyeballed me judgementally, as if a grown man fielding cricket balls by himself in a sports museum was odd. I figured that was a good time to *pull up stumps*, to borrow a cricket phrase, and made my way to the exit.

...

On a sunny Saturday afternoon, the journey to the MCG for a big game of AFL football is as authentic of an Aussie experience as you can have. If you come on foot through Richmond, that means you probably pre-gamed at a pub, and there are plenty to choose from. You could stop off at the Richmond Club Hotel, enjoy the sunny rooftop at the Corner Hotel, or drown a couple pints on the wide space of The Precinct. If you're ambitious, and a bit of a planner, maybe all three. They will all be crowded, along with the bevy of other haunts in the area

Most of my AFL football experiences at the MCG started with a walk from my apartment across the Yarra River to one of the establishments mentioned above. On one particular Saturday in September 2012, a few months after I moved to Melbourne, I decided to tag along with a couple of coworkers and attend my first game of finals (playoff) footy. Their team, a huge Melbourne club called the Hawthorn Hawks, was hosting the Adelaide Crows in a preliminary finals match. A trip to the Grand Final (the Granny) was on the line. Like a good ex-journalist, I kept notes on my phone as the day progressed/disintegrated, so that I might someday share the experience. For the sake of accuracy, it's a good thing I did.

Early Afternoon: It's a sunny, T-shirt temperature day and Swan Street, the main road through Richmond, is awash in the yellow and brown team colors of Hawthorn—also known as "piss and shit" to rival fans. Most *supporters* are wearing their team's *guernsey* (game jersey/tank top) or scarf. In many cases, they wear both. A few out-of-town Adelaide fans are mixed in as well, including two young men who are carrying a six-pack of Corona in one hand and drinking from open bottles with the other. I'm new here, but I'm fairly certain that's not legal. As I stroll deeper into Richmond, the crowd noise swells, the unseasonably warm temperature and cloudless sky delivering an added, if unnecessary, catalyst for pregame lubricating.

I turn off Swan Street onto the more residential Lennox Street and make my way to the London Tavern. Inside, the pub's giant main room is packed and the atmosphere is on par with the streets outside. Nearly everyone is holding a pint of Carlton draught and I'm careful not to bump into one that I will wear for the next twelve hours. I meet my coworkers on the sun-splashed back patio, which is *chock-a-block*. I was expecting the place to feel like a men's locker room, but it looks to be about 40 percent female. (I learned later that many young girls bond with their fathers over the footy and become lifelong supporters of their dad's favorite club.) Before I've even finished meeting the extended group, someone hands me a pint of beer. Before that one is finished, I'm given another.

After two beers in fifteen minutes: To keep the ship—my ship—from going adrift, I make for the bar and order a Chicken Parma, the staple of Aussie pub food. A *parmy* consists of breaded chicken (known here as a chicken schnitzel) topped with tomato sauce and parmesan cheese. It's served on a bed of *chips* (fries), as opposed to pasta, with a side of salad. Sometimes they throw a slice of ham between the sauce and the cheese. It's fabulous.

4:30 p.m. – Parma consumed and with less than an hour until the opening bounce, we begin the pilgrimage to the *ground*. The walk to the entrance gate at the MCG takes about ten minutes, across Punt Road and through Yarra Park, which serves as a parking lot on game days. The G, with its six light towers that stand fourteen stories high, towers above everything, including most of the buildings in the nearby CBD. Hawthorn fans are chanting, singing, and whistling. Some are slurring words despite the fact that the game's starting time is still forty-five minutes away. In Yarra Park, we pass an entrepreneurial twenty-something young lady playing the Hawthorn team fight song—which sounds just like "Yankee Doodle Dandy" (seriously)—on her bagpipes. She's got a little cap in front of her to collect donations. My new friends tell me she plays the fight song of whatever team is playing that day and they like to drop their phone numbers in her money collection bin, rather than money. In my defense, they are more like coworkers and friends of friends than actual friends at this stage.

5:10 p.m. – We buy our first beers inside the stadium. For games that start after 6 p.m., the sports venues in Melbourne serve only mid-strength beer. That is, beer with less alcohol. I guess they figure no one drinks to get drunk during the day. They would be wrong. As this is a 5:15 p.m. start, we'll be drinking full-gas beers. Again, good thing I'm taking notes.

5:13 p.m. – The national anthem of Australia is played while the two teams stare at each other, arms locked together, in the middle of the oval as a late-afternoon sun splashes over the MCG. The entire crowd of 70,000 sings along to "Advance Australia Fair" in what is described by someone near me as "the best part of the game," which I guess means we should all go home now. That would save me a headache tomorrow.

5:15 p.m. – The anthem ends and the crowd around me breaks into song before the opening bounce. The umpire bounces the ball at the center of the ground and a collective roar signals that we are underway. Either that or they just dropped the price of beer.

5:29 p.m. – A generous courier delivers our second round of stadium beers, but who's counting? I should be, actually. The beverages have been delivered by the person with the weakest bladder. The rule, it seems, is if you go to the bathroom, you come back with beers. Beer No. 2 is also a Carlton Draught, if you're scoring at home. And if you are scoring at home, get a calculator. You're going to need it.

5:48 p.m. – Two more Carltons arrive in a little cardboard carrier (which costs an extra $1) for me and my mate, Phil. Riding shotgun to the beers are two ten-ounce Jim Beam and Cokes. There is absolutely no reason for those right now. None. Zip. Zero. We both drink them both.

6:02 p.m. – Hawthorn has started slowly, so the fans are frustrated. At the moment, they're taking it out on an Adelaide player named Taylor "Tex" Walker or, more specifically, his famous mullet. From behind me, I hear: "Fuckin 1980s hairstyle, fuckin' get in there…fuckin el!" (Which means fucking hell.) Not sure where he was going with that.

6:04 p.m. – On the flip side, the fans are comically well mannered in tone when complimenting the play of one of their own. Normally it's a subtle, "Well done, Buddy!" or "Good on ya, Sam."

6:06 p.m. – The Hawks kick a goal when goals seem hard to come by. This comes at 14:06 of the second quarter and the player who scored is named Luke. The Hawthorn crazies immediately break into song: "Luke, there it is! Luke, there it is!" It's a hometown variation of the 1993 No. 2 billboard hit "Whoomp, There It Is" by the legendary musical group Tag Team. What planet am I on right now?

Halftime arrives – And with it, another round of Carltons. The Hawthorn faithful around me are in full panic mode. I can sense this because I'm a lifelong Boston Red Sox fan. We invented sports panic, and it usually arrives three games into a 162-game baseball season. During halftime, I'm not surprised to learn that the crowd seems to be populated with a healthy amount of "experts" who are confident that they have the secret strategy to help their team win if they could just get into the locker room and share this information. Sports fans are sports fans, wherever they are.

Sometime late in the six o'clock hour – Someone must have let the super-smart Hawks fans into the team room to share their brilliant tactical ideas. In the third quarter, they put on a clinic to storm back from six points down and take a twenty-point lead. The mood of the home fans changes drastically. Thirty minutes ago, they were frantically yelling, "Ohhh, shit...get the fucker!" Now, in an almost calming tone, they are saying things like, "Oh geez, he's done well to get there, hasn't he?" to no one in particular when a player makes an effort-driven play.

Wait...is it really not even 7 p.m.?

7-something p.m. – Someone hands me another beer and I think about how I love going to the footy. I've temporarily moved up to the second level to say hello to a friend who provided me with my ticket. He's in the company of two of his mates, one of whom has brought his young daughter. She looks to be about five years old and she's wearing her Hawthorn game jersey. When it comes to the footy she is *switched on*. Undoubtedly, she will grow up sharing a love for Hawthorne with her father. Now, she's climbed over my friend, grabbed the open seat next to me, and proceeded to dish out several high-fives in my direction while yelling relentlessly for a supremely talented Hawthorn player of Indigenous descent who she calls "Spiro Ravioli" despite his name being Cyril Rioli. I'm digging the high-fives, but would feel better about myself if I had consumed five fewer Carlton Draughts prior to this interaction.

7-later-something p.m. – A massive umpiring call goes Adelaide's way with just over nine minutes remaining and they cut the Hawthorn lead to 84-79. Hawthorn supporters jump from their seats and raise their collective arms up and out in the international signal for "WHAAAAT? Umpire, you blew the call!" It's the same gesticulating used by fans in stadiums the world over.

Approaching 8 p.m. – As a thanks for the ticket, I buy a round of beers for my mate and his mates. I momentarily consider omitting myself from this round, but that would be rude (although so would vomiting in front of a five-year-old). On the field, out of nowhere, Adelaide scores from forty meters out to take the lead, 85-84. An upset is brewing. I couldn't care less who wins, but I'm conscious of the fact that a loss by the hometown Hawks would put a damper on what is shaping up to be a memorable evening that none of us will remember. So I guess I do care. "Come on, the Hawkahs!"

Still not yet 8 p.m. – How is it not eight o'clock yet? Moments after the Adelaide goal, the Hawks strike back, with Rioli leading the way. My little friend next to me yells "Spiro" repeatedly and pumps her fist. I decide it's time to rejoin the hooligans downstairs before the five-year-old starts judging me.

8-ish p.m. – The Hawks hold on to win, 97-92, in a game that was much closer than anyone expected. Despite the victory, my Hawk-supporting mates look emotionally destroyed. It could also be the Carlton Draughts and Jim Beams, but it's difficult to tell on account of my vision being blurred.

Just after 8 p.m. – The crowd empties out of the MCG and we make our way to a local pub, where they will have something besides Carlton draught and Jim Beam, I presume.

8:32 p.m. – Yep, they have rum. I feel a little full on beer; let's switch to rum! Solid choice. (Sunday morning addendum: You may be surprised to learn this, but switching to rum was not the high point of my decision-making for the day.)

8:47 p.m. – We encounter a supremely friendly young lady who has definitely been out longer than us, or at least trying harder, if that's even possible. She's tenuously holding a glass of very red wine. "That's going on someone," I say to Phil, before backing up a couple of steps and looking briefly in the opposite direction. Four seconds later, I turn back to see that the white shirt being worn by one of the guys in the group is now covered in red wine on the shoulder and chest. Called it.

11:30 or so p.m. – Gee, it feels later than 11:30. A taxi driver rakes us over the coals and charges us, if my notes are correct, $7 apiece to drive four minutes to an area of town called Chapel Street, with late-night bars and clubs. This is what is known as "chasing the night" and it's stupid. Time seems to be going by slowly at this point. Money, on the other hand, is evaporating into thin air.

1-something a.m. – It's well past my bedtime. I'm not writing down anything that happens at this point. It will be too hard to decipher tomorrow and I'm resisting the urge to text friends in the US who are probably going about their adult Saturday morning routines of taking the kids to soccer practice or mowing the lawn. I should go home.

Fifteen minutes later – It's nearly 2 a.m. and I'm dancing to "Rump-shaker." Aussie rules football…what a game.

Shrine of Remembrance on Anzac Day

Chapter 20: Livin' in Mel-bin

Like ghosts, 30,000 Melbournians drag themselves from a restful slumber in the wee hours of April 25 and assemble in the pre-dawn darkness to stand in silence around the Shrine of Remembrance. The figures appear from the trees nearby and the crowd stretches hundreds of meters in all directions. It's made up of veterans, their families, and ordinary citizens who feel compelled to show their gratitude and respect at the Anzac Day dawn service every year. Important people say important things to honor more important people. Someone recites something called "The Ode," a passage taken from a poem called "For the Fallen" by English poet and writer Laurence Binyon in 1914.

They shall grow not old, as we that are left grow old;
Age shall not weary them, nor the years condemn.
At the going down of the sun and in the morning
We will remember them.

On Anzac Day, you don't have to be from Australia or New Zealand for the eyes to get a little misty as the sun rises over the Shrine.

Opened in 1934 as a place for Australians to honor those who died during the First World War, the Shrine of Remembrance in Melbourne is today a war memorial to those who have served on behalf of Australia. Of the 89,000 Victorians who served overseas in WWI, 19,000 were killed. Because many were buried overseas, the Shrine was created to give locals a place to pay their respects. Appropriately, it was designed by two Melbourne soldiers who returned from serving overseas to become architects. On the day of its opening in 1934, a crowd of 300,000 people came to pay their respects, and a collection of Shrine Guards have stood by it ever since. Not the same guys.

Today, you can take free tours of the Shrine and it's well worth the price. The first floor is home to an exhibit area as well as a crypt and sanctuary. At the top, an outside viewing area offers a magnificent view straight down St. Kilda Road to Federation Square and the Melbourne CBD. In front of the shrine, an eternal flame honors those killed in World War II.

Outside the Shrine entrance a simple passage reads:

ANZAC IS NOT MERELY ABOUT LOSS. IT IS ABOUT COURAGE
AND ENDURANCE, AND DUTY, AND LOVE OF COUNTRY
AND MATESHIP, AND GOOD HUMOUR
AND THE SURVIVAL OF A SENSE OF SELF-WORTH
AND DECENCY IN THE FACE OF DREADFUL ODDS.

The inclusion of "humor" always struck me as a uniquely Australian word choice for a war memorial, and yet it makes perfect sense. On Anzac Day, thousands of people gather at dawn at similar memorial sites across Australia and New Zealand to pay their respects. Anzac stands for Australia New Zealand Army Corps, and the April 25 date marks the anniversary of the day in 1915 that a group of *diggers* (soldiers) from Australia and New Zealand set out to capture the Gallipoli peninsula in World War I. They were met with great resistance and the fight continued for eight months until the allied forces were evacuated at the end of the year. More than 11,000 Australians and New Zealanders died.

On Anzac Day afternoon, after a veterans parade and probably a *kip*, attention turns to the MCG on the other side of the Yarra for the Anzac Day football match between local rivals Collingwood and Essendon. The game can draw up to 100,000 spectators. In a pregame ceremony a solitary bugler plays the "Last Post" as the crowd stands in complete silence. It has been said that you can hear the flags flapping in the wind. Even if you watch the game in a pub, the patrons fall quiet. Sydney journalist and former Australian rugby player Peter FitzSimons wrote that he had "rarely seen something so impressive in the world of sport. As they played 'The Last Post' and the national anthem, the 100,000-strong crowd uttered not a peep, whispered not a murmur. The atmosphere was electric and the general mood in the air one of reverence for the diggers and anticipation of the game to come.... Somewhere, someone has done a superb job organising that landmark day in Australian sport."

Across a small road from the Shrine you can join the Tan, a 3.8-kilometer mostly gravel pathway that encircles a green parkland called the Kings Domain. For me, a more healthy Melbourne weekend often began with a Saturday morning run along the Tan. On a gorgeous Saturday morning it can feel like half of Melbourne is there getting their weekend off to a healthy start before popping into a café nearby.

Rising up a hill above the south side of the Yarra River, Kings Domain is one of my favorite places in Melbourne and serves as a gathering place for the city's inhabitants. They picnic there, see concerts, relax on the great lawns, and exercise in and around it after work and on weekends. At one end of this parkland is the Sidney Myer Music Bowl, an outdoor concert and arts venue with 2,000 covered seats and a rising lawn that holds 11,000 more. Built in 1959, it hosts everything from the Melbourne Symphony to the traditional "Carols by Candlelight" Christmas concert to an afternoon rave or a rock concert. I once saw the Dave Mathews Band there and, from the lawn, the backdrop of the stage against the Melbourne skyline and the setting sun place it on par with a venue like Red Rocks in Colorado.

The venue is named after businessman and philanthropist Sidney Myer, who immigrated to Australia in 1899 as a poor Russian Jew. He started selling towels and sheets door-to-door—imagine trying that one today, fellas—and grew his business somewhat rapidly, opening Myer stores in multiple locations, until his death in 1934. The business continued to thrive and Myer has enjoyed a long history as one of the major department stores chains in Australia.

Opposite the Shrine of Remembrance is a Children's Garden, where I presume the little *tackers* grow tomatoes and zucchini. There is also a small museum, an Aboriginal Heritage Walk, and the Melbourne Observatory. At one time, the observatory was used for weather forecasting and other technical scientific information you can now obtain on your phone in three seconds. Today, the observatory offers reserved nighttime tours where they presumably point out the Southern Cross and refrain from making sad, pathetic comments about Uranus, like I was unable to stop myself from doing just there. If you keep walking into the park, you'll find yourself inside the Royal Botanical Garden, a wonderfully landscaped area of thirty-one plant collections that takes up more than ninety acres. Outside of some time assisting my mother and father with planting them around their house, my knowledge of plants and flowers begins and ends with the fact that women like receiving them and they need varying amounts of water and sunlight to survive.

If you fancy yourself a planstman, anthophile, or wannabe botanist—yes, I just looked up two of those words—what I can tell you about the Botanical Gardens inside Kings Domain is that they have a little bit of everything.

257

Sunset on the Yarra River

On warm days, the canopy of the Australian Forest offers cool shade, and there is also a Fern Gully collection, bamboo, cacti, and a "world-acclaimed" Camellia Collection, which I'm sure must be a big draw for people around the world who adore camellias.

On summer evenings, one of the lush green lawns in the garden plays movies on a large screen and folks bring blankets, sit under the stars, and have themselves an evening. Still, most of the traffic you see around Kings Domain is people exercising. On a warm night after work or a bright weekend morning, the area is filled with runners who come by foot from the nearby neighborhoods of Richmond, South Yarra, and Toorak or even after work from the CBD to make a loop or two around the Tan and tackle the Anderson Street hill.

Alexandra Avenue borders one side of the Tan and separates it from the Yarra River and its bright green banks. Locals spend their free time rowing on the Yarra and barbecuing and picnicking along its banks, but no one swims in it because you will probably spend the next few days shitting liquid akin to the river itself. A bike path runs along both sides of the river, which the locals use to commute to work from the nearby eastern suburbs, even on inclement days.

If you follow the river toward the city from the Botanical Garden, it will take just a couple minutes by bike and ten or fifteen minutes on foot to arrive at Melbourne's CBD and Federation Square. A bustling bit of real estate, Fed Square is what they would call a piazza in Italy, but with fewer people talking with their hands. It's built above the working rail lines that enter and exit Flinders Station just across the street. Melbourne didn't really have a central gathering place until Fed Square "opened" in 2002. Today, it hosts more than 10 million visitors each year. At one time or another, the area had been home to a railway yard, a fish market, corporate offices, and the city morgue. Tourism-wise, this is an improvement, as morgues don't seem to attract many visitors unless they go there horizontally and permanently. Also, morgue photos don't play as well on Instagram.

The architecture of the buildings, one of which houses a very in-depth visitor's center with a super-helpful staff, is ultra-modern, with a large open space that is well used by street entertainers and for various organized events. There is also a large video screen, in front of which people gather to watch things like World Cup soccer matches, the Olympics, and the Australian Open. It's less than a mile walk from Fed Square to the National Tennis Center (and the Melbourne Cricket Ground) via a pathway and footbridge, but those who can't get their hands on tickets often gather at Fed Square to watch the tennis on the big screen. When a marquee match is on the schedule, they arrive early to claim one of the lounge chairs that are available on a *first-in, best-dressed* basis (first-come, first-serve). On one such weekend night, I found visitors from France, the U.S, and Germany and locals from Melbourne who had found a chair or simply plopped onto the ground—small picnic and a couple of sneaky cocktails in tow—to watch Roger Federer dispatch whatever poor schlep was across the net from him.

The Australian Open is regarded as one of the best-run sporting events on the planet, with live music acts nearly every day, a party-like atmosphere, and, oh yeah, world-class tennis. The middle Saturday is always a festive occasion, with 60,000-plus fans filing through the gates. When I attended on the middle Saturday of the 2013 tournament, it also happened to be Australia Day (January 26), which seemed to elevate the level of revelry just a smidge.

Australian Open tennis in the shadow of the Melbourne CBD

261

Barely out of earshot from the courts, on what was then called the Heineken Live stage, Aussie music icon Daryl Braithwaite belted out his biggest hit, "The Horses," while the sun-drenched, alcohol-infused crowd sang along, jumped up and down, batted beach balls, and danced with life-sized inflatable kangaroos, as you do. By shifting your attention to a big screen that towered above the crowd, you could even watch the tennis, if you were so inclined. While it bears mentioning that the seats inside the tennis arenas were filled, for the crowd gathered in front of the music stage, one of the sport's four biggest events was just an excuse to sing along and party in the sun. It's all splendidly done.

When the sun went down, I adjourned to Fed Square and met friends at a bar called Transport. I assume, judging by the cost of a beer and the amount of people in there, they are still very much in business, and likely thriving. A night match was being shown on the big screen outside and on the TVs inside the bar. The place was buzzing and tall glasses of Heineken were flowing freely, and by "freely" I mean for $11 apiece. The crowd was largely Australian, but with a few international tourists and tennis fans mixed in. Outside, in perfect weather, the crowd oohed and aahed at each big point. It was a perfect example of how a sports-passionate city like Melbourne gets behind events like this. If you plan on having a big night out in Fed Square, bring your kids' college savings because this is tourist central and the prices reflect that. When our group's bar tab arrived at 1 a.m., I thought my vision was blurry—and it may well have been—but I was still seeing the number correctly. It would have been cheaper (and healthier for sure) to buy court-side seats at Rod Laver Arena, but I'm not sure it would have been more fun.

From Fed Square and Flinders Station, you can either go north and dive deeper into the CBD or cross the picturesque Princess Bridge to an area called Southbank. There, along St. Kilda Road, are a number of museums, theaters, and other art-centric attractions. Among them are the Arts Centre Melbourne, the State Theatre, the National Gallery of Victoria, Federation Hall, and the Victoria Barracks.

Opposite Flinders Station along the south side of the Yarra, the Southbank Promenade is lined with restaurants and bars. The centerpiece to the area is the Crown Casino, which hosts galas, award shows, and other highbrow events. The most entertaining stroll of my time in Australia took place along this very promenade in 2013. Dressed in a suit and tie, I was on my way to some kind of swanky function at the casino about three hours before the British & Irish Lions rugby team was to take on the Australian Wallabies at the nearby Docklands Stadium. The English, Scottish, Welsh, and Irish supporters (there's a combination to put on one side of things, huh?) were *priming the pump* for the game at the riverside pubs along South Bank. Imagine several thousand middle-aged rugby fans on a boys-only adult spring break who have not seen the sun in three months, or years. Several were dressed like queens. Don't take that as some sort of homophobic slur. I mean they were going to a rugby match dressed as Queen Elizabeth II. They wore royal dresses of some kind with the full wig and the white gloves, using one hand to wave the queen's slow wave to passers-by while holding a pint in the other.

In the middle of the river, accessible via a pedestrian bridge, is a floating bar called Ponyfish Island, which is a fun location to have a drink as the sun goes down on the Melbourne skyline above. From Fed Square, the CBD stretches north away from the Yarra River in a more traditional city grid. While most of the action in the CBD takes place during the week—with people commuting to and from work and sometimes sticking around for dinner and drinks—there are still theaters, restaurants, and bars in the downtown area. One of the unique highlights of Melbourne's CBD is the laneways. Instead of letting them become dark, dirty alleys where you don't want to find yourself when the sun goes down, Melbourne's laneways are lined with take-out eateries and small restaurants with loads of outside seating. Lunchtime has a very European feel, as if half of Melbourne is eating in them.

The laneways that aren't occupied by businesses are where the city's street artists come to ply their trade. While it is still technically illegal (best as I could determine) to create graffiti on property that is visible from a public place unless you have the owner's consent, the street art of Melbourne's laneways has become one of the city's biggest tourist attractions. Nobody seems to bother stopping the artists, and people come from around the world to view their work. On weekends, you might even catch an artist doing his or her thing while perched atop a stepladder. I occupied many a Saturday *arvo* walking from one art-covered laneway to another, stopping for a pint here or there along the way. There are plenty of art-covered laneways, but check out Hosier Lane, Blender Lane, AC/DC Lane, Duckboard Place, Union Lane, Centre Place, or Croft Alley if this is your thing.

Graffiti art, Melbourne laneway

The Bourke Street Mall, a wide promenade that runs through the center of the CBD, is home to all of Melbourne's biggest department stores. It's here and on Chapel Street, a few kilometers away, that Melbournians who seek the newest fashions come to empty their wallets. Like any significant city gathering place, Bourke Street Mall is also home to a fair few *buskers* (street musicians), which is a nice way to pass time if the person you're with is inside trying on dresses. If you want to see the central parts of Melbourne and walking miles upon miles isn't your cup of mocha chai latte or cappuccino, the City Circle Tram will take you on a loop around the CBD for free. The trams on the City Circle line are all painted in a throwback manner in maroon and green with yellow and gold trim. Onboard, you can listen to audio commentary that explains sights you are gliding past—the City Museum, Parliament House, the Docklands area, Fed Square, the Melbourne Aquarium, the Princess Theatre, and the place where English guys dress like the Queen of England and skull pints.

The best way to interact with the Yarra Trams of Melbourne is to ride on one because they are a nuisance for drivers. In fact, when the trams first came online in 1889 they were probably a nuisance for horses and pedestrians. Seven years later the trams were tossed aside, only to make their permanent comeback in 1907. Today, there are more than 250 kilometers of tracks around Melbourne and its suburbs. It's the largest network of tram tracks on earth, God help us. Seventy-five percent of these tracks are shared with automobiles, and by "share" I mean you sit in your car behind them and try to seize a safe moment to pass. Despite the fact that trams have been a part of many Melbourne roads for more than a century, the locals don't always seem fully accustomed to them being there, to say nothing of the tourists on foot.

Online, I stumbled upon a report published by an organization called Transport Safety Victoria revealing that there were 962 collisions between vehicles and trams in 2016, 977 more in 2017, and 1,138 in 2018. Essentially, in 2018, a car collided with a Yarra Tram 3.1 times per day, on average. The high rate of tram-related accidents is not due to a lack of warning. Yarra Trams have undertaken various advertising campaigns to create awareness, though why that would be necessary I haven't the first clue. My favorite campaign was the one that depicted a rhinoceros riding a skateboard and said:

"If a rhinoceros on a giant skateboard was heading your way, you'd get out of the way, right? Well guess what, a tram weighs about the same as 30 rhinos so it's not something you want to get hit by."

First of all, if a rhinoceros on a skateboard is coming toward you, go to rehab. Secondly, if you need to envision being run over by thirty rhinos on skateboards to comprehend that getting hit by a tram might be bad for your personal business, well, maybe you deserve to be hit by a tram.

Assuming you are not one of those people, the biggest concern you should have about trams is getting stuck behind one and not getting home in time for whatever you have going on three days from that moment. I haven't measured the distance between tram stops in Melbourne, but it feels like they move approximately twelve meters before they stop and let people on and off. I'm all for public transportation, but you should be expected to walk past the end of your driveway to get to it, right? A friend and golfing buddy who has lived in Melbourne for the better part of three decades once told me, "I have driven into those goddamn trams more times than I've hit my 4-iron!"

I had a fair few days of cursing the trams myself while stuck in Melbourne's congested commuter traffic, but neither the trams nor the weather was ever enough to sour me on the place. After my very first visit to Australia, which included that initial visit to Sydney and a few days in Melbourne, I left thinking that if I ever had the chance to live in the country, Sydney would be the spot. It was just flashier and life seemed almost dreamy. There was constant sun, and people took ferries to work and then went surfing or jogging along the beach when they got home. Half the people looked like Instagram models. Besides all that, it was similar to the life I was living at the time in San Diego, without the Instagram models.

A year later, with an eye toward potentially working there, I visited Melbourne for a week and got to know the place, which is when I first fell in love with it. That feeling only increased during my time living there. Melbourne has, for me, just the right mix of Old World European charm and American convenience, but with that unique Aussie character...and characters. The people are genuine, but with an edgy wit that I appreciate. You know where you stand with them. And, it bears repeating, there is never a dull moment on the calendar. It's a city for people who seek out life's little adventures in their daily lives. For nearly three years, I never ran out of new things to discover. I guess you call a place like that "livable."

UNSOLICITED ADVICE: MELBOURNE

MUST DO:

On a sunny day, walk or jog the **Tan** and then poke your head into the Botanical Garden… If you are here from the end of March through September, **a game of footy at the MCG** is a must-do. Pre-game at a pub in Richmond… There are some fun **happy hour spots along the river** near Finders Street Station, and when the sun goes down, spend your night in any of the neighborhoods I mentioned… The **pubs of Richmond** were my favorite because I could walk home, but north of the city are some fun **music spots**… Melbourne is perfect for combining your touring with socializing. Walk a bit, find a **beer garden**, and socialize with locals. In St. Kilda there are spots that get packed during the day, but beer gardens are scattered around the city. Just build a stop into your tour to make it feel like you've immersed yourself in life as opposed to just observing it.

UP TO YOU:

If you prefer to plan your visits around events, the **Australian Open** in January is supremely well organized and fun no matter how well you know tennis… Likewise, the spring horse racing carnival is a once-in-a-lifetime experience. Throw on a suit/dress, some sunscreen, and your best drinking shoes. Check the schedule for dates at each track… If you **play golf, the Melbourne Sand Belt** may just have the greatest concentration of top-notch courses on the planet. Many are on every golfer's bucket list. Most are private so the cost to walk on as a non-member is not cheap, but they are spectacular… I loved walking the **South Melbourne Market** (or another one) on weekends, and that will give you a local feel… For a daytrip (or an overnight), **Mornington Peninsula** has beaches, wineries, and cool coastal towns that feel a bit like Cape Cod, Nantucket, or the Hamptons. I've never attended the **Portsea Polo** down that way, but that is a see-and-be-seen summertime event… The **Yarra Valley** is a slightly closer drive if you fancy tasting wines.

NEXT TIME:

As I spent nearly three years here, it's difficult to say what I've missed. There are various excursions from the city itself, such as a drive toward Geelong and then out the **Great Ocean Road**, but you'll need a bit of time to attempt that… If outdoor adventure is your thing, look into trips to places like **Grampians National Park** (three hours from the city)… Melbourne also has a number of **country towns** an hour or two from the city that will give you a taste of small-town Victoria.

PART VIII:
TASMANIA

Tasmanian road signage: Beware of the devil

Chapter 21: Road Trippin' in Tassie

The airport in Launceston, near the North Coast of Tasmania, feels more like a bus terminal than a place that planes fly in and out of. There's a little statue of a small Tasmanian Devil in the middle of the baggage claim area urging visitors to make a coin donation to help keep this native animal alive in the wild, but other than that you could be at a Greyhound terminal in New Mexico. It's not an off-putting place in any way; it's just not Heathrow or Charles de Gaulle.

After collecting the keys to my rental car from a desk at the airport, I spent the next fifteen minutes attempting to decipher how to open the trunk/*boot* of said vehicle. The fact that I was searching around like a bomb-sniffing dog at the American embassy in Baghdad attracted a fair bit of attention from passers-by.

"Whatcha doing there?" the first lady asked, with a bit of chuckle.

"I'm building a bridge, actually!" is what I prevented myself from snapping back with, before taking a deep breath and reining myself in. "Believe it or not, I'm trying to figure out how to open the boot," I said, laughing in an attempt to cover my frustration.

She was the first of several kind travelers who stopped to help, and before long we had a small empathetic gathering at the rear of the vehicle. Though no one had the answer, I must admit it felt better to be befuddled with company and I was struck by how many people stopped to help. Good first impression, Tasmania! A couple of people helped for a minute or so, giggled a bit, then marched on with their lives, not that I could blame them. Finally, an older gentleman came strolling down the sidewalk, noticed the search party, and stepped toward the rear of the car. Barely breaking stride, he pushed the logo on the trunk/boot and...voila...it popped open.

"Nice job!" I said. "Thank you. I'm sure I tried that earlier, but..."

We all had a bit of an uncomfortable chuckle together, while the locksmith strutted away silently like he'd just sorted global warming. (A little too smugly, if I'm being honest, but I was thankful nonetheless.)

Most people probably don't get their first impression of Tasmania in Launceston because most people fly to the bigger city of Hobart, a few hours away by car on the southeastern part of the island. I chose to fly across to Launceston from Melbourne, which takes about an hour, because a point-to-point road trip to Hobart seemed like the easiest way to see a good slice of the island.

Tasmania was always so close to Melbourne during my time living there—and before and after I lived there, one would presume—but for some reason I put off a visit for quite a while. This was odd because it suits me well. I had heard it described as a baby New Zealand, and the landscape of the place actually makes it look more like New Zealand than Australia. Outdoorsy types like me could spend a couple of weeks poking around Tassie. There are legitimate mountains, coastal hikes, unspoiled beaches, and great mountain biking. More than two-thirds of the island consists of protected national parks and nature preserves. It also has winemaking regions, whiskey distilleries, and breweries. Clearly, these highlights would require some investigating on my part as well.

With parts of five days to explore, my plan was to head out from Launceston, do a little mountain biking at the famed Blue Derby trails a couple of hours away, then make my way to the East Coast and plot my way south from one scenic spot to another over a couple of days. Eventually, I would arrive in Hobart, where I planned to spend a couple of nights. I was foregoing a trip to the more mountainous areas to the north and west of the island, including the famous Cradle Mountain. This is a decision I'm sure Tassie aficionados will give me shit for, but having walked all over the French Alps for the previous few years, the beauty of the coastline just seemed more appealing.

Tasmania sits 240 kilometers off the south coast of Victoria and has a rich history as a penal colony for European settlers in the 1800s. Originally, it was named Van Diemen's Land by Abel Janszoon, an ass-kissing explorer from the Dutch East India Company who called it that in honor of his Dutch superior Anthony Van Diemen. The name Tasmania evolved over time and eventually became official in 1856, mostly to remove the tarnish of it being a place for convicts. One can understand how that kind of PR campaign would be important to real estate value even in the 1850s. For the record, the Aboriginal people called it Trowunna, Trowenna, or Loetrouwitter before it was Tasmania or Van Diemen's Land.

In the morning, I packed up and moved the car 500 meters into the central business area of Launceston. It would have been quicker to crawl because parking meters on the main streets of Launceston required me to use a smartphone app that, as a tourist, I didn't have. Brilliant. So, I gave up my premium spot and drove around for ten minutes until I found pay lot. I had enough coins for forty-five minutes, so we were looking at a forty-four-minute walking tour of Launceston, which seemed like it might be enough. I walked up Charles Street, which intersected with a rather lengthy pedestrian mall that was called The Mall, according to a sign I saw.

Considering the creative names of everything else in Australia, that seemed the equivalent of having a kid and calling him The Son. The Mall—turns out it's called the Brisbane Street Mall, but I like the son joke so I'm leaving it—was lined with all kinds of small businesses, banks, and chain stores that were just coming to life at 9 a.m. Up ahead, The Mall intersected with George Street, where I found Samuel Pepys Café. *The Diary of Samuel Pepys* was once a favorite of mine, so I decided to pop in for some eggs and toast, which were tasty and served up by friendly people. With fifteen meter minutes remaining, I strolled George Street, where there was a record shop, coffee shops, and chocolate shops. For the sake of my wallet and my waistline, I needed to get out of here.

I returned to the car with two minutes to spare and pointed my rent sled out of town through green farmlands and into the Tasmanian countryside. Eventually, I joined up with the Tasman Highway under threatening clouds and past a sign welcoming me to an area called Dorset. The road wound its way up a mountain through a dense forest over something called Billycock Hill. Now THAT would be a name for your mall, Launceston.

An hour and twenty minutes after departing the dam, I arrived in the tiny town of Derby. For mountain biking fanatics, a visit here to the famed Blue Derby Trails is on the life bucket list. The main part of town is only about 400 meters long and reminded me of a place you might see in a western like *Tombstone*, except instead of seeing Wyatt Earp's trusty steed hitched to a post, there were hundreds of mountain bikes hanging by their seats in front of cafés, bars and bike shops. In front of the few establishments in town, bikers sat and chatted over a coffee, a beer, or a sandwich, presumably about mountain biking and the "sick shit" they rode that morning.

I picked a bike shop, got set up with a half-day bike rental, and, for $11 extra, reserved a spot in the next shuttle to the top of the trails. The young woman in the bike shop kindly offered to switch my breaks to match my bike at home, which I took her up on. Let me explain:

A few years earlier, while mountain biking with my friend, André Caron, near Lake Taupo on New Zealand's North Island, I had seen firsthand how not "switching the brakes" could lead to an unpleasant riding session. You see, in Australia and New Zealand, the brakes on bicycles are normally on the opposite sides of the handlebars (rear brakes on the left, front brakes on the right). When André and I rented our bikes in New Zealand, I listened attentively as the shop manager explained that the brakes would be the opposite of what we were used to. André listened less intently. When I stopped a kilometer or so down the trail, I found myself waiting a couple of minutes for him to arrive. When he did, it was with ripped pants and a slightly bloody scratch on his leg.

"You all right?" I asked.

"Yep, just took a little spill," he said.

At the next stop, his pants were slightly more sullied, and at the third stop he was filthy and his arm was bruised.

"What are you...drunk?" I asked, as a concerned friend would.

"Hey, are your brakes the opposite?" he asked. "Like, is the rear brakes on the left? And the front brake on the right?"

"Yeah," I said. "He told us that at the shop."

"Yeah, I didn't hear him say that," he said, catching his breath from picking himself off the ground three times in a mile.

"So you were squeezing the front brake and throwing yourself over the handlebars?" I said laughing.

"I was," he said, not laughing.

"And you did this three times before you noticed?" I asked, laughing more.

"I did. Okay, that's good to know," he said, never one to complain about a thing. "Left is back, right is front. Cool. Let's go."

And off we went.

Derby, Tasmania

Today, in Derby, I was wise enough to spend twenty minutes on the flat trails in town familiarizing myself with the bike. A few minutes later, I was inside a four-wheel-drive van surrounded by people with accents from around the world who, when you consider what it takes to get to Derby from anywhere not in Tasmania, had to be admired for their dedication to the sport. Out the windows, the occasional rider would appear on a trail through a gap in the trees and then disappear again. After fifteen minutes, the shuttle dropped us off at the end of a long dirt road in front of a huge trail map that detailed Blue Derby's 125 kilometers of manicured single-track (mountain biker speak for trails that are wide enough for only one bike). Trails descended into the woods in all directions.

The trails at Blue Derby are as mellow or death-defying as you want them to be. Because I like my teeth in my mouth and my bones inside my skin, I heeded the advice of the woman at the bike shop and chose a fast, flowy, "more difficult" trail called Flickity Sticks that weaved through eucalyptus trees, over pavers, and around immaculate berms. The place was mountain biking heaven. I spent three hours exploring a few trails, enjoying the downhills, then pedaling back up. Occasionally, I would come across teenagers with zero care for their well-being launching themselves twenty-plus feet in the air. Toward the end of the day, I was feeling comfortable on the rental bike and decided to finish the session with a twenty-minute downhill ride back to town on a trail called Return to Sender, which the shuttle driver told me I "had to ride before I leave Derby."

A few kilometers into Return to Sender, I whipped around one of Blue Derby's berms just a smidge too fast. A split-second later, the bike—and, by extension, my body—were suddenly horizontal. After a flight you could have served drinks and pretzels on, we both landed in a sizable pile of branches, twigs, and leaves about fifteen feet from where we took flight. Apart from a bruise to my ego and my left shin, all my bits were where they were supposed to be and my rental bike was fine, too. Knowing that other riders were coming behind me, I hurried to my feet and continued on. Twenty seconds later I was at the end of the trail, which deposited me just behind the Derby town post office.

I returned the bike just before closing time, then headed across the street to the bike washing stations and frigid public showers to clean up. During a quick stop at the Federal Tavern on the main street for iced tea and a snack for the road, I made an ambitious plan for the last few hours of daylight. I would drive an hour to Ansons Bay on the East Coast, then south along the water through an area called the Bay of Fires and, eventually, to St. Helens. As I pulled out of Derby at 5:15 p.m., the staff members of the bike shop were beginning an evening group ride.

The winding road out of town was absent of any traffic at all, and the only people I saw were six kids who eyed me somewhat curiously as I drove through their street scooter session. One of them gave me the "hang loose" sign. It was the sort of interaction you have with passing cars in places where you don't get many passing cars. Not long after the kids was a fork in the road where I needed to veer right toward Ansons Bay and drive another twenty-eight kilometers. About 300 meters farther on, the road turned from pavement to rugged gravel. I drove on for a few minutes trying to convince myself that the loss of cell phone service, rumbling roadway, and apparent nothingness that lie ahead was no big deal. It'll probably turn back to pavement here soon, I told myself, though a sign had clearly warned me otherwise. Another sign warned drivers to watch out for Tasmania devils, which made me want to keep driving on the off chance I might see one.

Finally, when it became apparent that the car might not withstand the beating it was taking for another half-hour, I pulled over. There were no driveways around, so I executed a three-point turn just in time to avoid a lunatic in a *ute*—which is basically a pickup car, as opposed to a pickup truck—steaming along the gravel at mach 2 as if he was Lewis freaking Hamilton in his Formula 1 car if Lewis Hamilton drove around in a dirty *singlet* (tank top) and a mesh trucker cap. Back at the fork in the road, I consulted the map sprawled out on the passenger seat to my left and found a new way to the coast. It would mean backtracking (which I hate) for a few minutes and probably missing the Bay of Fires.

I waved hello again to the scooter gang and gave them my best I'm-not-lost-I-was-just-having-a-look-at-the-area face, but I don't think they bought it. At some point down the road, I broke out the package of Tim Tam cookies I had bought at the store in Launceston the night before and ate roughly all of them. Tim Tams, if you are unaware, are like the Oreo of Australia. Aussies might not like that comparison, but I struggle to think of another. They are coated in chocolate fudge with chocolate biscuit (or cookie material or whatever you call that) inside. In our office in Melbourne, a guy named Timmy Palmer used to walk from desk to desk distributing two packages of them to us, his coworkers, every Tuesday afternoon for what he called Tim

279

Tam Tuesday. (Get it? His name is Tim. They are called Tim Tams. It was Tuesday.) Despite my weekly protests that I should get two Tim Tams because my name was also Tim, he never budged. He worked in finance.

As I polished off way more Tim Tams than Timmy Palmer ever would have given me, the landscape turned almost jungle-like. The air outside felt refreshing, almost tropical, and I was enjoying driving with the windows down on a warm spring evening. I was in something called the Luthier Forest Reserve and then, a few minutes later, climbing over a mountain pass, where I stopped for a quick nature break. When I got out of the car, it was cold and windy, completely different than thirty minutes earlier. To the left, in the distance, I caught a glimpse of the coastline, where I was headed. The sun was setting off to my right behind some mountains, which almost made freezing my ass off tolerable.

About a half-hour before St. Helens, I pulled off the Tasman Highway onto St. Columba Falls Road to investigate a small town called Pyengana, set among some sun-splashed cow pastures. A kilometer down the road, past the local football oval, was the Pyengana Dairy, "The home of Australia's heritage farmhouse cheese." It was closed, which disappointed me, because they had a nice café and a deck and offered cheese tastings. Nearby was the Pub in the Paddock, which has existed here in one form or another since 1880 and is something of a Tasmanian icon. The sign outside invited visitors to "come meet our beer drinking pig," which piqued my interest because I'm a human.

Unfortunately, the pig had finished her drinking for the day and was likely passed out somewhere with a bag of Doritos on her lap because the Pub in the Paddock had closed an hour earlier. Further online research led me to discover "Priscilla, the princess of the Paddock," the pig who drinks beers straight out of the bottle through the fence of her pen. Right there on the pub's website, people are holding bottles to her snout, and Priscilla is guzzling away. I explained the photos just in case you were wondering how Priscilla can hold a bottle to her snout with hooves. She can't. She's a pig for chrissakes. "You simply cannot visit the Pub in the Paddock and not share a beer with Priscilla," the website says. Needless to say, I was more devastated to miss Priscilla after the fact than I was when I was there.

Thirty minutes later I arrived at the Comfort Hotel Bayside in St Helens. There wasn't much else open in town so I had dinner in the front of the restaurant where the TAB was. The TAB is basically an off-track betting parlor where you can watch and *have a punt* on horse racing, dog racing, or other things you might be inclined to wager on. Throughout Australia, small hotels like this one often have a restaurant on one side, a TAB on the other, and a bar in the middle that serves both. The man behind the bar made it clear that I was to eat in the TAB, not the restaurant, so I ordered a *chicken parmy* and a James Boag's Draught (brewed in Launceston) and sat and watched dog racing for an hour while I ate. There were ten screens. Seven were dedicated to dog racing and two more to horse racing. One screen had a human on it, and she was delivering the nightly news.

My parmy was tasty, but served on a plate that was curved on one end and sloped in the other direction, as if it wanted to be a bowl, but never quite achieved this lofty status. As the No. 6 dog took Race 4 on TV No. 7, I chased my chicken down the plate/bowl and onto the table with my fork. It was a weirdly stressful eating experience that I dealt with by ordering a second schooner of Boag's.

Wineglass Bay, Tasmania

Chapter 22: Freycinet

To spare myself from another meal spent watching dogs race around a track on television, I went to breakfast at the Bay Café, a small brekkie joint on the main drag in St. Helens. Their delectable egg and bacon panini sandwich was the perfect start to the day, and a piping hot English breakfast tea had me *traveling* in the right direction. While I waited to pay, another customer was busy conducting the Spanish Inquisition about a piece of cake sitting under the glass in front of us.

"Is it fresh?" asked the man.

"Yes," the teenage girl behind the counter said cheerfully. "Mom made it this morning."

And then he continued with an interrogation you might conduct with a used car salesman before considering the purchase of a $40,000 BMW rather than a $3 piece of cake. It was as if he knew I wanted to get going, and was intent on doing everything in his power to prevent me from doing so.

"Are those sprinkles on top? Is the cake gold of chocolate? Is it sweet?"

It's a cake, mate. It's not gonna be bitter! It's gonna taste like a cake!

A scenario played out in my mind in which I delicately removed the cake from under the glass display and violently force-fed it into his face while laughing aloud and high-fiving the poor girl dealing with him. Instead, I waited impatiently until The Decisive One had finished paying—after not ordering the cake—then took my breakfast outside and ate it in the warm morning sun. While egg yolk oozed across my fingers, St. Helens was springing to life. Across the road an older woman was setting up to sell "100% pure Tasmanian honey" in front of the Portland Memorial Hall, which had a "Lest We Forget" sign and what looked like a WWII cannon in front of it. A mural on the side of the building depicted the faces of military veterans through the years.

I didn't have a newspaper handy so I pulled out my phone to learn a bit about where I was currently stuffing my face. Among the factoids I picked up are that St. Helens is an old whaling town. Today, it's tourism and fishing that drive the local economy. If I were a fisherman, this is where I would have gone out on one of those charter boats where everyone in the party envisions a day battling a marlin and drinking copious amount of James Boag's in the sun, but instead they spend twelve hours vomiting overboard. I'm not a fisherman, so instead I was driving south to Freycinet National Park to do the famous Wineglass Bay hike.

If standing on a boat, or the shore, with a pole in your hand waiting for your Moby Dick moment is not your thing, the beaches on this part of the Tasmanian East Coast are hard to beat. This was quickly apparent as I made my way south for ninety minutes. On the radio, a sexy-sounding woman was finishing the national traffic report. Yep, *national...traffic...report*. I caught the part where she referenced something going on in Humpty Doo, which is a place I traveled through with Jack the Talker tour guide outside Darwin on the way to Kakadu. Humpty Doo is about 4,300 kilometers away from St. Helens, in case you were curious, or fifty-one hours by car then boat then car. So this was not exactly what we call "localized content" in the marketing world.

It was a safe bet that the traffic situation in Humpty Doo wasn't going to affect my leisurely journey along Tasmania's Great Eastern Drive this morning. Neither was the weather, which was *just magic*, as they say in these parts. I stopped here and there to visit a couple of beaches, which were mostly empty. The ocean was calm and turquoise. Opposite the Tasman Sea, the occasional vineyard appeared in the hills to my right and a "Penguin Crossing" sign reminded me where I was. If my math is correct, I was only a thousand miles farther from Antarctica than I was from Humpty Doo.

At the welcome center at Freycinet National Park, an older gentleman explained where to go, what it cost ($24 for a one-day car pass entry), and the best things to see in an afternoon. In five minutes, I had the next few hours mapped out without doing much thinking at all, and being told the best plan of attack was a welcome respite from having to decide everything myself. If you happen to be married and/or used to traveling with children, I understand that this notion might be incomprehensible. I apologize. My new mate at the welcome center told me to drive four kilometers to the car park to access the trail to Wineglass Bay and that the water was 14 degrees Celsius, which was cold but "tolerable if I was man enough" to take a swim. Challenge accepted, kind sir.

After a short search through a crowded car park, I raced to get ahead of a massive crowd of Chinese tourists. When they all stopped to take pictures with and feed a small kangaroo (which you shouldn't do) in the parking lot, I made my move to the front. The hike to the viewpoint, which overlooks Wineglass Bay, is supposed to take about forty minutes. Usually these posted estimated travel times are for people of average health and, I guess, allow ample time to stop and take photos or have a heart attack. I'm no Kenyan distance runner, but it took me eighteen minutes to get to the top, not that I was counting. The trail was more like a firm dirt sidewalk, and weaved through large red rock formations with a reddish hue. Freycinet is a large peninsula, so as you stroll to the top, you can look back behind you at Honeymoon Bay and beyond. The *choice* views, however, are on the other side of the hill, which is why you make the walk.

From the observation area at the top, the dark blue waters of Wineglass Bay turned turquoise as they met the white sand beach far below. The lookout was crowded with tourists whose labored breathing gave the impression that they don't do a ton of hiking or running or walking or standing up from the couch. The beach below was too tempting, so I decided to make my way down the 1,000 steps of the path that led there. As one might expect, the trail to the beach was 90 percent less crowded than the trail to the top had been. I'm *tipping* this was due to the sign at the top, which warned: "You should only choose to continue down to Wineglass Bay Beach if you are properly prepared and physically capable of walking down—then back up—around 1,000 stairs. (That's a lot of steps!)" It also said that the young, unfit, and those unaccustomed to bushwalking might find the walk challenging.

The nice part about a place that takes a little effort to get to—or in this case, get back from—is that there aren't many people there when you arrive. After twenty or so minutes of downhill walking, I was on the beach with a handful of other people who were not kids, "unfit," or couch potatoes. I plunked down in the sand for a few minutes, dipped my toes in the ocean, and enjoyed the view. There seems to be some debate as to how Wineglass Bay got its name. Is it because the water is as clear as a wineglass or the bay is shaped like one? Regardless, it is one of the most famous beaches in the world. I suppose if they want to decrease the tourist traffic, they can always change the name to 1,000 Steps Bay.

The walk back up was twice as difficult as 500 steps sounds. To be honest, I was more concerned with stepping on some kind of poisonous snake than the climb itself. I was back on top in thirty or so

Wineglass Bay Beach

minutes and then descended back down the other side toward the car. In the car park, the same small kangaroo was still mugging for photos and letting people pet him. Young tourists were crowding around him taking selfies. He should have been charging.

On the advice of the old mate at the welcome center, I moved the car a short distance to another parking area at Honeymoon Bay, where the rocky coastline sloped gradually into the ocean. It was the perfect place for a dip, aside from the fact that I could have placed my testicles on the side of a milk carton afterwards because they went missing after plunging into the frigid water for two minutes. Still, the swim left me refreshed and ready for my afternoon drive to Orford, about an hour and a half away.

A few hundred meters past a place called Coles Bay, I sped by a café and ice cream joint called The Pondering Frog. The large sign above the entrance had a drawing of a frog lying on his side. He appeared to be, umm, pondering. What he was contemplating I couldn't tell,

286

but it seemed worth investigating and I was hungry. I made a *uey* at the next crossroads and headed back to see what was on the frog's mind. The dusty parking area was dotted mostly with camper vans. Everywhere—inside and out—were frog figurines. Stuffed frogs, ceramic frogs, paintings of frogs—there were hundreds of them. They should have just called it The Lily Pad.

A sign on the grass said there was also a working bee display, which seemed somewhat random. The owner, a man named Lester, was a *pisser* (a character). While Lester got to work fixing my chicken tenders and fries, I listened to him advise (tell) tourists how they should spend their afternoon and evening.

"Do you have wine? Do you have dinner in the camper?"

"No," they said.

"Well, why not?" he asked, which seemed like a fair question. He pulled out a small map. "Here's what you're gonna do. You're gonna go down here five kilometers up the road and turn right. And you're gonna camp there for free."

"Okay," the retired couple said, seemingly afraid to disagree with Lester.

"Or...orrrrr," he continued more loudly, "you're gonna get your wine and drive to here (he pointed to another place on the map), and go to the pub for dinner. Orrr you're gonna drive all the way to here (he pointed again) and get a pizza. Does that sound good?"

"Yes," they said, sounding as if they were getting directions from their father.

With Lester busy doling out advice like he was the head of Tourism Tasmania, I didn't dare interrupt to ask about the history of The Pondering Frog. Later, on their website, I learned that Lester and Collette, whom I guess is his other half, found the property on a visit here back in 2013. Lester owned and operated a large, popular tourist facility in New South Wales, which he built up from a shed on the side of the road into a restaurant, retail outlet, and manufacturing facility that supplied products to some big Australian supermarket chains. He also had a large cherry orchard. Lester was a mover and a shaker, it seems, not just a local tour guide. Collette, the website said, is the "frog lady." Naturally. She has been collecting frog figurines for years. As you do.

287

"On the way down to Tasmania in 2014, Lester's daughter gave Collette the large ceramic pondering frog as a house/business warming present," the website says. They were unable to decide on name for their new business until a customer walked in and asked what the frog was thinking about. Collette told him that he was pondering what to call the place, and there you go.

Though his manner of offering advice was rather direct, I wanted to be friends with Lester. He may never see the folks who visit him again, but he wanted them to have a good time in his backyard even if he would make no money from the rest of their day…unless he owned the pub and the pizza joint, too, which seems plausible now after reading his story online. As I pulled out of The Pondering Frog, I had a smile on my face and a bag of warm chicken tenders in the console. I "pondered" what it is that stirs people to make this sort of extra effort for visitors. Maybe it's just civic pride, but people like Lester make certain places in the world more fun to visit.

Now, there was only one way to finish the day: go wine tasting. As luck would have it, there were a couple of wineries between me and where I planned to sleep.

Before the balmy plunge at Honeymoon Bay, I had looked online to find a couple of wineries that were open past 5 p.m.—Why does this sound familiar?—and made a plan. The first stop was the Freycinet Vineyard, located at the end of a short road off the one I was traveling on. Freycinet Vineyard has been here since 1979 and they do their own winemaking right there on site. I chatted with the pleasant lady behind the bar, bought a bottle to enjoy in my hotel room over the next couple evenings, and drove up the road a couple minutes to stop No. 2, Devil's Corner Vineyard cellar door. Devil's Corner was set on a hill overlooking some farmland that eventually arrived at the sea in the form of Moulting Lagoon well off in the distance below. Across the water, the Hazard Mountain range looked back from Freycinet Peninsula, where I had just come from. In addition to the free wine tasting room, which I visited, the Devil's Corner cellar door also had a wood fire pizza and oysters on offer. Patrons were enjoying all of the above on the deck and on blankets out on the grass. I stayed a while, enjoying a bit of pizza, a glass of Pinot Noir, and the view.

I chased the wine and pizza with a cup of tea and an unnecessary, but tasty chocolate chip cookie for the road, which left me quite content for the eighty-minute journey to Orford, located where the

Prosser River meets the sea. For the second consecutive night, I was staying in a casino disguised as a roadside motel. That's a slight exaggeration because, in all fairness, the Orford Blue Waters Hotel did have a very nice bistro. It also had a room full of *pokies* (slot machines) that would have left my mother with tendinitis in her right shoulder the next morning. I arrived with plenty of time to spare before dinner, so I settled into my spacious digs and did a bit of reading for the next day's adventures. The rooms at the Blue Orford were set up like mini townhouses—and I'm using that term loosely here—with two units sharing a wall. Next door to me, an older couple had parked their tandem bicycle outside, probably hoping someone would steal it. Gee, the prospect of that looked fun; sitting on the back seat staring at your spouse's ass all day while he or she farts in your face for three or four hours.

With time to kill before dinner, I went for a short stroll behind the hotel near the mouth of the river. The tide was low, which left seaworn tree trunks half-submerged and a multitude of boat docks six feet above the water line. After a few minutes, it started to feel a bit chilly so I strolled up to the bistro, grabbed a table, and sat down for a *feed*. I ordered a steak, which arrived about fifty minutes later. The place was *chockas* (packed), which probably had something to do with them needing to go find the cow before bringing me my steak. At any rate, the waiter was apologetic and the grub was worth the wait. On my way out I consulted with the guy at the front desk, who also happened to be the bartender, about the best route to Port Arthur, the old penal colony tourist spot I was planning to see the next morning.

"Yeah, mate, make sure don't take the shortcut to Port Arthur because it's a dirt road for a long way," he said.

I pulled out my phone and pointed to the most direct road on the map, the one I had fully planned to take.

"Yeah, that one," he confirmed. "Don't take it! That road is shit and it'll take you all morning."

"Good tip," I said. "Ta."

Where was he two days ago on the way to Ansons Bay? Never mind. I know where he was. He was right here, standing behind this bar, probably saving some other tourist a few hours.

I woke up well rested, but slightly dry-mouthed after capping the

289

evening with a couple of glasses of red from the bottle I'd purchased at Freycinet Vineyard. The first half of the ride to Port Arthur the next morning was a fairly entertaining one, thanks again to the Australian roadside signage. There was Break Me Neck Hill, which preceded Bust Me Gall Hill. There was "Sheep Poo" on sale for $5, leading me to assume that someone nearby had the shittiest job in Tasmania, and a poorly paid one at that. One small town was asking for nominees for the Australia Day awards, including Citizen of the Year. Australia is funny with giving awards like this to grownups as if they are in a high school graduating class. They actually give out an award called Australian of the Year, honoring one person as the best person in the whole of Australia for that year. I would have officially, or unofficially, nominated the guy who opened the trunk of my rental car in Launceston, but he was too smug to stick around. His loss.

A little while on I saw a *chook shop*—a shop that sells chicken— called Legs and Breasts, a name that would likely be deemed unlawful or "offensive" in half the states in America today. At Dunnaly, I followed the road onto the Tasmanian Peninsula and began the winding drive south through farmland and a few small towns. An hour or so later, I arrived at the Port Arthur Historic Site, where tourist busses and carloads of retirees and families with kids who already wanted to leave were marching from the parking lot to the ticket desks. Ideal.

The lady at the front desk—and everyone else lurking around the entrance in Port Arthur Historic Site uniforms—seemed in quite a rush to explain the various tour options to me, as if she wanted me to commit to the experience before I changed my mind. This should have sounded alarm bells. My fault there.

"G'day. Do you want the harbor cruise and the walking tour?" she asked me before I could even open my mouth.

"Hello. I don't know. What's on the tour?" I asked. "I didn't come here with a ton of information."

This honesty was also a mistake I would later regret and she was trained to pounce on uninformed folks like me.

She explained my options and the schedule of tours happening over the course of the next couple of hours. Port Arthur Historic Site, in case you were curious, offers "access to more than 30 historic buildings, ruins, restored houses, heritage gardens and walking trails." It is a fully restored tourist trap...err, destination...that offers a glimpse at life in the area during the 1800s. It began as a timber station back in 1830, relying on convicts to do the labor. Three years later it evolved into what the guidebook calls a "punishment station for repeat offenders from all the Australian colonies." It was strange in that prisoners, military officers, and civilian officers and their families lived in this one community, though their quality of life varied, as you might expect.

The prison shut down in 1877, but the place didn't become a tourist destination in a historical sense until a century later when people realized the money it could bring in....I meant to say they realized its "significance." Today, Port Arthur Historic Site covers 360 acres (146 hectares, whatever those are) and is one of eleven sites across Australia that make up the Australian Convict Sites World Heritage property. Five of them are in Tasmania. It should be noted that when you read about these things in Aussie books, in tourism pamphlets, or on signage while traveling, they are almost always written with a prideful tone. It must be a strange thing for your country heritage to be so deeply connected to criminals. Then again America was stolen from Native Americans, so I guess we're mostly all in the same boat.

Port Arthur Historic Site

291

My $42 ticket for the day offered the chance to take a forty-minute guided walking tour, a twenty-five-minute boat cruise and a walk around the grounds. The schedule was such that I couldn't get the guided tour and the boat tour.

"I don't have a boat, so I'll do the boat tour," I said to the lady behind the counter.

She didn't crack a smile.

"So you don't want the guided walking tour?" she said to me.

"I'd prefer not to wait around for an hour to get started," I said politely. "Are there signs so I will know what I'm looking at?"

"Yes, but you won't get the same stories," she said.

"Thanks, yeah, I'm okay with that," I said.

"Okay, fine," she said, seeming mildly offended.

She handed me a five-inch stack of cards, papers, and ticket vouchers and I made the short walk to the boat docks, where a group of us traded places with a similar-looking lot of disembarking tourists. The boat was a two-story ferry-type craft that went out into the harbor and did a little spin while a woman on the microphone told us what we were looking at, which was a small island and, well, the ocean.

She explained that back in the day ships were built and repaired here, mostly by convicts, sometimes standing in water up to their necks. For criminals who were sent here from Great Britain, the journey took six months. From 1834 to 1849, child criminals were sent to the Point Puer Boys' Reformatory on a sliver of peninsula we were now cruising past, where they were subjected to harsh discipline and stern punishment. They also received an education and learned a trade of some kind.

A mildly ambitious swim from Point Puer was the Isle of the Dead, a small island that was—as the name might suggest—the burial place for 1,100 convicts, military officers, and their family members. From where we were floating, it is an eight- to ten-hour trip by sailboat to Hobart, which was just a couple of hours by car. The tour guide told us that this area of the Tasman Sea is ripe with marine life, and that it is not uncommon to see southern right whales, humpback whales, and orcas. Today, we saw none of those things.

After thirty minutes we returned to the dock and I started my self-guided tour around the grounds, which felt a bit like a country club with no golf holes or beverage carts. The lawns were well kept, and paths made of crushed stone guided visitors from one "attraction" to another. The penitentiary, the hospital, the asylum, the church—there was an endless list of buildings to pop your head into, read some signs about life in those times, and then walk on. The entire place was very well presented and well-kept. Little tip here: Stay on the paths; there is more goose shit than grass on the grass. I'll come back to that momentarily.

While strolling, I learned that by 1840 Port Arthur had 2,000 residents and it was a major industrial hub that produced everything from bricks to ships (in neck-deep water, by the way) to furniture. Basically, it was the IKEA of the 1800s for Tasmania. In 1853, transportation to all of Tasmania (then known as Van Diemen's Land) ended, which stopped the flow of convicts and turned Port Arthur into an institution for aging and physically and mentally ill patients. In 1877, it became the last penal settlement in Tasmania to close. Many of the buildings were later destroyed by bushfires or taken down as the locals attempted to erase the convict branding of the area. In the early 1900s tourism became a thing here and by the 1920s some of the buildings became museums and attractions. It wasn't until the 1970s and 1980s that real conservation of the area began.

In more recent times, Port Arthur gained notoriety for being the site of the largest mass shooting in Australian history. On April 28, 1996, a deranged gunman killed thirty-five people and wounded nineteen more, including both visitors and staff members. Walking the grounds as a tourist it is unfathomable to imagine what that day must have been like for the poor people who simply happened to be working or visiting that day. Not far from the visitor's center is a memorial garden honoring their memories, and a page in the visitor's guide dedicated to the Memorial Garden explains that it "incorporates the shell of the Broad Arrow Café, where twenty of the victims were killed during the massacre." To Australia's credit, they have successfully prevented such an incident from happening again by strengthening gun control laws in the wake of the tragedy.

I made my way to the prison and had just begun reading descriptive plaques when I felt a small drop of something on my hair. I looked up to see a flock of seagulls circling above. The white gooey substance on my fingers confirmed what I'd hoped was false: for the

293

second time in my life, I'd been shat on while touring a former prison. About five years earlier, while standing on the dock at Alcatraz off the coast of San Francisco, a different seagull (I presume) shit on my favorite Boston Red Sox hat. The Sox went on to win the World Series that year, so I have since come to accept that this was a stroke of good luck. I am not expecting the same good fortune to shine on my hairline in the years ahead.

There was a bathroom nearby where I did my best to wash my hair and, in the process, earned a suspicious look from an older gentleman who walked in while I was turning the bathroom sink into a salon.

"Bird shit on my head," I said nonchalantly.

"Ahh," he said, and walked to the urinals.

Hair rinsed, I regrouped mentally and decided to give the place another chance. For protection, I pulled a baseball cap from my backpack and plopped it atop my dome. The pathway to the asylum was covered by trees, which I surmised would offer protection from the threatening skies above. Somewhere along the way, I concluded that the whole place was essentially a park with moderately old buildings. There were other tour options on offer at Port Arthur—a nighttime ghost tour, the After-Dark Package, the Escape from Port Arthur, the Isle of the Dead Cemetery Tour—and I'm sure I would have found those add-ons more exciting, but today was dragging on. I had been here for an hour and a half and, with the bustling metropolis of Hobart waiting an hour and a half away, I decided to take my shitty new hairdo and *pull the pin.*

Hobart waterfront

Chapter 23: Hobart

My first reaction upon arriving at the MONA museum was one that I imagine is shared by many, which was to wonder what the hell kind of place I had walked into. Of course, I knew a bit about the reputation of the Museum of Old and New Art (MONA) as a modern art experience that was not to be missed if you were to find yourself in Hobart. In the end, it was unlike any place I have ever been to or heard of. It's not a museum and it's also not an art gallery. It's a few hours of sensory overload. It's difficult to build a day destination for tourists and locals alike, but MONA seemed to be just that. Even if you live in Hobart, it's a place you'd go back to again and again, especially because it's free for the people of Tasmania. Before I try to explain why, a gentle reminder that I don't know shit about art and can't draw a straight line with a measuring stick, but that seems to be just fine at MONA.

Escaping from Port Arthur to Hobart meant I had to drive north and then south for ninety minutes or so around a rather large body of water, then past the downtown area of Hobart via a series of bridges, off-ramps, and on-ramps. The MONA driveway led up a small hill past a modest-sized vineyard, part of the Moorilla Winery, which the museum sits within. You can also get here via a super-cool-looking fast ferry from the waterfront in Hobart and on a rather *schmick*-looking Mona Roma bus. If I did it again, I'd take the ferry because this is the way that MONA founder and owner David Walsh intended the place to be accessed. Plus, as a general transportation rule, you should choose ferry over bus ninety-nine times out of 100. The exception, of course, is party buses for things like bachelor and bachelorette nights, which you should never, ever say "no" to. I love a good party bus. But I digress. Anyway, next time...ferry.

Walsh grew up in a poor area not far from where MONA stands today. He dropped out of university to become a professional gambler and was very good at it thanks to a *Good Will Hunting* kind of gift for mathematics. He won a lot of money—like a shitload—lost a lot, won some more, spent a shitload, and started collecting art despite not being a real art aficionado. To make a long (and fascinating) story short, he took a lot of his money and built this private art museum. MONA is "dedicated to sex and death" according to a fantastic Walsh profile written by Aussie author Richard Flanagan in *The New Yorker* in 2013, which I highly recommend. Side note here: Don't be scared off from visiting MONA if you don't like sex (okay, sure) or death (more likely). You might be offended in spurts, but get over yourself. MONA, the visitors' pamphlet says, is "a temple to secularism, rationalism, and talking crap about stuff you don't know much about." If you want to know more about MONA's reason for being, Walsh wrote a book called *Monanisms* that explains why he built the place.

The short walk from the car toward the museum leads through a plot of open space the size of an athletic field with a stage at one end. Just beyond that is a wine bar and a cellar door for wine tasting. A few meters beyond that is a tennis court with no fence around it that randomly serves as the centerpiece of an open plaza, which sits atop the hill and looks out over the River Derwent. The whole property sits on the smallish Berriedale Peninsula. From here, the river flows past downtown Hobart just to the south and then into the Tasman Sea. The campus, for lack of a better term, is outrageously modern and will probably feel that way for years to come.

The museum is the centerpiece of the elaborate complex, and the entrance to that is just off the doubles alley at one end of the tennis court. I paid my entrance fee of $28 (because I'm not from Tasmania), which felt like a steal compared to the $42 I paid to have a bird shit on my head at Port Arthur, but let's get past that. The next five minutes were spent trying to find my way inside the bunker that is the MONA museum. A long spiral staircase descended at least three levels down into the earth and, in the middle of the staircase, a modern elevator flew past me filled with lazy people. This feeling of being lost was, for me anyway, part of the entire experience at MONA, and I mean that in the best way possible. I was never quite sure where I was or what I was looking at, but that didn't really matter.

Once I found my way to the start, a woman handed me a small device the size of a mobile phone called the O, which stands for orgasm, I learned. The O contained everything I could want to know about the place. Incidentally, if orgasms guided visitors through more museum tours, folks would probably be a lot more inclined to visit them. There are no signs on the walls at MONA, but even for someone who doesn't really understand or "get" art (raising my hand again here), the O makes it easy and interesting thanks to interviews, descriptions, and even music. It seemed ironic that MONA had found a way to use our human reliance on mobile devices to draw us into appreciating art. The descriptions on the O device are all written with a healthy amount of attitude, so it doesn't feel at all stuffy; quite the opposite, in fact. Still, for uppity art types, the O has a tab called Art Wank, which pokes fun at *wanky* art types while giving them the deeper descriptions they might crave for each exhibit. The Art Wank icon was a drawing of a penis with two testicles. We call that "attention to detail."

The first exhibit I visited at MONA was the toilet. When I walked in, a projection of a short film played between my feet, nearly causing me to piss down my leg. There was an augmented reality room, exhibits on worker fatigue by the Caterpillar construction company, and a waterfall that spelled out Google search terms as it fell from the ceiling. Even if there was nothing hanging on the walls, the building would be a cool place to visit. There were tunnels and mazes and places where they did crazy things with light. The art exhibits felt like stopping points on a journey through a building from a James Bond film.

One of the most interesting exhibits is Wim Delvoye's "Cloaca Professional," which consists of six tanks suspended above the floor across an area about a quarter the size of a basketball court. (I'm not a building contractor or a realtor so I can't give you a square footage/meters estimate.) Each tank was connected to a long, silver pipe that ran the length of the display above. A series of hoses ran down from the pipe into the tanks, inside of which a variety of substances seemed to be mixing. There was a distinct smell in the area.

"What's this meant to be?" asked a woman who had strolled up to my left.

"I think it's a human digestive system," I said because I had read the description on the O that was also hanging around her neck.

"Ah, right," she said, then turned and walked away after four seconds, which I thought was a weird thing to do when you see an exhibit of a working human digestive system in front of you.

A woman in a white lab coat was milling around with the hoses of the tanks.

"If you're still here in ten minutes or so, I'm going to feed it," she said.

"I'm sorry?" I said.

"It gets its afternoon meal at 4 p.m."

"Ahh, of course it does. Okay, thanks. I'll come back."

I spent the next eight minutes wandering around in the nightclub light of the museum looking at other exhibits and wondering if this was the only museum in the world where you had to feed the artwork. In one dark room a large video screen was playing clips of lions and other animals having sex. In front of the screen was a moving—umm, sculpture, I guess you would call it?—of two skeletons boning (get it?), missionary style. A loud creaking sound rang out in rhythm with Skeletor's hip thrusts, as if they were on an old bed.

"She's a little too thin for my liking," I muttered to a stranger who didn't seem to have a sense of humor.

All right, that's eight minutes.

When I sauntered back to Dave the Digestive System (my name, not theirs), the woman in the white coat was feeding something that looked like shepherd's pie into Dave's mouth, which looked like a food processing type machine at one end.

"We give it pills to help break down fats because it doesn't have a pancreas and can't do that," is what I think she was saying. "The temperature is the same as the human stomach, about 36 degrees Celsius, and the feeding schedule is 11 a.m. and 4 p.m. each day. Pooping time is at 2 p.m."

Talk about being regulated.

Aside from that account of the eating art exhibit, I don't want to ruin the element of surprise that MONA offers by detailing what you might encounter on a visit, including Dave's Dump at 2 p.m., but it is a sensory experience of art and optical illusions and mind-benders and even science experiments disguised as art. If you aren't into art or museums, go anyway. Really. If I didn't convince you that the $28 is worth *a go*, there is plenty more outside the museum. The place was described somewhere by Walsh himself as Disneyland for adults. There is live music on weekends, a library of Walsh's personal collection of 14,000 books (he must read quickly), a craft brewery, the winery, a couple of restaurants, and the aforementioned wine bar.

I stayed until closing time at 5 p.m. and then headed into downtown Hobart at rush hour, which was the dumbest thing I had done

MONA Digestive System

since spending two hours at Port Arthur. Just kidding, Port Arthur. The Airbnb I had reserved was on a main street in Hobart, so finding a place to park my car was far less enjoyable than anything those two boning skeletons at MONA were probably getting up to after hours. Eventually, after circling the block four times, I nabbed a spot, paid the meter for the remainder of the evening, and easily opened the trunk and removed my luggage all by myself, I'm proud to say.

While the locals hustled home from work, I spent an hour or so settling into my new digs, a contemporary studio one floor above

301

a loud, bustling city street. As the clock hit 7 or 8 p.m., the streets were almost desolate and suddenly quiet. The contrast from an hour earlier was stunning. Australian cities all feel this way to me. It's as if no one really lives in the downtown (CBD) areas so they bubble to life at 8 a.m. and feel like a ghost town twelve hours later. In this case, it meant the construction zone outside my window had come to a halt, which made me simultaneously happy for the present and dreading the morning.

On the walk from the car, realizing I hadn't eaten lunch, I had stopped to grab a quick pie at a place called the Pilgrim Pie Shop. Next door was a live music venue and an outdoor beer garden that looked inviting, so I started my evening stroll in that direction. An American musician I hadn't heard of was doing a sound check, and his guitar picking wafted out the front door into the evening air. The complex, called The Hanging Garden, had an outdoor space between two buildings, plus the music venue. It was cool. The outdoor area, where people presumably convened for drinks before and after a show, was covered in AstroTurf that you could have built a mini golf course on. Twenty or so people were having a happy hour drink, but the place had room for hundreds.

Salamanca Market is the most noted building in Hobart's waterfront area so I pointed myself in that general direction to see if it was a bit more lively. About ten minutes later, I was standing across the street from a cruise ship terminal and looking at a row of bars and restaurants along Salamanca Place. Some conversational noise and laughter was emanating from a bar called The Whaler and five or six other spots with outdoor seating, but overall it was pretty tame for a Thursday night. Down a pedestrian walkway on an open plaza was the Salamanca Market, which springs to life on Saturdays, right after I would be departing town.

A bar called the Brick Factory was going with the tallest Smurf advertising strategy, promoting that they had "the world least crap trivia night." There was also a whiskey bar, a rug studio, another bar, a wool shop, an arts center, and a guy parading around in a skin-tight white dress shirt and skin-tight white Lycra pants who would make Freddy Mercury look reserved.

At the far end of the plaza were the Kelly Steps, which I remembered reading something about. There appeared to be a lot of them, so I decided this adventure would be best saved until tomorrow. The trees above were filled with chirping birds, which gave me a case of

PTSD from the episode at Port Arthur, though I did ponder lurking beneath them for a minute to see just how lucky, or unlucky, I could be. If being shit on by a bird once is good luck, twice in the same day might mean I'm about to meet that woman my father always warned me about—the millionaire nymphomaniac supermodel whose father owns a liquor store.

I was distracted by that notion when a guy not in white Spandex strolled by carrying a sweet-smelling box of pizza and reminded me that I was starving. Because I had it in my mind that I was going to visit a brewery or two in Tasmania, I made the decision to walk my famished ass back up the hill, past my Airbnb to the Shambles Brewery, about fifteen minutes away on foot. Hobart is a hilly little goddamn place, by the way.

The crowd at Shambles was sparse, but the beer was tasty, which is probably a good thing if you are in the business of brewing and selling it. I ordered a Dirty Copper Amber Ale with a Shamburger and fries, then washed it all down with a pale ale of some other catchy moniker. I rolled myself back down the hill to my Airbnb as a fair wind blowing off the water cooled things down considerably. Back at the Hanging Garden, the concert was ending and I decided to treat myself to a nightcap in the open air.

"How's your night been, mate? All right?" the bartender asked in an overly friendly manner, if one can be overly friendly.

"Yeah, not bad at all, thanks," I said. "I'll just have a schooner, please."

"Here you go. Thanks, mate," he said, sliding the beer across the bar. "You enjoy your beer, okay?"

"Yes, yes I will," I said, wondering if he thought perhaps I had the deciding vote in the Employee of the Month contest or was just the nicest person in Tasmania. It's a good sign when people are so friendly that you wonder what's going on.

I grabbed a seat, watched the last few patrons stand and disappear into the night, and reflected on a very full day. Tomorrow would be my last day in Tasmania, and I was a little sad to be leaving.

I awoke to the soothing, delicate sounds of a jackhammer blasting through concrete fifty feet from my eardrums. As alarm clocks go, that's right up there with a someone lobbing a warm cup of urine on your head (just guessing here). I moved the car to a pay lot, which was pleasantly inexpensive, and thought about how the cost to park your car somewhere is still a good indicator of whether or not you are in an overpriced city.

Hobart, which is Australia's second oldest city behind Sydney, has become quite a popular place for visitors in recent years, but it doesn't feel *exy* (expensive) like other places in Australia can. Nice restaurants, the draw of nearby nature, a few spectacular golf courses, a rather chilled out attitude, and things like MONA have made it a destination not only for mainland Aussies, but international travelers, too. Tourism Tasmania reported that international visitors jumped by 21 percent from 2017 to 2018. Of the 626,000 tourist visits to Tasmania from September 2018 to September 2019, nearly 300,000 of them came from overseas, mostly from the US and China.

Today, the temperature was climbing to about 30 degrees Celsius (86 degrees in my language). The lack of clouds made for a warm morning, but offered a clear view of 4,000-foot Mount Wellington to the west of the city, which Charles Darwin climbed in 1836. I chose to walk downhill instead, in the direction of the waterfront again, past the state Parliament House where folks were lounging on the grass in the shade of a few big trees. A nice breeze was blowing in off the water. Near Salamanca Market I found a breakfast spot called Machine Laundry and popped in for a bite and a look at the local newspaper, *The Mercury*.

The big story of the day was the sale of the State Cinema by independent owner John Kelly to a big corporation. The cinema is a Hobart landmark that has been entertaining crowds in North Hobart for a century, with eleven movie screens and a rooftop cinema. Kelly had been running the place for eighteen years and, on a radio interview I heard the day before, was doing his best to calm the fears of locals by saying that the new owners would maintain the "essence" of the place.

Another *Mercury* news story reported that an "ex-stripper was jailed for drug trafficking." It seems that the pole-dancing Pablo Escobar was flying back and forth from Sydney to Hobart quite frequently before the authorities caught on and found her with 150 grand worth of ice and cocaine in her bra. If you are wondering how a stripper could have space in her bra to smuggle that much drugs, we are on the same page here. She was going off to jail for sixteen months now, so evidently you cannot do it discreetly. Machine Laundry makes a solid omelet and a nice English breakfast tea, and also offers coin laundry machines. It reminded me of how, at one point, I had the idea of opening a laundromat/bar in a university town called Suds and Buds, but never got around to it. By "never got around to it" I mean I came up with the name and the idea, then stopped. So it's fair to say that, in this case, even the drug-smuggling stripper from Sydney had more entrepreneurial follow-through than I did.

Salamanca Place, Hobart

Outside of Machine Laundry, the shops of Salamanca Place that were mostly *shut* the previous evening were springing to life. There were plenty of art galleries and places to make art, which followed a theme I noticed along the streets of Hobart, which had an abundance of record shops, musical instrument stores, and signs advertising music lessons for hire. Even *The Mercury* had a healthy art and music section, which is always a good indicator that a place has some shit going on.

A couple of minutes after breakfast, I was standing at the bottom of the Kelly Steps, which took me up into a delightful Victorian residential neighborhood called Battery Park. The steps deposited me onto Kelly Street, where every house was adorned with flowerbeds or flowerpots. It immediately reminded me of the affluent areas of Melbourne and was clearly the high-rent district of Hobart. Every house was built just feet from the street on small plots of land that were magnificently kept. Kelly Street ended at Hampden Road, the main street through Battery Park, but even that road was fairly quiet, with only the odd car passing through. Hampden runs up the hill away from the harbor on one end and into an area with a few corner stores, including the popular Jackman & McRoss with its cakes and breads.

Further down the road was the Pollen Tea Room, a Kathmandu themed restaurant (which I didn't know was a thing) and a Thai restaurant with a pedicab in front of it. All were well adorned with flowers, and the whole street in springtime was bursting with colors. Everything seemed to blend perfectly into the 150-year-old neighborhood. I strolled off Hampden down Runnymede Street, which passed through a small, immaculately landscaped circular park with a playground at the center. A couple hundred meters away, I walked through an ivy archway into Princess Park, which offered some welcomed shade under old oak trees as well as a panoramic view of the River Derwent, which looked liked the ocean. In the 1800s there were cannons up here to protect Hobart's harbor. Today, only a few children played with their parents in a well-appointed playground. Hobart, it seemed to me, was a miniature combination of Sydney and Melbourne. They might not love that kind of talk around here, but looking down at the harbor while standing in a Victorian neighborhood sure made it feel that way.

I made my way back to Salamanca Place and continued my walking tour along the waterfront, past the various piers from which you can grab a ride on numerous tour boats and ferries. The camouflaged (and quite visible) high-speed MONA ferry arrived at one terminal looking as extravagant as the museum itself. Across a small drawbridge the marina became populated with sailboats, fishing boats, and smaller tour boats that were more modest in appearance than MONA MR-I and MR-II. Wilderness journeys, simple day cruises, and even sea plane rides were on offer.

At the other end of the waterfront was something called the Jam Factory, where a guy named Henry Jones once ran the largest and most modern jam factory in the world, according to a sign. Fruit, it said, was delivered here by trucks and river steamers. It was canned here on the spot and shipped all over the world. Jones, according to another historical sign, started on the factory floor at the age of thirteen and was constantly *flat out like a lizard drinking* (busy working hard). He was also—I surmised from reading between the lines—a real dick to work for. His personal motto was: "I excel at everything I do." Except modesty, it seems. Today, the Jam Factory houses restaurants, an arts center, and some office buildings and apartments.

I spent another hour or so meandering the streets of Hobart, and pondered making a drive south toward what my *National Geographic* travel guidebook said is the "picturesque heart of Tasmania's apple orchard district." You can be there in a half-hour or so, but an evening flight out of Hobart had me a little nervous about being back in time. Instead, I decided to make the day more educational by immersing myself in two of Hobart's old and new industries—brewing beer and making whiskey.

The Cascade Brewery in South Hobart is an easy fifteen-minute drive from downtown through some neighborhoods to the foothills at the base of Mount Wellington, and it seemed like the perfect place for a mid-afternoon lunch. Cascade is Australia's oldest brewery, dating back to 1824. The same guidebook says the brewery itself looks like a French chateau, which I probably should have noticed after living in France for four years. The large, granite structure stands five or six stories tall and towers over a bend in Cascade Road, which delivers you to it. I'm not exactly Gustave Eiffel, but on closer inspection, I'll be damned if it doesn't look a bit like a French chateau. A small stream called the Hobart Rivulet flows past and is the main reason the brewery was constructed here. That and be cause people like beer.

Cascade was started by two English immigrants, Peter Degraves and his brother-in-law Major Macintosh, both of whom arrived in what was then Van Diemen's Land in 1824. Degraves—who studied engineering, architecture, and law—was of French heritage. Hence, the chateau thing. He played a vital role in the early days of Hobart's development, building local saw and flour mills, backing the construction of the Hobart Royal Theatre, and even helping to build the city's water supply. Two years after he landed on the island, the forty-eight-year-old horny father of eight was forced to serve time in the Hobart Gaol (jail) for some sort of issue with creditors back in England. To his credit, Degraves didn't just spend his prison time lifting weights and bartering for cigarettes. Instead, he made plans to use the clean waters "cascading" from Mount Wellington to make beer on the plot of land where his sawmill was sitting. The construction of the place was done by convicts of the day.

Degraves sounds like he was a pretty driven guy, so he likely would be disappointed to learn that that the electricity was out on the day I arrived at the Cascade Brewhouse. No power meant no tour of the brewery itself across the road (the chateau-ey place) and, even worse, no food. It didn't mean, however, that there was no beer and no fun. The brewhouse sits on three acres and includes a restaurant and resplendent garden out back. With the kitchen unable to power up, I ordered a schooner of Cascade Pale Ale, the oldest continuously brewed beer in the country, by the way, and strolled out to the garden. There were picnic tables with umbrellas, fountains, flowers, and a bright green lawn that was freshly mowed. I took a seat on the grassy slope and sipped my beer in the sun. The working brewery peaked above the trees from across the street and Mount Wellington towered above behind that, while a couple to my right argued vociferously about the pageantry of their pending baby shower.

Although it doesn't hurt, you don't necessarily need to like beer to visit Cascade. The menu is well beyond pub food and the grounds of the place are relaxing, contentious baby shower discussion notwithstanding. They even host wedding receptions here. When I went back inside, the electricity was back on, so I ordered a pizza and a second small beer, a lager this time. The food was good and I was happy.

I still had a couple of hours to burn before my flight out of Hobart that evening, so I took the advice of my buddy Leighton and decided that the brewery visit would pair nicely with a stop at one of Hobart's now famed whiskey distilleries. Before you get overly judgmental, this was indeed an educational sojourn. Whiskey has become a *full-on* industry in Tasmania in recent years, which I didn't know until

I started planning my visit there. A quick Google search turns up thirty-one whiskey distilleries in Tasmania alone, despite the fact that micro-distilleries were not even legal in Australia until the 1990s.

The one I settled on was on the way to (and not far from) the airport, which was convenient if I planned on doing a bit of tasting, and why would you visit such a place and not have a taste? (That's a rhetorical question. You would not.) Sullivans Cove distillery, which sits behind a chain-link fence on a two-lane road outside of town, looks like any modest warehouse you might come across on the edge of any mid-size city. You would never suspect that this small Hobart distillery won the coveted top prize for World's Best Single Malt at the World Whiskies Awards in 2014. That honor made it then, and still to this day, the only Australian whiskey ever to win World's Best. Prior to that, the World's Best awards almost always went to Scottish distilleries.

The victory by Sullivans Cove was a landmark event in the business of whiskey-making, especially in Tasmania, where it turned locally produced whisky that was mostly imbibed by thirsty Aussies and the occasional visitor into an internationally desired beverage. And another reason to visit. In 2018, Sullivans Cove won more hardware. This time, it was their American Oak Single Cask that took the prize for World's Best Single Cask Single Malt. They followed that up a year later by winning the 2019 World's Best Award for their French Oak Single Cask, becoming the only distillery in the world to ever win the award twice. That's a bit like a guy from Australia coming to America and winning the MVP of the National Football League…three times.

For some reference, Sullivans Cove opened in 1994 and is minuscule in comparison to a massive company like Jameson, which opened in 1780. That was according to Ally, the young woman who was our tour guide. After a brief introduction she took our small group up some stairs to a platform that overlooked the area where the magic happens. There were tanks below us and rows of whiskey barrels stacked to the ceiling on the other side of the space. I don't know enough about whiskey to give you an educated report, but we tasted a few drams and they were unbelievably smooth. Ally told us a few stories and a fair bit about making whiskey that I won't bore you with here, except to say she didn't give away the company secrets. All I got was that they rely on local brewers to brew their barley and that the pot still used to distill the whiskey is named Myrtle.

Ally told us that when Sullivans Cove won their first World's Best Award back in 2014 they had sold all of that year's edition, which meant they had to call around to buy back bottles of their own products if they wanted to have some on hand. They got three. 3. Like, 03. Their run of success has led to the place we were now standing in becoming overrun with tourists clamoring to get a look at where the champion whiskey was made.

"People had to stop working so that they could give tours," Ally said. "So we built the little visitor center."

Toward the end of the tour, it became clear that, despite the awards, Sullivans Cove was still a down-home Tassie business. Bottles were coming into a small room through a window from the warehouse floor and a woman named Tammy was cleaning, filling, labelling, polishing and packing every single bottle by hand. Just for fun, I looked up the cost of a Sullivans Cove Single Cask French Oak Whisky on the website of Dan Murphy's, a large liquor store chain in Australia. Their website said there was a two-bottle limit, which didn't matter because they were out of stock, and the cost was $449 AUD per bottle. Tammy better be sure-handed.

I passed on purchasing a bottle at the distillery—only because didn't have room in my bag, obviously—and headed to the Hobart airport with a warm (but legal) glow about me. My flight into Launceston five days earlier arrived two hours late and in the dark. Now, on a clear evening from a window seat on my departing flight, Tasmania looked positively spectacular. The plane flew north and west over the center of the island toward my nest stop, Adelaide, back on the mainland. In the distance was the coastline, its rocky sections contrasting with its white sand beaches and turquoise water. Inland, there were big mountains, green fields, and dense forests. Behind me was a charming and walkable Victorian city with breweries, whiskey distilleries, and a world-class museum. I had seen only some of Tasmania over parts of five days, but it seemed to have a bit of everything. It was, as I had been told, a small version of Australia that looked a bit like New Zealand. And that, I'm sure, is how you offend the inhabitants of four islands in one sentence.

UNSOLICITED ADVICE: TASMANIA

MUST DO:

MONA in Hobart was clearly a highlight for me, and is *the* reason many visit the city in the first place. Take the twenty-five-minute MONA ferry from the terminal in Hobart, which is like a twofer tourist excursion—a boat trip and a museum visit. And remember, if you time it right, you get to watch a fake human digestive system take a No. 2 at 2 p.m (that's two twofers if you're keeping score)... Also in Hobart, the **Cascade Brewhouse** was a fun place to have lunch and sit on the lawn with a frothy. It's a short drive from downtown and I bet it's a cool scene on a weekend. Go when there isn't a power outage... The stroll through **Battery Point** was an hour well spent... The **winery** stops along the entire trip were a nice way to break things up.

UP TO YOU:

Freycinet was a beautiful area if you like a nice, approachable walk, depending on your definition of approachable. If you go and are fit, bring a sandwich, make a half day of it, and hike down (and back up) the 1,000 steps to the beach itself on the other side... The Sullivans Cove **distillery tour** in Hobart was interesting, but a little steep at $50 or so. There are others, too... If you like mountain biking, **Blue Derby** was incredible. It'll cost you $100 or so for the bike and helmet, unless you somehow bring your own gear. Just know that there isn't much else in that neck of the woods... Don't try to drive from Orford to **Port Arthur** to MONA to Hobart in a day unless you are a lunatic like me... I clearly wasn't enamored with Port Arthur. I'm not sure if I was just tired and looking forward to getting to Hobart or if it was just boring.

NEXT TIME:

I chose to skip **the Northwest**, which pained me. If you love hiking, that's your spot. I love hiking, too, but time was short... I didn't find much on offer in **Launceston**, but if you want to do a point-to-point road trip or see the Northwest area and **Cradle Mountain**, it's a good starting point... Overall, I wish I got to Hobart sooner, used a day walking the city, another day taking the ferry to MONA, and then explored the **Huon Valley Drive** and beyond that into **Hartz Mountains National Park** and the **Southwest Wilderness area**.

PART IX:
SOUTH AUSTRALIA

Goodman Crescent Lawns, University of Adelaide

Chapter 24: "Radelaide"

When I first met Simon Bartold, I had already moved out of Australia a year earlier. The two of us were working for the same company in France, and my job was to help market the running shoes that he was developing as a well-respected podiatrist. Knowing I had lived in Australia for some time, a colleague told me I should meet "the Aussie guy who worked on the other side of the building."

I distinctly recall that the third or fourth sentence out of Simon's mouth was that he was from Adelaide, which he described as "The Athens of the South."

"Umm, Georgia isn't much to brag about," I said, assuming he would understand that I was pretending he meant Athens, Georgia in the US.

"Greece, mate!" he said, realizing I was *taking the piss*. "Fucking Athens, Greece. Not Athens, Georgia in America. Fucking Yanks..."

I knew from that moment that we would be mates.

When I told Simon that day that I had never been to Adelaide despite having lived in Melbourne for three years, he acted as if I had gone to base camp at Mount Everest and forgotten to look up at the mountain. I didn't have a good reason for having never gone to Adelaide, other than the fact that no one I knew in Melbourne ever seemed to go there for fun and things just got in the way. Even my then-coworker Matt Knowles, who is from Adelaide, wasn't exactly urging me to visit the place. Reports of its coolness had been somewhat conflicting. Some said it was a fun little city with nice beaches and access to some of the best wine regions in Australia, which it does indeed have. Others told me it was not as cultured as Melbourne and Sydney, and that it was a "big country town." People told me the same thing about Canberra so you can understand that my expectations were rather tempered when I arrived on a Friday night to spend four-plus days *sussing out* the place.

Simon, and I am pointing this out only because it will annoy him, is in his mid-sixties. He and his American wife Lisa have two young children and had since moved back to Adelaide when I arrived for my visit. This meant two things. First, I would likely be getting a home-cooked meal because Simon loves to fire up the *barbie*. Second, I'd have a tour guide whenever my old chum could break away from his considerable adult responsibilities and act like an adolescent with me. Turns out, that was day one.

"I'll pick you up at 9:30 tomorrow morning," he told me, "and we'll go wine tasting in either the Barossa Valley or McLaren Vale."

I looked at my watch and recognized that our 9:30 a.m. meeting meant 10 a.m. Australian Eastern Standard Time. I mention this because South Australia and the Northern Territory have the peculiar status of existing on Australian Central Standard Time, which is 30 minutes behind the Eastern Time Zone that Victoria, New South Wales, Queensland, Tasmania, and the ACT exist on. (Western Australia is two hours behind the East Coast.) You may be wondering why thirty minutes. Well, much like the entire existence of Canberra, the thirty-minutes-later time zone thing is the result of a compromise. In the colonial days, South Australia was on central time, which was an hour behind the eastern time zone. In the late 1800s, when pressure came from the Chamber of Commerce to get Adelaide on the same time zone as the bigger eastern cities, the government came up with a compromise that put clocks thirty minutes behind. Interestingly enough, my research tells me that the origins of the half-hour time measurement can be traced back to the fourth-century in Greece.

The Athens of the South it is then.

Simon is an oenophile, which is a fancy way to say he likes fancy wine, and one of the many charming things about Adelaide is its close proximity to several world-renowned winemaking regions. Simon grew up here, thirty minutes behind the people of Sydney and Melbourne, went to university here and has spent most of his adult life here. He loves Adelaide, as you may have gathered from the ancient Greece comparison that I think he may actually believe to be true.

"Did you get some breakfast?" Simon asked me, as we strolled to the car from a café near my hotel, morning beverages hand.

"I ate a massive breakfast at midnight," I said, explaining how I was starving when I arrived the night before and went searching for grub like a twenty-one-year-old drunken university student. "I found this place called the Pancake Factory, about a ten-minute walk from here, and *smashed* some pancakes, eggs, bacon, and hash browns. I'm still full."

"You went to the Pancake Factory last night? At midnight?" he said, laughing. "I used to go there in Uni."

"Pancakes existed back when you were in Uni?" I said.

He looked at me without uttering a word, and we drove off.

After debating between McLaren Vale and the Barossa Valley, Simon settled on taking me to the Barossa, about an hour and fifteen minutes north of downtown Adelaide. As we began the trip, I got my first peak at the city in the daylight. It is a vibrant place and was devoid of traffic at about 10 a.m. on a Friday. The River Torrens curled its way alongside the downtown area, its green banks surprisingly unpopulated with people, which would become a theme for the week.

An hour later we were rolling along a highway, up and down dry hillsides, with a lengthy view across valleys that stretched in all directions.

Turkey Flat Vineyard, Barossa Valley

319

The Barossa Valley is known for red wine, and Shiraz is its calling card around the globe, as Mr. Wine Spectator himself was telling me. We entered the valley via Tanunda and its picturesque tree-lined streets, and made our way—after a couple of u-turns, if I'm being honest—to a tasting room to try the wine of a friend of Simon's. The room didn't have the drop Simon was after, so we drove over to one of his favorites, Turkey Flat Winery.

"These are some of the oldest vines in the world," Simon said of the vineyard in front of the building.

"Oh, what did the place look like when you planted them?" I asked.

Just kidding. I didn't say that.

"These guys make an absolutely wonderful Shiraz," said Mr. Fancy, who proceeded to buy a case of it after a couple of tastings served to us by the young French lady behind the bar. I walked out with a sweet after-dinner wine from their reserve barrels of Pedro Ximénez, whatever the hell that means.

We headed back into Tanunda for lunch at a delightful café called the Four Seasons of Nosh, which was set in an old flour mill. The building's exterior was such that it just made you want to look inside and the food backed up our curiosity. We walked through a small-ish entryway, which then opened into two spacious rooms, and an upstairs dining area. Behind the counter, a friendly bloke took our orders. We ate lunch at a sidewalk table out front and Simon laughed at me as I ate a monster Caesar salad and meat pie.

"It's a good thing you exercise like crazy, mate," he correctly pointed out.

In my defense, I'd eaten *brekkie* thirteen hours earlier and the food looked too good not to go for broke. If you find yourself near Tanun-da, I highly recommend the Nosh Café. The meat pie/salad combo lays a nice base for an afternoon of tasting more reds.

When I said Simon liked his wine, I wasn't being a smartass...well, I was, but he knows his stuff and is the perfect vineyard guide. With what remained of the afternoon, he had a special treat in mind. We drove ten minutes or so to Rockford, one of the area's oldest vineyards and makers of some of Australia's most popular and premium wines.

The place is set in an old brick courtyard that dates back to German settlements from the mid-1800s. The courtyard is surrounded by old stone buildings with industrial-looking tools that people operated by hand in order to exist back in those times. At the main tasting room, Simon flashed a small coin-type thing on his keychain that had a number on it. He was particularly proud of the number, which was 02, because this meant he was an early member in the Rockford Stonewall group, which doesn't have many of them.

The keychain seemed to surprise the guy behind the bar who was busy serving wine to the mildly intoxicated group taking up most of the space in the room. A couple minutes later, on account of Simon's dog-tag thing, a woman arrived to escort us across the courtyard through a small doorway and into an exclusive tasting room to see a Heritage winemaker named Robert O'Callahan. There, in a members' only area, we would have access to a selection of wines far too good for my less experienced pallet, but nothing I was going to turn down.

Five minutes later, in the members' tasting room, the five-star treatment was *well and truly* underway. The wines were exquisite and the list of what we could taste seemed endless. Being the guest and non-driver on the day made me the primary beneficiary of this experience. While Simon chatted about the science of cork and the merits of his 1988 bottle of whatever the hell he had at home and will never open, I kept on drinking the wines the friendly woman was putting in front of me. I lost track at seven and, for a second, started to feel guilty about doing the bulk of the tasting.

"Have whatever you want, mate," Simon said. "I'd be right there with you if I wasn't driving."

Doesn't Simon sound great? Yeah, I think so, too.

While he was busy buying up a case of this or that from exclusive selections that are only available to members, I was trying to decide what I felt comfortable spending and what would fit comfortably in my luggage. Luckily, the second element was going to curtail the first. I walked out with two or three bottles, including a 2016 Basket Press Shiraz that I'm supposed to put away for some number of years. We'll see how that goes. I also had a mild buzz that lasted most of the ride back to town.

Simon took the scenic route back through the Adelaide Hills, which is today a rapidly developing winemaking region, according to my tour guide. We started on something called Eden Valley Road, which carried us through several small towns with names like Eden Valley,

Springton, and Mount Pleasant. The road met up with Torrens Valley Road, which wound past still more vineyards and up and down some substantial climbs that are popular with road cyclists. Along the way I spotted cherry farms, a random roadside hut with free produce and books inside, and trees that Simon told me are likely a couple of hundred years old.

"You can see in the trees where the native Aboriginal people have taken a segment of bark so they can build a canoe from it," he said. "And they did it so that the tree lives. It's really quite remarkable."

Suddenly, I've gone wine tasting with Sir. David Attenborough.

Because this is Australia, rather out of the blue we came across the world's biggest Rocking Horse, towering above the road in Gumeracha, forty minutes from Adelaide. Australia is famous for big shit like this that they build by the side of the road to attract people driving by. I believe they have a Big Banana, a Big Scotsman, a Big Penguin, and the list goes on. When I came across the world's biggest Rocking Horse, I started researching big things in Australia and my favorite one has to be the Big Bogan in Nyngan, New South Wales, about seven hours east of Sydney. The Big Bogan was designed specifically as a tourist attraction in 2015. It's a six-meter-tall statue of the quintessential Aussie *bogan* (redneck), a long-bearded guy dressed in a tank top and *thongs* (sandals). He's holding a fishing rod and standing with an *esky* (cooler). The pictures of it online are thoroughly unspectacular and I cannot fathom someone driving a great distance to see it.

The world's largest Rocking Horse is a little more substantial and imposing. Standing eighteen meters tall (fifty-nine feet) and positioned up on a hill, it has been around since 1981 on the site of a wooden toy factory. It was all closed for the day now, as Simon and I drove by in early evening, but you can climb to the top of the rocking horse for $2 using a series of steps and then metal ladders if you are so inclined. Children under the age of three are free. How they navigate the ladders, I don't know. You do receive a certificate of achievement if you climb to the top. My certificates of achievement for the day were corked and lying in the back seat in cardboard boxes, which I carefully transferred from the car to my hotel room when we got back to town. My first day in South Australia was a success, thanks to Simon.

Left to my own devices for the evening, I went out on foot to explore what a Friday night feels like in downtown Adelaide. The logical choice

The Big Rocking Horse; Gumeracha, South Australia

was one block away on Rundle Street, which was *positively buzzing*. Much of Rundle Street is a pedestrian mall lined with shops big and small. The pedestrian-only part ends at Pulteney Street and that's where the nightlife begins. Both sides of Rundle are lined with restaurants and bars of all types, from *take-away* food options to more up-scale sit-down meals, cocktail bars, and beer halls. The sidewalks were full of people dining outside, though the temperature had cooled considerably since the afternoon. Like most Aussie cities, the variety of dining options was impressive. There were Thai, Japanese, Vietnamese, and Italian restaurants, as well as your traditional Aussie pub fare, all on the same block. It was difficult to decide what to eat.

The crowd seemed a mix of students and older professional types dressed in their button-down shirts after a day of work in the city. I made a little turn onto a side street called Vardon, and there were still more people packed in bars and gathering on the sidewalks over an evening pint at a place called the Belgian Beer Café. I remember thinking: Adelaide seems pretty cool; you'd want to live here. The buzz of Rundle Street ended abruptly at a street called East Terrace, and quiet parkland took over on the other side. Downtown Adelaide is surrounded by parkland, in fact, which makes for a nice drive in and out of the city and allows for an easy escape from what passes for a crowd in these parts.

I turned around and walked back up the other side of Rundle Street before deciding on an Italian restaurant called Sicily Pizzeria that had bar seating, perfect for solo dining. From behind the bar, a friendly thirty-ish Italian woman explained to me why she liked Adelaide so much since moving to Australia from Milan (the one in Italy) a year and a half earlier.

"Adelaide is a little less fancy than Melbourne, I think," was how she summed things up after I told her I had lived in Melbourne for three years. "You can get to the beaches and wineries easily and quickly. And they are better beaches and wine regions than Melbourne."

Her overall message seemed to be that Adelaide is a bit more approachable and convenient than Melbourne and Sydney, and that makes sense when you consider the population is about 1.3 million people as of 2020.

I finished up with a drink at a placed called The Distillery just up the street and spent a few minutes thumbing through a pamphlet for the Adelaide Festival, which was sitting on the bar. The Adelaide Festival is an arts festival that has been going on since 1960, and the schedule was loaded with ballets, opera, an international guitar competition, cabaret, literature, and plenty more. The whole thing takes place at various locations around town during the first two weeks in March and is part of what locals call "Mad March" because of the number of social happenings that occur then. Part of all this madness is the Adelaide Fringe, a festival that runs from mid-February to mid-March. On top of that is a Writer's Week, the horse racing of the Adelaide Cup, and the Tasting Australia food festival. When March comes to an end, Adelaide turns its attention to Aussie rules football with two professional teams and a passion for the footy that rivals Melbourne's.

While March sounded as exhausting (in a good way) as I currently felt, my first full day in "Radelaide" was the perfect introduction to the "big country town" and, after only twenty-four hours, the place was growing on me.

Old Albert pedestrian bridge over the Torrens

Chapter 25: Walking the Country Town

I woke up on Saturday morning and—after a much-needed workout in the hotel gym to burn off what had been an excessive Friday of food and alcohol even by my standards—set out on an old-fashioned *walkabout*. The first stop was Adelaide's central market, about twenty minutes away, which took me through Victoria Square and its well-manicured green space and small fountains. Tram tracks cut through well-mown grass. Around the square are the General Post Office, the Treasury building, the Supreme Court of Australia, and a Catholic church called the Cathedral of St. Francis Xavier. It struck me that everything seemed pretty well placed in Adelaide, with a nice blend of old and new.

Beyond Victoria Square, just to the west, was the Central Market, which has existed since 1869 and has all your market staples—fresh fish, fresh produce, butchers, cookies, bread, flowers, and the like. I strolled around for thirty minutes until happening upon a place at the other end called the Zuma Caffe, spelled with two Fs for some clever reason I couldn't grasp. I ordered breakfast, headed out to a sidewalk table, and plopped down my order number on one of those steel stand order number things that I don't know the name of. While pontificating over whether there actually is a name for those table number things, I overheard two sixty-something men in a fairly involved conversation about their overall health.

"...ever since I had my prostate operation" is how it all begin. He carried on saying something about needing to do something "ten hours a week," which seemed uncomfortable regardless of whatever it was he was referring to. From there, he began recounting a discussion about someone else's blood tests and how the results were "through the roof." Is this what happens when you get to your senior years? You sit around and discuss rare illnesses and test results? Delightful. I can't wait.

Ten minutes later, the health expert was detailing cancers and carcinogens and "when it's too late" and what means what. Meanwhile, his mate was fanning the flames by asking him questions as if he was an oncologist, which he surely was not.

"Well, my prostate was perfect," the other guy said.

All of this gave me great relief, as you can imagine, and I shoveled

327

another bite of a massive omelet and toast into my mouth.

"If they do (such and such), you are a goner," the expert said back to him. "Period. End of story."

I'd had enough of Derek Downer. I finished off my last piece of bacon and *pulled up stumps*. Bacon is good for the prostate, right?

From the market I strolled back in the direction I had come from toward the River Torrens, which is a cool name for a river, I think. It sounds like it could be dangerous if it needed to be, which fits with everything else in Australia. On the way was a rooftop bar called 2KW that I had read about online somewhere. As I'm always in favor of a bird's-eye view in a new city, I popped in for a look and to feel massively underdressed. When the elevator deposited me into the restaurant, there were scores of well-appointed people enjoying champagne and mimosas. The men were in button-down shirts and Aussie-fit tight slacks and the women were in summer dresses and high heels. There was a baby shower going on in one section. Dressed in my T-shirt, shorts, and small backpack, I walked through the restaurant to the open-air bar at the back feeling a tad out of place, although those skin-tight slacks didn't look comfortable on what was becoming a very warm afternoon. The terrace by the bar offered a sweeping view to the North over the river and the expansive green space around it. I ordered a small lager and wandered to the edge to snap a few photos and confirm that I was a tourist to anyone still unsure.

Beneath me was North Terrace, a road lined with museums, galleries, and the University of Adelaide. A kilometer or so away, just across the river, was the Adelaide Oval, where two AFL teams play. All looked worthy of a walk, so I charted my course from above, finished my small *frothy*, and made my way back downstairs. A tram ran down the middle of King William Road and I was struck by how spacious everything felt just a few steps from the heart of downtown. It seemed like some person gave thought to not building things right on top of the river, which made the city and all this open space seem worlds apart. I liked the feel of it all.

I wandered across the street past something called the Adelaide Festival Centre, where hundreds of senior citizens were exiting some kind of show. Beneath the Festival Centre a green lawn called Elder Park—maybe after the elders I saw—led down to the river, where a bike/walking path ran alongside the bank. Cyclists and joggers cruised by in all directions and people rented paddleboats from a small vendor at the edge of the river. Occasionally, a group would cruise down the river in something called a BBQ Buoy, a donut-shaped floating vessel with a barbeque in the middle that you and your mates sit around while grilling your own food. There was even a giant sun umbrella over the top of it. I wanted my own BBQ Buoy now. A little farther up the river, something called a Gin Cruise was getting ready to shove off later that afternoon. I wanted my own Gin Cruise as well.

The city side of the river was lined with buildings of varying shapes, all of which looked quite different from one another but somehow not out of place. It gave the entire area a sort of modern character and consistency despite its variety. I walked across the Torrens River Footbridge, which is ultra-modern looking as well. Opened in 2014, the 255-meter-long bridge cost $40 million to build. At eight meters wide, it is roomy enough to house two-way vehicle traffic, and it connects the Festival Centre with the southern gates of the Adelaide Oval, a 50,000-capacity cricket and football *ground* (stadium) that is home to both the Adelaide Crows and the Port Adelaide Power.

Adelaide Riverbank precinct on the Torrens

329

There has been a sports oval on this site since 1871 in some form or fashion, but the modern stadium that exists now is considered one of the best places to watch sports in the country, largely thanks to a $500-plus million upgrade that occurred from 2012 to 2014. In Australia, it's nice that many of the sports stadiums are easily accessible in the city by public transportation and/or a little walking. You can envision what it's like to go to the footy or cricket in Adelaide and then cross over the bridge and head into town, or vice versa.

On the other side of the stadium, a long walkway cut through parkland and took me into North Adelaide, an affluent residential suburb of the city, where the streets were lined with old trees and the Heritage-listed houses. I spent a bit of time wandering past the neighborhood's tiny work spaces, old mansions, new mansions, cafés, and little cottages. Eventually, I made my way to O'Connell Street, the main route through North Adelaide, which is chock-full of restaurants, shops, and old pubs with high ceilings. By accident, I stumbled upon Melbourne Street's upscale real estate. It was clear that, in some cases, the old structure had been knocked down and replaced by something shiny and new on plots that must have fetched a small fortune.

Melbourne Road led me to a huge parkland that houses Adelaide University's athletic fields, which I walked around carefully on account of the practice session that was taking place at the Adelaide Archery Club. Just out of range from where I might take an errant arrow to the chest from a wannabe Robin Hood or Lara Croft, I connected with a bike/walking path and then over another footbridge that led back across the river toward the city. Just off the path, a group of women were having a five-star picnic in the park. Dressed in sun hats and dresses, they were sitting on a blanket around a board about the size of a bedroom door. They weren't here to *fuck spiders* either (they weren't messing around). The board, which was propped up on stilts about six inches off the ground and functioning as their table, looked to be covered with a variety of cheese dishes and the like, along with vases full of flowers and bottles of what looked like champagne or rosé. It struck me how this is a decidedly female thing to do. If I called Leighton and Sully and asked them if they cared to meet for a wine and cheese picnic in the park, they would laugh and hang up the phone. And maybe never answer it again. If there was horse racing going on just outside the park, I suppose that would make it okay.

A little farther on, past the five-star Michelin picnic, the path took me past the entrance for the Adelaide Zoo and then into the Adelaide Botanic Garden, which Simon had told me was "one of the best botanical gardens going and much nicer than Melbourne's." If Adelaide had an Eiffel Tower or a Sistine Chapel, he would tell you those were the best ones going, too. Again, I'm no botanist but the botanic garden was just fine as far as botanic gardens go. It had plants and flowers and trees, and it seemed well used today.

At this point, I had put in close to ten kilometers on my unorganized walking tour, and was back in town. Much of the neighborhood near the world's greatest botanic garden is occupied by the University of Adelaide and the University of South Australia, which are right next to each other. Both are public universities with great reputations on well-presented pieces of property. The University of Adelaide, which opened in 1874 and is the third oldest university in the country, looks not unlike the highly esteemed university campuses you might find in northeastern US cities.

Just off North Terrace was a magnificent green space on the campus of the University of Adelaide called the Goodman Crescent Lawns, which we would refer to on an American university campus as a "quad." It was surrounded on three sides by spectacular sandstone buildings, and the grass looked like you could eat off it. The purple colors of jacaranda trees were in full bloom. A few steps away was the hustle and bustle of North Terrace, and then a block beyond that, was Rundle Mall. I found myself enamored with how quickly the vibe went from bustling city street to quiet green space in Adelaide. It was as if the noise of the city didn't penetrate the open space areas. I couldn't get my head around it. Still can't.

That night, I grabbed an Uber to the home of Simon and Lisa for a BBQ dinner and fine wine and to let their five-year-old son and two-year-old daughter beat the shit out of me, all of which exceeded expectations. As usual, Simon regaled me with stories about where he got the wine, the story behind it, and how good it would be, and did the same with the tri-tip or lamb or whatever it was that was filling his home with a delectable aroma.

"Next time you're here I'm going to serve you the Coat of Arms," he said to me.

"I'm sorry?" I asked.

"The Australian Coat of Arms, the national emblem, is the kangaroo and the emu," he said. "People make a meal called the Coat of Arms, where you serve up both of them. We might be the only country that eats its coat of arms."

"That's a good story, Simon," I said. "I look forward to that."

"You're quite well traveled, mate," he said to me. "You've only just got here, but I'm curious what are your impressions of Adelaide after a day?"

"It feels small, but not like a small city," I said. "I mean it feels like it has all the cultural attractions of a big city like Melbourne or Sydney, and the quality of life seems quite high. There doesn't seem like there is much traffic or other annoyances you get in a bigger city. It's a lot cooler than I thought it would be based on what I heard."

"Oh, there's no traffic at all compared to those places you mentioned," he said. "And I do think we have a lot more going on than we get credit it for."

I admitted that I didn't realize what a cosmopolitan place Adelaide seemed to be. For me, a city needs to offer cultural attractions like concerts and sports and restaurants and some kind of nightlife, of course, but the best ones also have places to escape to nearby—mountains, beaches, country towns, whatever you fancy. It's one of the reasons the San Francisco Bay Area or my hometown of Boston and even Denver have always been favorites of mine. You can hop in your car (or on a train) in any of those places and easily go explore something different for a day or two—mountains, beaches, wine country, or even another city. Melbourne, Sydney, and Perth all had that for me to some degree, and now Adelaide seemed to as well. You could be at a beautiful beach in thirty minutes or in the hills of a wine country in forty-five. When you throw in festivals and music and sport and universities, the latter of which always add a youthful mentality to a place, you've got a "livable" place to borrow from *The Economist*.

"There is always something going on here," Simon said. "I don't think I realized how good we have it in that area until I moved away for a few years and came back. Especially from February until April, when the weather is incredible and the festivals are nonstop. They do market all that locally, but when I show visitors around Adelaide they are surprised at how pretty it is. Maybe we just don't get the same attention that Sydney and Melbourne get when it comes to international marketing."

Eventually, when Lisa and the kids had gone to bed, Simon and I found ourselves opening a third bottle of one of his exquisite red wines, playing a little guitar, and sharing stories of the best concerts we had ever been to, as we often do when we get together. I talked about some of the great acts I had seen through the years—Springsteen, U2, Dylan, Dave Matthews Band, Jason Isbell, and Roger Waters—all of which are still alive. Then Simon shared some of his favorites from his years of concert-going—INXS, Led Zeppelin, AC/DC, Clapton, Beethoven, Bach, Mozart.

Then I took an Uber home and went to sleep.

Skyline Ferris Wheel at Glenelg, South Australia

Chapter 26: Adelaide and the Coast

It's fair to say I woke up a little *dusty* from the wine tasting and guitar session with Mr. Bartold, but I'm proud to say I shook off the cobwebs with a somewhat leisurely morning run (let's call it more of a jog) through and around several of Adelaide's parks and athletic fields. It's easy to link the city's green spaces by crossing just a few streets and then sticking to paved and dirt paths near the river and its bridges. Aside from some students training on the University athletic fields, I still couldn't understand why I didn't come across more people. Maybe they give away free prostate exams at the market on Sunday mornings.

I spent the afternoon poking around a few other parts of the city to see what I might have missed. On the recommendation of Simon, I started with a short walk to the Tandandya National Aboriginal Cultural Institute on Grenfell Street, which touts itself as Australia's oldest Aboriginal-owned and managed arts center. I was after a piece of Aboriginal art and Simon advised me that the place was legit. A not-for-profit organization, the arts center hosts events and attracts thousands of visitors every year to view the exhibits. All of the art I saw was also for sale, and it's nice to know that anything you purchase is directly benefitting the artist, not some middleman. There were handmade baskets, handbag-type creations, small paintings, and even large-scale murals on display. A woman working there told me that the baskets were created mostly by elder Aboriginal women who were taught the craft by their mothers and were now passing it along to their daughters and granddaughters.

I scoured the place for thirty minutes, searching for something that caught my eye and fit my budget, then settled on a small, one-square-foot canvas painting of a starry night sky that I kept coming back to. It's called *Seven Sisters Dreaming* by a young woman named Athena Nangala Granites. The Aboriginal name for the painting is *Napaljarri-warnu Jukurrpa* for all you Aboriginal art gurus out there. I know this because it came with a certificate of authentication. If you purchase Aboriginal art it's a good idea to get one of these so you know that it was truly done by an Indigenous artist, not some guy in a Hong Kong market with a paint-by-numbers kit.

The authentication letter also had a lengthy description of the painting, which I appreciated as an art neophyte. Now I will be able to blabber on about it like a museum docent when people walk into my domicile and examine my $100 painting that I tell them cost me thousands. It also made me curious about the artist. A quick internet search revealed that Athena Nangala Granites lives in a place called Yuendumu, a community of fewer than 1,000 people 292 kilometers northwest of Alice Springs in the Northern Territory. The most recent story I found about the place detailed how Yuendumu was in danger of running out of clean water in 2019, which indicates the remoteness of some Aboriginal communities. There is also a thriving artist community there, and Mrs. Granites learned to paint by watching her grandmother, her mother, and her sisters. When she is not painting and when the rain comes and it is cooler, she likes to go hunting with her family for honey ants, bush banana, goanna, and kangaroo. When the rain comes to my neighborhood, I like to take a nap or watch Netflix documentaries. So, yeah, different.

I dropped my new purchase in my hotel room and then took a stroll through the pedestrian-only shopping strip of Rundle Mall. It was infested with shoppers on a Sunday, and a few *buskers* jammed out on guitar. Beyond the pedestrian mall, Rundle turned into Hindley Street and, after a couple of minutes, I came upon a wide alleyway on the left called Peel Street. It was home to a few cafés, a tapas bar, cocktail bars, and lunch spots. A fit and dapperly attired couple in their fifties pulled up on their bicycles for lunch. He had a sweater draped over his shoulders, and she was donning a wide-brimmed straw hat. They looked like they were starring in the "before" scene of a Cialis commercial. I chose a place called Bread and Bone, walked up a short stairway from the entrance, and took a seat at the bar, where I would soon enjoy a beef brisket sandwich and an ice tea. It wasn't the cheapest lunch I've ever eaten, but it was tasty. Peel Street looked like it would be a fun place to spend a night out.

After lunch I headed west on Hindley Street, and 200 meters later the vibe turned from upscale to naked. There were strip joints all over the place with names that only the *rippahs* (strip joints) would go by—the Palace, Madam Josephine's, Strats, the Crazy Horse Revue, and more. I had just eaten a $25 brisket sandwich at a swanky lunch spot about a pitching wedge up the street and now I was smack dab in the middle of Adelaide's Red Light District, which Simon had warned me about.

"Not that you would, but don't go to that area at night, mate," Simon cautioned me a couple of days earlier. "It's nothing but trouble."

Admittedly, I wasn't really listening when he told me where the red light district was, but I didn't think it would be that easy to stumble upon that close to the Rundle Street Mall. Now, standing under a sign that said Destiny's Turn at 3 p.m. on a Sunday afternoon, the sidewalks were populated by drunks and rough-looking characters staggering around asking for money, which I didn't have on account of the brisket sandwich and iced tea. I'm sure Madam Josephine is a lovely old gal, but these weren't the people I was looking to spend the rest of my *arvo* with.

With the afternoon fading away, I hailed an Uber out to a beach town called Glenelg, about a fifteen-kilometer ride to the west. There was a market on Sunday afternoons that sounded interesting, and the pictures in my *Nat Geo* guidebook made Glenelg look both historic and sexy, which I admit is a combination that is difficult to pull off, though I am doing my best now in my forties. The downtown area of Adelaide, I should have told you earlier, sits about ten kilometers inland from the somewhat protected Gulf of Vincent. The city was established here, along the banks of the Torrens, because the first settlers thought the coastline at the mouth of the Murray River, about sixty miles away, was too treacherous. So it's the suburbs like Glenelg that are along the water on the gulf.

Glenelg is reachable via a tram from Victoria Square in central Adelaide, which is how I would return, but I thought the Uber out there would save me time. It didn't really, but my driver turned out to be a worthy investment. After appearing generally unhappy with life for the first five minutes of our journey, his local knowledge began to ooze out.

"I live in Glenelg, so it's on the way for me," he said, as if I should have been thrilled that I was doing him a favor by letting him drive me to his hometown for money.

After ten minutes his crusty exterior was gone and he was doling out travel advice like he worked for the Glenelg Chamber of Commerce. As I hopped out of the car he pointed out all the places he had referred to during the drive and sent me on my way. It was a nice evolution from *old cobber* to Helpful Bloke. I was proud of him.

For whatever reason, the lively atmosphere of Glenelg surprised me. The place was going off. Music blared out of bars, children danced through water fountains, people returned from an afternoon on the beach, and the old tram rolled into the Mosely Square

Station, which was at the center of it all. A large Ferris wheel towered over *take-away* shops, bars, restaurants, and the beach. Behind the Ferris wheel, the Glenelg Pier stretched impressively a couple hundred meters out to sea.

I walked out past the Ferris wheel toward the beach and wandered into the market, which consisted of about fifty or so stalls set up in rows along the grass. Uber Guy was right. Touring the Glenelg Sunset Market wasn't going to take long. Most of the visitors and merchants seemed to know each other, which gave it a nice community feel, and the majority of items on offer were of the beachy, hippie variety—T-shirts, artwork, vintage clothing, bracelets, scented candles, and jerky. Jerky seemed very popular with this crowd. Maybe it goes well with weed. I didn't find anything I could live without, then spent a few minutes walking the pier with an eye toward the sky, mindful of the Aussie pigeons and their affinity for honing their accuracy skills on unsuspecting tourists, or at least this one.

Around 7 p.m., I was rather *peckish* so, on the advice of Uber Guy, I headed in the direction of the marina restaurants. My walk coincided with a magnificent sunset over the pier. The Ferris wheel and four tall palm trees along the promenade framed the moment as children chased each other around in the sand, yelling and laughing. I crossed a small footbridge into the marina, where a number of expensive boats were parked, then walked the length of the Marina Pier. It was lined with several restaurants, many of the seafood variety, which doesn't help someone (me) allergic to seafood.

At the end, I discovered The Sunset Bar and strolled in with the intention of grabbing dinner. At the back, where the place opened to the ocean, a group was gathered outside having drinks and watching the last of the sun disappear below the horizon. Before checking out the menu, I ducked into the men's bathroom. As I stood at the urinal trough staring at the wall, minding my own business, a bloke from the group outside walked in and attempted to stand next to me and do the same thing I was doing.

"Are you *spewing*?" he said in a drunken slur, while fighting to maintain his balance and urinate at the same time.

"Huh?" I said.

Spewing means throwing up—and can sometimes mean *to be mad*—but I'm fairly confident he was asking if I was vomiting in

338

the urinal trough. It was obvious that he'd had a *skin full* (of booze). I was doing what you do at a urinal. Unless he'd seen a man vomit from "down there" before, I'm not sure where the confusion came from.

"Oh, have a look at my cock, why don't you?" he then said/asked somewhat angrily.

This was a rhetorical question, I assume, as I had no plans to look at his penis and it didn't appear that he actually wanted me to, though he seemed to be intimating that I had done just that. Now I was annoyed.

"What did you say?" I said, with bit of anger in my voice.

He said nothing, except "Pfft!" Then struggled to pull up the zipper on the jeans he had pissed all over, didn't wash his hands, and staggered back into the bar.

I'd be lying if I said you don't run into a fair few blokes in Australia who are properly *pissed*; the kind of drunk that will give you a two-day hangover. The Aussies like a drink. That stereotype exists for a reason. I'm not sure where the drinking culture comes from but it's probably why the legal limit for drunk driving is very, very low. (As in: if you're going to have more than two beers, don't drive!) Far be it from me to cast a stone at anyone who likes to blow the frost off a couple cold ones now and again, but outside of a sunny spring Saturday afternoon I once spent in York, England, I've never been any place where people get so utterly wasted before the sun is down like they do in Australia. Maybe it's got something to do with the hole in the ozone layer.

Given the state of the clientele, I decided to explore alternative dining options and settled on a sushi restaurant back up the pier. Now officially famished, I sat down at an outdoor table and ordered so many things that the waitress looked at me as if I had made a mistake. As she walked away, I called to her and asked for a small, airplane-size bottle of red wine. I hadn't planned on drinking any alcohol today but, aside from nearly having a *blue* (argument) with the guy now standing in piss-soaked jeans a few minutes earlier, the whole Adelaide experience had gone pretty perfectly. I was in a somewhat celebratory mood.

When I finished cleaning my plate(s), I walked back in the direction of the Ferris wheel to catch the tram back to town, but not before treating myself to a small ice cream cone at a shop up the road. The area was heaving with young folks who were out partying their

Sunday evening away. I finished the cone just in time to hop on the tram, which provided an easy and relaxing ride back to town.

The next morning began with some morning exercise to work off the guilt of the ice cream, wine, fried vegetables, barbeque brisket, and gallon of Teriyaki sauce. (It doesn't feel good to list it out like that; I'm not doing that again.) I followed more advice from Simon and rented a car for a day excursion to the coastal town of Victor Harbor, about an hour away. The road passed through the village of McLaren Vale, the heart of another wine region, which I would cruise through on my way back. Except for the fact that I have ridden skateboards with more horsepower than the rental car I was driving and the engine sounded like a lawn mower, the ride was easy. The green vineyards set against dry hillsides reminded me of the wine region of California's central coast, north of Santa Barbara. Along the way, I passed farm stands, fields of vegetables, and then a business that employs people who have chosen what is surely one of the most underpaid occupations on earth (and I have no idea of their salary).

The sign for Snake Catchers of Adelaide featured the head of a giant, ferocious-looking snake that, if you saw it near your home, would make you want to phone them immediately, and that was probably the point. I didn't have a snake problem, so I didn't stop in for a chat, but I did spend a fair bit of time on Snakecatchersadelaide.com.au later just because this seemed like a fascinating choice of occupation. I learned a whole host of things like snake myths and snake bite first aid, and I even spent fifteen minutes combing through the galleries of reptiles and wildlife they had helped remove from properties and homes. I also learned that the eastern brown snake, which the website said is the second most venomous land snake in the world, causes more snake bite deaths in Australia than any other and is the most common snake found in South Australia. On the off chance you are ever bitten by an eastern brown snake—and this would take a great deal of misfortune from wherever you probably are sitting now—Snakecatchersadelaide.com.au said you can expect the hours immediately following your shit luck to go like this:

First hour: Headache, irritability (no shit!), confusion, vomiting, diarrhea, and loss of consciousness (also known as mercy)
Hours 1-3: Abdominal pain, hypertension, cranial nerve paralysis, hemorrhage
Three hours after: Limb and muscle paralysis leading to respiratory failure, peripheral circulatory failure, and eventually death

While it was unfortunate to read that the eastern brown snake is known to visit "many backyards in and around Adelaide's suburbs," it is comforting to know that most snake bites occur when people simply don't leave them be. So if you go to Australia and see a snake— and I can't believe anyone would need to be told this—leave it alone.

The head snake catcher was a guy named Rolly Burrell, and doesn't that name just sound like a guy who would be a head snake catcher? He wasn't going to be named Chester Kennedy III, now was he? The most surprising part of the entire website visit was learning that Rolly had somehow managed to find ten other people who wanted to work on his staff. Rolly should be giving TED Talks on employee recruitment strategy.

In all my years of living and traveling in Australia, the closest encounter I had with a snake was on a golf course on the Mornington Peninsula down the coast from Melbourne. As myself, my buddy Nick Coulthard, and two of his mates walked off the fourth tee box dragging our *buggies* (pull carts), I watched one of them—rather causally, in my opinion—alter his stride ahead of me, stepping ever so slightly to the left of his intended path and continuing on. Lying in the thick green grass between the tee box and the start of the fairway was a baby tiger snake, a highly poisonous and often aggressive breed. The casual nature of my playing partners astounded me.

"Watch your step there, mate," one of them said. "There's little tiger snake there."

"Okay, thanks," I said, doing my best to hide what I was thinking, which was: You can't be serious!

This bloke had stepped over this poisonous snake like it was a pile of dog shit lying in the grass. I walked a little farther to the left—by about two miles—and felt uneasy for the next fourteen holes. Any ball I hit that was remotely close to any tall grass, and there were plenty that day, was a goner as far as I was concerned. I think I shot 142 and went through ten golf balls.

A few minutes up the road from Snake Catchers of Adelaide, I reached the ocean at the town of Victor Harbor, which sits on Encounter Bay and is the largest town out here on the Fleurieu Peninsula. It's about fifty miles from Adelaide and on weekends crowds file in from the city. The town felt like most beach towns, and on a Monday it was relatively quiet. Just behind the main downtown, adjacent to a 1980s-style mini golf course where you putt through a shark's mouth and under a lighthouse, was a small horse-drawn tram. The big Clydesdales that do the tram-pulling were chilling out in their stable a few feet away, so I went over and had a brief chat with them. And wasn't that enlightening...for them, I mean.

The tram was sitting on tracks that ran out a long causeway to a place called Granite Island, about 600 meters away. The whole journey on the horse-drawn tram is almost two miles to a visitors center at the other end. I didn't stay long enough to ride the double-decker tram out to Granite Island, but evidently there is a colony of fairy penguins out there that draws a fair crowd.

Victor Harbour Causeway, South Australia

342

On more advice from Simon, I drove five minutes along the coast toward a small town called Port Elliot, past a gathering of old-timers out playing lawn bowls in the midday sun. Simon was adamant that I go to the Port Elliot Bakery and get myself "the greatest pie you will ever have in your life," and that is a tip I don't need to be told twice. Built in the 1860s, the small building on North Terrace has been a bakery for more than 100 years, still with its original wood fire oven. The current owners have been making their products onsite since 1989. The Port Elliot Bakery smelled like heaven. I ordered two steak pies, another pie that I think had pork in it, and, for later, one of their chocolate glazed donuts that looked like it might kill me instantly, though it would've been a good way to go.

I took my three pies and dessert donut and drove a minute down a small street called The Strand. It led to a scenic overlook called Freeman's Knob, which was either named for the way the peninsula jutted out into the sea or some guy's pecker. It sat up on a small cliff and had sweeping views of Horseshoe Bay, where you can spot migrating whales at certain times of the year. Today, it was just the perfect place to fend off seagulls who love meat pies.

When my pies were *done and dusted*, I pointed my four-wheel scooter back in the direction of Adelaide, turning off after about thirty minutes onto Old Willunga Hill Road. It was a twisting, turning one-lane country road. A cyclist struggled up what I assume was Old Willunga Hill, a steep section that is used in the Tour Down Under professional cycling race. At the bottom of the hill I found myself in Willunga, a scenic town that claims a welcoming Saturday farmer's market, restaurants, pubs, and the kind of scenery that comes with being in one of the world's best wine-growing regions. Just up the road are the inviting B&Bs and culinary delights of the town of McLaren Vale, which is the centerpiece to this entire wine-growing region that goes by the same name. The McLaren Vale region has vines that are more than 100 years old and it's home to about ninety wineries, most of them of the boutique variety. Shiraz is the dominating varietal of the region, in case you are not as smart as Simon on these topics.

A couple minutes up the road, I pulled into a winery called d'Arenberg, which Simon had recommended...I think because it was expensive. There were a few buildings on the property, including something called the Cube, a five-level building that a sign told me had a "sensory room, a virtual fermenter, a 360-degree video room and many other tactile experiences." There was also some kind of

Salvador Dali sculpture in front of it. I just came to try a couple drops of vino. This was all more trouble than I was after at the moment. It was $15 to walk in the door, which seemed an expensive cover charge for a sensory room unless they had an exhibit of two skeletons *rooting*. Instead, I walked across the parking lot to the restaurant and café, bought an iced tea for the road, and got back in my rocket ship.

On my way back to the highway, I came across a family winery called Maxwell. "Be rude not to," I thought. I tried three wines in the tasting room of the family-owned winery, and then hit the road back to Adelaide for a late afternoon arrival. A few minutes up the road, my phone rang. It was Simon.

"How was your day?" he asked.

"Great! Very cool area," I said. "And those pies were unreal. I couldn't decide which two to have…so I had three."

"You ate three pies?" he said. "Holy shit!"

"Yes, and I have a donut here riding shotgun," I said. "And I just hit a couple wineries on my way back."

"Righto. Good day then, mate," Simon said.

"Yeah, but no koalas," I said, lamenting the fact that I had spent years of my life in the country and still never seen one in the wild.

"You and your koalas," he said.

"Been all over this country and the only place I've ever seen a koala is at the Sydney Zoo," I said. "I'm starting to think koalas are all a bunch of bullshit you Aussies made up to attract tourists. They're like Bigfoot."

We hung up and I drove on a few more miles in the direction of Adelaide. Five minutes later, Simon rang me again.

"Mate, you can't leave Australia again without seeing a koala in the wild," he said. "I'll tell ya what: be ready at 8:30 tomorrow morning. I'll pick you up with Henri and we'll show you a damn koala in the wild."

"Seriously? All right, but don't make promises you can't keep," I said to him.

"Mate, there are koalas everywhere here. Just be ready at 8:30. I've got shit to do."

"I'll be ready," I said.

The next morning Simon, Henri, and I drove out of town toward Morialta Conservation Park, five or ten minutes from his home and only twenty minutes from my downtown hotel.

"I hear koalas are endangered," I said. "I read an article on the plane about it."

"Koalas are NOT endangered, mate," Simon said.
"They are everywhere."

"Yeah, we'll see," I said.

We drove on a couple minutes farther, chatting away with Henri about things five-year-olds talk about. For the record, he was also adamant that there were plenty of koalas in the area.

"Well, I'm really pleased that you liked Adelaide, mate," Simon said to me. "And I'm absolutely *chuffed* that you made it here for a visit. It's a nice little town we've got here."

"I'm glad I made it, too," I said. "There are still plenty of places I haven't been in AUS, but I think this is a good place to finish with for now."

"You've seen more of this bloody country than nearly every Aussie I know," he said. "Would you move back here? It seems like you have a real affinity for Australia."

"I do," I said. "And I would. The quality of life is great here and I do feel a connection with the people and the places. It's just awfully far from home at the moment."

I told him how I liked that you tend to know where you stand with Aussies, and that you can be friends pretty quickly with them, too. I like that they have a strong work ethic when it's time to get shit done, but they love to blow off steam and have a laugh, too. They are rivaled only by the Irish and the Italians, in my experience, when it comes to their general welcoming attitude toward strangers. And they love sports, which makes them okay in my book. And, probably because I'm from Massachusetts, I like that they will *take the piss* with you and that this means you can do the same with them, and that if you can bust each other's balls a bit like that, this means you'll *get on* just fine. I guess what I really like is that, broadly speaking, Aussies take things seriously, but not themselves.

And I like that after countless miles of travel by plane, by car, by boat, and on foot over nearly a decade, you can be standing in the cul-de-sac of a road fifteen minutes from a city on a Tuesday morning with your good mate and his five-year-old son searching for a koala like a couple of morons. (It's not Henri's fault he got dragged into this.)

"Simon, I don't see…" I started to say.

"Right there!" Simon said proudly, pointing to the tree in front of us. "Koala. Told ya."

And there it was, a young koala climbing ass-first down the limb of a tree thirty feet away.

"Holy shit!" I said, laughing like a kid. "It's a koala."

"Well, no shit it's a kola, mate," Simon said.

"Koalas are normal here, Tim," the five-year-old added. "This is Australia."

Thanks, mate.

The elusive koala…finally!

UNSOLICITED ADVICE: ADELAIDE

MUST DO:

Adelaide is a very walkable place, but **having a car** to transport you to the places an hour or so out of town in various directions is a plus. If you have a "Simon" to cart you around, all the better... I enjoyed the trip out to the **Barossa Valley**, and the lunch in Tanunda was perfect. Spend a day there and return the long way through the **Adelaide Hills**, leaving time to stop here and there... I feel the same way about **McLaren Vale**; the drive along **Epicurean Way** deserved more time and stops than I gave it... Sometimes I go on a "tourist run" to familiarize myself with a new place. If you do, too, then **a jog along the River Torrens** and from park to park is ideal.

UP TO YOU:

With a little effort, you can see most of the city of Adelaide on foot in a couple of days, so **leave time to explore beyond town**... There are plenty of outdoor things, like nature preserves, just ten to fifteen minutes from downtown if that's your thing. You'll probably see a **koala**... A quick tram trip out to **Glenelg** is a relaxing way to spend an afternoon and/or evening. Go early via the tram, take a swim, grab some food, and tram it back... **Rundle Street** is your best bet for nightlife... If wine is your thing, **Claire Valley** and **Coonawarra** and the **Murray River Valley** are additional options farther from Adelaide.

NEXT TIME:

I'll make a time to rent one of those BBQ buoys or Gin Cruises on **the River Torrens**... Rundle Street was fine for a night or two, but next time I'd spend a night trying the **pubs on O'Connell Street in North Adelaide** and a night in the swankier spots on **Peel Street**... I'd love to be in Adelaide during **Mad March** for one of the many events on the calendar, like the **Fringe Festival**... The beginning (March/April) or end (August) of the Aussie rules football season, when the weather is generally perfect and there is a game of **footy on at the Adelaide Oval**, would be great, too... I only skipped through McLaren Vale on my way back from Victor Harbor and Port Elliot. Next time, I'd spend a couple of nights doing a combo trip from Adelaide through **McLaren Vale**, then continue to **Port Elliot** (for the pies), **Victor Harbor**, and **Jervis Bay**. From Jervis Bay, you can catch a forty-five-minute ferry to the scenic nature preserves of **Kangaroo Island** and spend the day checking out the wildlife. The island was badly damaged by wildfires in early 2020, but is on the road to recovery.

THE POINTY END

Chapter 27: The Pointy End

My most recent visit to Australia culminated with a short stay in Sydney. I spent a night on my way out of the country at the home of my old pal Richard Ennis, the Northern Irishman who had arrived on these shores about the same time I did, and his wife, Dee. It was late 2019 and the bushfires that would be broadcast around the world were just beginning to rage out of control. As my short flight from Melbourne to Sydney descended into Kingsford Smith Airport, the smell of the smokey air outside was evident inside the plane. Out the window, a gloomy haze darkened another Sydney sunset as winds pushed the inland smoke all the way to the coast. In the end, these fires would go on for months, destroying thousands of homes and businesses and claiming many lives. Much of the areas I drove through on my road trip from Sydney to Canberra to Melbourne just a few weeks earlier were burned to the ground. When it comes to natural disasters, Australia doesn't do things *in halves*.

In the weeks and months following the bushfires, the various Aussie tourism organizations on the national and state levels did a wonderful job of reminding potential tourists that the best thing they could do to help Australia get back on its feet was to "come and visit us." Not long after that, the COVID-19 pandemic swept the planet and, from far away, Australia looked even more isolated, which might've been a good thing.

On my final day in Australia, with that smokey gloom hanging over the most picturesque cityscape on the planet, I made my way back out to Bondi Beach and commenced the coastal walk from there to Coogee, the same walk I took on my second day in Australia nearly a decade earlier. I thought about the time that had passed since I first stood jet-lagged and lost in the rain on that street corner in Sydney chatting with the policeman. I thought about that broken suitcase, the excitement that came with not knowing what would come next, my thirty-three months living in Melbourne, and the countless places and people of Australia that I'd come to know, all because I had said YES to a wedding invitation and then YES to a job offer. Thanks, Leighton (and Jungy!). I thought about the unlikeliness of all that happening to a kid from the suburbs of Boston who got curious about the funny accents from the distant land he saw on TV, and then had the good fortune to end up living it.

"Greatest country in the world, mate!" is what an Aussie would say right here.

I don't know how you judge that sort of thing, but AUS—it's not Oz—has been pretty good to me, so it seems appropriate to first say: *Ta*, which means thank you.

Like my first trip to Australia, the main reason for this return visit was for the Melbourne wedding of a good mate. This time it was my former colleague, Jonno Lindsay, who was marrying his now-wife, Belle. In addition to doing an absolutely *spot-on* impression of Sir David Attenborough, Jonno is the type of guy who, if you're not an Aussie, is a little difficult to understand the first time you meet him. He's a smart, well-educated bloke, but he talks faster than an auctioneer and he uses Aussie-isms that he doesn't even realize are flying out of his mouth at warp speed. It helps to know what they mean if you want to have the first clue what he's talking about. If you've understood all the *italics* I've used, you should be fine if you happen to run into Jonno someday.

When I chat to Jonno, it always reminds me of my first few weeks living in Australia, when every day felt like a day at the MONA museum—sensory overload in all directions. There was plenty about the big move that I *envisaged*, as they say here, and much that I did not. Learning to drive on the left side of the road, starting a new job, buying a car, insuring said car, finding a place to live, insuring the contents of said place to live, setting up a bank account, and then spending money from said bank account like a drunken sailor on shore leave at IKEA and Target in an effort to fill said domicile with items you just sold in the US on Craigslist for 10 percent of their original value. After a few months I came to the realization that I had underestimated the amount of busywork that comes with relocating to a new country. It wasn't exactly like uprooting to Somalia on the culture-shock scale, but it was more of a transition than I expected. Rewarding for sure, but man was it frustrating at times.

Everything I did took so much longer than it would have in the US. It wasn't Australia that was to blame and it wasn't my fault either, though the entire experience did teach me to better cope with life's little inconveniences. Mostly, it was just new processes, new places, and new ways of doing things. Tasks I had done in the blink of an eye back home took planning and research. At some point, you accept it and just *get stuck into it*. Then, without even noticing, life in a new country starts to feel like…home. Learning the difference between a *schooner*, a *pot*, a *pint*, a *stubby*, and a *jug* helps, I must say.

In the days leading up to Jonno and Belle's wedding, I found myself eager to experience some of the more routine things of my former life in Melbourne. I went for a run along the Tan and around the outside of the MCG, strolled down Chapel Street on a Sunday afternoon, and visited my old colleagues at the office. I played golf at the magnificent Kingston Heath Golf Club with a Scottish mate named Daniel Pollack, whom I had befriended during my time here. I laughed my ass off over happy hour pints with Paul Moynes at an Irish pub in Southbank, and chatted about the footy over pints with my old mates Leighton, Phil, Mykey, and Timmy at the London Tavern in Richmond, which turned into a pint at another place and a pint at another place and a kebab before a taxi home. (These things happen. If you haven't judged me by now, the late-night kebab isn't going to be the straw that breaks the camel's back.)

To get a pre-wedding haircut, I even went to my old barbershop, a hipster spot called Dr. Follicle's in Richmond where they blast obscure Bob Dylan tunes and give you a Coopers Pale Ale while you wait. The place had been remodeled into something a bit more refined, but the people and the attitude remained unchanged.

"How did you like living here?" the woman with the scissors asked me.

"I loved it," I said. "It's awesome to be back. I've missed it."

"Would you come back to Melbourne?" she asked.

I hadn't considered the question until Simon had posed the same one a couple of days earlier in Adelaide.

"Yes," I said. "Absolutely. It's a great city and this is a great country. I think the quality of life is very good here, whatever that means."

Everything isn't perfect, mind you. Since I first moved to Australia, it appears to me that the politics have become increasingly divisive, as if it's just a few years behind the US in that regard, which is a shame. There are also heated discussions over immigration and race and the cost of living and the future of the planet. Just because you are far away from the world doesn't mean the problems of the world don't exist on your doorstep.

Some of my affinity for Australia probably stems selfishly from the impact it has had on me since I first visited about a decade ago. Living abroad does wonders for personal growth, confidence, and perspective on the world. While it's true that what you see of a place on TV from afar often doesn't live up to expectations in real life, what I learned from *having a go of it* Down Under is that sometimes it can be *heaps* better. Today, Australia remains exotic to me, but now it's also familiar and so are many of its people. While I will always cherish the memories of cruising the croc-infested Yellow Water billabong in the Aussie Outback, strolling the coast from Bondi to Coogee, or standing in silence at the Anzac Day dawn service in Melbourne, the characters I met along the way are what made the stories worth sharing. And today, many of those characters are my good mates. Except the Taekwondo-fighting hot dog vendor in Byron Bay. I stayed away from that guy.

On my last day in Melbourne, I had lunch with Leighton and his young son Angus, who was wondering what was going on with my funny accent. After lunch, before I headed to the airport, we said goodbye as we have done in various locations around the globe over the fifteen years of our friendship. Leighton seemed slightly more sentimental than usual, which caught me off-guard.

"Good to see ya back in AUS, buddy," he said. "You need to move back. This is your home!"

"Feels good to be back, mate," I told him.

"Friends for life, mate," he said, offering a man-hug and then repeating himself, "friends for life."

"Absolutely," I said, a little surprised at his warm and fuzzy send-off. "See you soon."

Leighton placed Gus into the back seat of his car, closed the door, and looked up. I searched for some poignant words to express my gratitude for the role he had played in this Australian journey of mine, then noticed the wonderful Yarra Trams clogging the roadway he was about to set off on.

"Righto," I said, motioning to his car and the road. "*Onya bike, son.*"

ACKNOWLEDGMENTS

This book would not have been possible without the kindness of so many individuals. An enormous thank you to David Aretha, who edited the book and convinced me to keep believing in the project. A true professional! Thanks as well to Natalia Olbinski, who designed the cover. Seeing her first sketches had me feeling like a child on Christmas morning. It was becoming a real thing! And now it is. Antonina Konopelska did a masterful job on the internal layout, delivering original and creative design ideas with an impressive attention to detail that pulled this whole thing together. Thank you.

My friend Scott Goryl read numerous chapters along the journey. He encouraged me to keep writing, asked for more of my Aussie stories, and shared some of his own (Hemp Olympix, anyone?). His support was *massive*, as they love to say Down Under. Thanks, Scott.

Friend and accomplished filmmaker Mike Douglas read the entire book as I was finishing it, offering final advice and support. Thanks to the "Godfather of Freeski" for his time, his storytelling expertise, his honest feedback, and for letting me use a quote from one of his text messages on the cover.

So many friends and acquaintances read bits and pieces along the journey and inspired me with notes like: "Send me more!" Your generosity was crucial. I will forget someone, I'm sure, but a heartfelt thanks to Janet Sweeney (my mom), Ed Sweeney (my dad, who has since passed), Chris Sweeney (my brother, who has always kept me sharp with his witty barbs), Daniel Pollock, Paul Moynes, Simon Brizard, Anssi Makela, Saila Hanninen, Majell Backhausen, Marilyn Glasheen, Betty Filkins, Mike Ambrose, Damian Shutie, Aaron Gallagher, Cindy Woods, Angie Jacques, Paul Griffin, Brian Eustis, Loïc Bailliard, Paul Griffin, and the always supportive Stuart MacDonald.

Andre Caron, a loyal friend for more than 25 years, contributed a handful of photos where I didn't have any of my own. When he is not fixing people as a physical therapist and canning beers at a brewery, he takes fantastic outdoor photographs and shares them @peaceoftrail on Instagram.

In Australia, so many mates made a lasting impact on me during my time there. Thanks to Richard and Dee Ennis, Eric Watterson, Will and Anna Spraggett, Simon and Lisa Bartold, Tim "The Shermanator" Sherman, Sam Graham, Scott McLean, Nick Coulthard,

Jonno Lindsay and family, Phil Wokulski, Mykel Rugers, Matt Knowles, Matt Sullivan, Bruce Flint, Timmy Palmer, Marc Lord, Natacha Johnston, Jenny Burford, Dan Clark, Matt Tudor, and Siobhan Anderson. And thanks to Scott Jungwirth for helping me land on the shores of Australia. And a huge "ta" to all my former colleagues at Callaway Golf South Pacific. If I've forgotten anyone, I'll thank you in the next book. Sorry!

To Leighton "The Wiz" Richards, Laura Richards, and the entire Richards *family*, you welcomed me since I first turned up on your doorstep, bags in hand for the big wedding. Thank you for your treasured friendship, even from afar. I hope you got a few laughs from these stories.

Finally, to the people of Australia whom I met on airplanes and trains and buses, in pubs and restaurants, at sporting events and vineyards, and, yes, even in museums, a most sincere thank you. I don't ever remember feeling unwelcomed wherever I stepped in your magnificent country. And I miss it. I'm sure I left some stuff out and missed a few of your favorite spots, but it's good to leave a few places to explore down the road.

See you soon, *you beauties.*

-Sweens
January 2023

BIBLIOGRAPHY

Bibliography

I wrote mostly from notes scribbled into my notebook (or onto the occasional cocktail napkin) and typed onto the Notes app on my phone, or from the iPhone photos I snapped of museum and exhibit displays. Later, I used the following sites and articles for fact-checking and research. My sincere apologies if I missed anyone along the way.

Lennon, Troy. "Black Sunday 1938: Hundred washed out to sea on Bondi Beach as freak waves kill five, injure dozens." (2005 Feb 15). The Daily Telegraph.
https://www.dailytelegraph.com.au/news/black-sunday-1938-hundreds-washed-out-to-sea-on-bondi-beach-as-freak-waves-kill-five-injure-dozens/news-story/2f584af7365abc298d039d42e5f2ddf1

Spicer, David. "Bondi Beach lifesavers commemorate 80th anniversary of Black Sunday drownings with re-enactment." (2018 February 4). ABCNews.net.au.
https://www.abc.net.au/news/2018-02-04/bondi-black-sunday-lifesavers-commemorate-80th-anniversary/9394930

Kuranda Village in the Rainforest
https://www.kuranda.org/kuranda-visitor-information-centre/indigenous-culture/

The Woolshed website
http://www.thewoolshed.com.au/

Nimbin Mardigrass
http://nimbinmardigrass.com/hemp-olympix/

NT.gov
https://nt.gov.au/emergency

Maddocks, Tom. Darwin's Inpex legacy: riding the boom and avoiding the bust. (2018, Sep 29). ABC.net.au
https://www.abc.net.au/news/2018-09-29/inpex-legacy-riding-boom-avoiding-bust-nt-economy/10236158

NT.gov.au. Litchfield National Park.
https://nt.gov.au/parks/find-a-park/litchfield-national-park

Matt.ExperienceOz.com.au. Top 10 sunsets in Australia.
https://www.experienceoz.com.au/en/the-top-10-sunsets-in-australia

Davidson, Helen. Man killed by crocodile at Cahill's Crossing in Kakadu national park. (2017 Jan 19) The Guardian. https://www.theguardian.com/australia-news/2017/jan/20/man-killed-crocodile-cahills-crossing-kakadu-national-park

Dutter, Barbie. 14-ft crocodile kills backpacker. (2002, Oct 24). The Telegraph. https://www.telegraph.co.uk/news/worldnews/australiaandthepacific/australia/1411154/14ft-crocodile-kills-backpacker.html

Shepard, Briana. Fremantle needs to reclaim identity to reverse 'downward slide', think tanks says. (2015 Dec 1) ABC.net.au https://www.abc.net.au/news/2015-12-01/fremantle-needs-to-reclaim-identity-think-tank-says/6988602

Freemantle.wa.gov.au. Aboriginal history. https://www.fremantle.wa.gov.au/council/about-city-Fremantle/aboriginal-history

Harry's Café de Wheels website https://www.harryscafedewheels.com.au/

Miller, John. The $200,000-a-Year Mine Worker. (2011 Nov 16). Wall Street Journal. https://www.wsj.com/articles/SB100014240529702046219045770161723508693l2

Cullen Wines.com.au https://www.cullenwines.com.au/cullen-wines/

ABC News (Australia). NSW Bushfires: On the ground in Batemans Bay (2020 Jan 1) https://www.youtube.com/watch?v=eMj7WE0v1yA

AIATSIS. Land Rights. https://aiatsis.gov.au/explore/articles/land-rights

AIATSIS. The Mabo Case. https://aiatsis.gov.au/explore/articles/mabo-case

Australian Bureau of Statistics. Census of Population and Housing: Characteristics of Aboriginal and Torres Strait Islander Australians, 2016. https://www.abs.gov.au/Ausstats/abs@.nsf/7d12b0f6763c78caca257061001cc588/656ea6473a7580bbca258236000c30f7!OpenDocument

National Archives of Australia. Australia's Prime ministers. https://www.naa.gov.au/explore-collection/australias-prime-ministers

Atelj, Adrien. These Are the Fastest Growing Suburbs in Australia. (2020 Jan 5) Homes.com.au. https://www.homes.com.au/news/these-are-the-fastest-growing-suburbs-in-australia/

CNBC.com. Why Starbucks Failed in Australia. (2018 Jul 26). https://www.youtube.com/watch?v=_FGUkxn5kZQ

AFL.com.au. The History of Australian Football. https://www.afl.com.au/about-afl/history

Nauright, John. Australian rules football. Britannica.com. https://www.britannica.com/sports/Australian-rules-football

Transport Safety Victoria. 2018 Annual incident statistic: Victorian Tram Operators. https://transportsafety.vic.gov.au/__data/assets/word_doc/0014/402152/Tram_incident_statistics_annual_2018_final.docx

Anzac Day Commemoration Committee. https://anzacday.org.au/words-of-remembrancehttps://fedsquare.com/history-design#:~:text=Construction%20of%20what%20was%20then,various%20tenancies%20and%20major%20sponsorships

Flanagan, Richard. Tasmanian Devil: a master gambler and his high-stakes museum. (2013 Jan 13) The New Yorker. https://www.newyorker.com/magazine/2013/01/21/tasmanian-devil

Flanagan, Richard. The Gambler: At home with David Walsh. (February 2013) The Monthly.com.au. https://www.themonthly.com.au/issue/2013/february/1366597433/richard-flanagan/gambler#mtr

Patterson, Kate. Blending science, art and other excrement. (2016 February 11) TheConversation.com. https://theconversation.com/blending-science-art-and-other-excrement-54584

Bergman, Justin. 36 hours in Hobert. (2019 Dec 5) NYTimes.com. https://www.nytimes.com/2019/12/05/travel/36-hours-in-hobart-and-environs.html

Tourism Tasmania. Visitor Statistics. https://www.tourismtasmania.com.au/research/visitors/

Downie, David. Cascade Brewery. Australian Beers.com. http://www.australianbeers.com/history/cascade.htm

UTAS.edu.au. Peter Degraves. University of Tasmania. https://www.utas.edu.au/library/companion_to_tasmanian_history/D/Peter%20Degraves.htm

Risen, Clay. In the New World of Whiskeys, Australia Strives to Stand Out. (2019 Dec 3) NYTimes.com. https://www.nytimes.com/2019/12/03/dining/drinks/australian-whiskey.html

Sexton, Mike. Time zone shift favoured by business in south Australia but opposed by some west coast residents. (2015 April 12). ABC.com.au. https://www.abc.net.au/news/2015-04-12/business-backs-sa-time-zone-shift,-but-some-regions-worried/6385030

Cartwright, Mark. Ancient Timekeeping. (2012 Aug 30). World History Encyclopedia. https://www.ancient.eu/Timekeeping/

Barossa.com. https://www.barossa.com/visit/towns-and-villages/krondorf

Warlu.com. Warlukurlangu: Artists of Yuendumu. https://warlu.com/artist/athena-nangala-granites/

Beavan, Katrina. Yuendumu in Central Australia at 'severe risk' of running out of water. (2019 Aug 13) ABC.com.au https://www.abc.net.au/news/2019-08-13/remote-community-yuendumu-running-out-of-drinking-water/11405024

Snake Catcher's Adelaide. https://snakecatchersadelaide.com.au/ https://www.portelliotbakery.com/history

Port Elliot Bakery website https://www.portelliotbakery.com/

These three books have been on my bookshelf since I first started traveling in Australia, I relied on them on many occasions.

Smith, Roff Martin. National Geographic Traveler: Australia (Fourth Edition). National Geographic.

Thomas, Karoline. The Rough Guide to Melbourne. Fourth edition. (Published 2009). Rough Guides.

Hunter, Jenny. The True Blue Guide to Australian Slang. (New Holland Publishers, 2004)

OnlyMelbourne.com. Sidney Myer - Simcha Myer Baevski. https://www.onlymelbourne.com.au/sidney-myer

ABOUT THE AUTHOR

The author in full tourist mode in the Northern Territory

Tim Sweeney was born and raised in Massachusetts. He graduated from Eckerd College in Florida and began his professional career as a newspaper journalist in Colorado, where he won the award for Best Serious Column Writing from the Colorado Press Association at age twenty-three. He has written for numerous magazines and worked as a radio and TV sports reporter, a magazine editor, and an advertising copywriter. As a marketing professional, he's held roles for premium sports brands in the US, Australia, and France. He's also hosted a YouTube series, developed adventure films, and dabbled in podcasting.

Follow his travels on Instagram **@tesweens**
Website: **TimSweeneyLive.com**